Hammond Innes has now written twenty-seven hugely successful novels. He has also written two travel books, a history of the Conquistadors and a fictional history based on Captain Cook's last voyage. He was awarded the CBE in 1978 and more recently Bristol University has awarded him the honorary degree of Doctor of Letters.

A Scot born in England, he wanted excitement and he wanted to write. He had both during the Battle of Britain, writing *Attack Alarm* while a gunner defending Kenley fighter station. It was in the early fifties, with books like *The Lonely Skier*, *Campbell's Kingdom*, *The White South*, all of them filmed, that he achieved international fame. His work developed steadily with such books as *Atlantic Fury*, *Levkas Man*, *The Big Footprints*.

New editions of every book he has written are constantly appearing in various countries.

In addition to his life of writing and travelling, Hammond Innes is deeply committed to forestry. His knowledge of the sea, so evident in his books, comes from his very considerable experience of ocean racing and cruising. He married Dorothy Lang, an actress who later turned playwright and who more recently has written three books about their journeys and their homes. They live in Suffolk.

Hammond Innes

MEDUSA

FONTANA/Collins

First published in Great Britain by
William Collins Sons & Co. Ltd, 1988
This Continental edition first published by
Fontana Paperbacks 1988

Copyright © Hammond Innes 1988

Printed and bound in Great Britain by
William Collins Sons & Co. Ltd, Glasgow

To
My wife's cousins,
the John Langs, father and son,
who, when in command, have done so
much over the years to involve
me in the work of the
Royal Navy.

CONTENTS

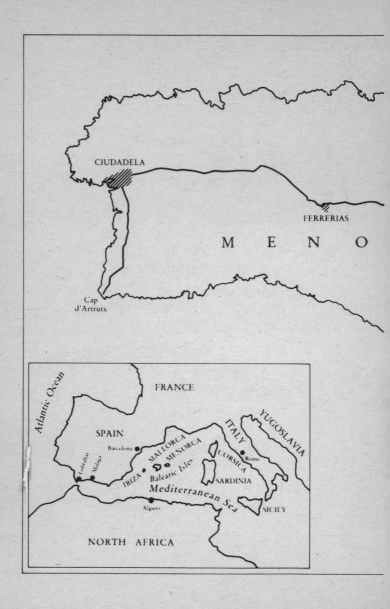

CIUDADELA

FERRERIAS

M E N O

Cap
d'Artrutx

Atlantic Ocean

FRANCE

SPAIN

YUGOSLAVIA

Barcelona

MALLORCA

ITALY

IBIZA

MENORCA

CORSICA

Rome

Gibraltar   Malaga

Balearic Isles

SARDINIA

Mediterranean Sea

Algiers

SICILY

NORTH AFRICA

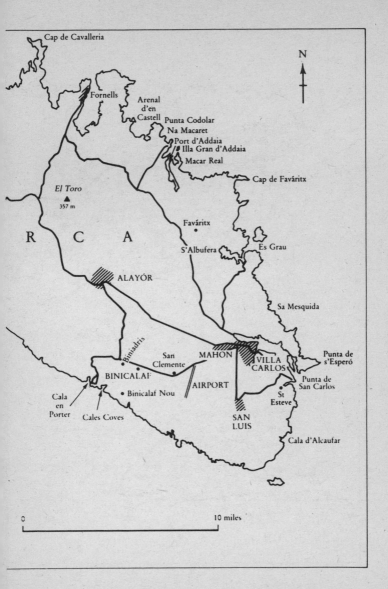

N

Cap de Cavalleria

Fornells

Arenal
d'en
Castell

Punta Codolar

Na Macaret

Port d'Addaia

Illa Gran d'Addaia

Macar Real

Cap de Favàritx

El Toro
357 m

Favàritx

S'Albufera

Es Grau

R   C   A

ALAYÓR

Sa Mesquida

Biniadris

San
Clemente

MAHON

VILLA
CARLOS

Punta de
s'Esperó

BINICALAF

AIRPORT

Punta de
San Carlos

Binicalaf Nou

St
Esteve

Cala
en
Porter

Cales Coves

SAN
LUIS

Cala d'Alcaufar

0   10 miles

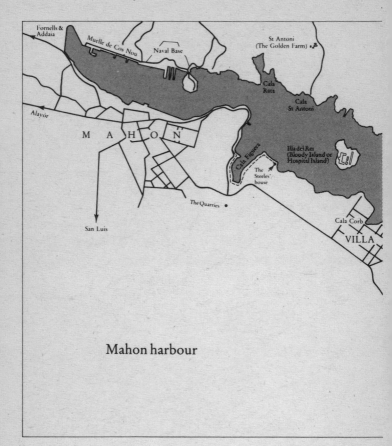

Mahon harbour

I

THUNDERFLASH

CHAPTER ONE

I was at the office window, looking out over the still waters of the harbour and watching a small boat break the reflection of Bloody Island's hospital ruins, when he drove up. It was our first real spring morning, the air fresh and clear, red roofs shining in the sun of the promontory opposite and the sounds of the port coming with great clarity across the water. He was driving one of those small Italian cars hired out to tourists and I watched idly as he backed it into the raw parking lot we had recently bulldozed out where the roadway stopped abruptly at the water's edge.

The local people had thought us mad to set up shop in this cul-de-sac on the east side of the Cala Figuera. It was so far from the main waterfront highway and almost overhung by the cliffs on which the small town of Villa Carlos was built. But we were close to the Atlante, one of the best restaurants in Mahon, and we had found that people liked an excuse to come to this rather wild little spot that gave them a totally different view of the harbour.

I glanced at my watch, looking down at him, still idly, as he got out of the car and stood there in the sunshine, gazing out to the small motor boat now clear of Bloody Island and cutting a broad arrow as it headed towards Cala Rata on the far side of the harbour. It was not yet eight, early for anybody to visit us on business, and at that hour you don't expect the arrival of somebody destined to shatter your whole life. Nevertheless, there was something about him, his hesitation perhaps, or the way he held himself – I couldn't take my eyes off the man.

He seemed to brace himself, closing the car door and

turning abruptly. But instead of crossing the roadway, he stood there, still hesitant, his hair gleaming black in the sun. He had the sturdy compactness of a climber, or a man who played games, and he was good-looking; neatly dressed too, in blue trousers, white short-sleeved shirt open at the neck, and his bare arms had the paleness of somebody who had spent the winter in the north. He glanced up at the open window where I was standing. It was a big bay window we had built out over the roadway to give us more room in the tiny office. He could not help seeing me and he began to cross the road.

But then he checked, stood staring for a moment at the chandlery, then turned quickly and strode back to the car.

The door below me slammed shut and Carp came out, walking across the road to his motor bike, which was parked as usual against one of the old bollards. He was dressed in overalls with a thick cardigan over the top, the bald patch at the back of his head catching the sun.

Carp was the only Englishman we employed. He was an East Coast man, and that cardigan, or some form of woollen pullover, was never discarded until it was hot enough to melt the tar on the Martires Atlante opposite. He looked after our boats. His full name, of course, was Carpenter and he always left for the naval quay about this time of the morning. But instead of starting off immediately, he paused after jerking the bike off its stand, turning to look back at the driver of the Fiat.

For a moment the two of them were quite still, facing each other. Then the visitor reached out and opened the door of his car, ducking his head inside, searching for something, while Carp began to prop the bike up on its stand again. I thought he was going to speak to the man, but he seemed to think better of it. He shook his head slightly, half-shrugging as he kick-started the engine.

As soon as he was gone the visitor came out from the car's interior and shut the door again, standing quite still, watching until the motor bike disappeared round the bend by the restaurant. He was frowning, his rather square, clean-cut features suddenly creased with lines. He turned slowly, facing towards me, but not looking up, and he just stood there, still frowning, as though unable to make up his mind. Finally, almost reluctantly it seemed, he started across the road.

Our premises were the only buildings there, so I called down to him and asked if he wanted something from the chandlery.

He checked abruptly, head back, looking straight up at me. 'Am I too early?' He said it as though he would have been glad of an excuse to postpone his visit.

'The door's not locked,' I said.

He nodded, still standing there. Only a few years separate us in age, but at that first meeting he seemed very young.

'What is it you want?'

'Just a chart.' He said it quickly. 'Of Mahon and Fornells. And one of the island as a whole if you have it. Admiralty Charts 1466 and 1703.' He rattled the numbers off, then added, all in a rush, 'Are you Michael Steele?'

I nodded, looking beyond him to the sharp-cut shadows of the old hospital, the peace of the harbour, resenting his intrusion. It was such a lovely morning and I wanted to get out on the water.

'I think you know a Mr Philip Turner.' He said it hesitantly.

'Phil Turner?'

'Yes, owns a yacht called *Fizzabout*. If I could have a word with you . . .' His voice trailed away.

'All right, I'll come down.' Two years back I had skippered *Fizzabout* in the Middle Sea Race and Phil had laid up with us the following winter.

It was dark on the stairs after the sunlight. The bell over the door rang as he entered the chandlery and Soo called out to me from the kitchen to check that I was answering it. Ramón usually looked after this side of the business, but I had sent him over to Binicalaf Nou with the materials for a villa we were repainting. 'So you're a friend of Phil's,' I said as I reached the trestle table that did service as a counter.

There was a long pause, then he muttered, 'No, not exactly.' He was standing just inside the door, his back to the light and his face in shadow. 'It was Graham Wade suggested I contact you. He and Turner, they both belong to the Cruising Association. Have you met Wade?'

'I don't think so.'

Another long pause. 'No, I thought not.' And he just stood there as though he didn't know how to proceed.

'You wanted some charts,' I reminded him. 'The large-scale chart of Port Mahon and Fornells also gives details of the passage between Ibiza and Formentera.' I knew the details of it because there was a regular demand for that particular sheet. I produced it for him, also Chart 1703 which covers the whole of the Balearics. 'Where's your boat?' I asked him. 'At the Club Maritimo?'

He shook his head, and when I asked him where he was berthed, he said, 'I haven't got a boat.'

'You on a package tour then?'

'Not exactly.' He produced a wad of peseta notes and paid for the charts, but he didn't leave. 'Wade said you'd been living here quite a few years. He thought you'd be the best person to contact – to find out about the island.'

'What do you want to know?' I was curious then, wondering why he wanted charts when he hadn't got a boat.

He didn't give me a direct answer. 'Your wife, she's half Maltese, isn't she?' He said it awkwardly, and without waiting for a reply stumbled quickly on – 'I mean, you must know Malta pretty well.'

'I was born there,' I told him.

He nodded and I had the feeling he already knew that part of my background.

'Why? Do you know it?' I enquired.

'I've just come from there.' He glanced out of the window, his face catching the light and reminding me suddenly of Michelangelo's David in Florence, the same straight brows, broad forehead and the wavy, slightly curling hair. It was an attractive face, the classic mould only broken by the lines developing at the corners of mouth and eyes. 'Grand Harbour,' he said. 'It's not so big as Mahon.' His voice, still hesitant, had an undercurrent of accent I couldn't place.

'No. This is one of the biggest harbours in the Mediterranean. That's why Nelson was here.' I still thought he was connected with sailing in some way. 'It's not as big as Pylos on the west coast of the Peloponnese, of course, but more sheltered. The best of the lot I'd say.'

His eyes, glancing round the chandlery, returned to me. 'You've done a lot of sailing, have you? I mean, you know the Mediterranean?'

'Pretty well.'

He didn't pursue that. 'Wade said you rented out villas.'

'Depends when you want to rent. Our main business, apart from boats, is villa maintenance. We only own two villas ourselves and they're fairly well booked. I'll get my wife down if you like. She looks after the renting of them.'

But he was shaking his head. 'No, sorry – I'm not wanting to rent.'

'Then what do you want?' I asked, glancing rather pointedly at the clock on the wall.

'Nothing. Just the charts.' I had rolled them up for him and he reached out, but then changed his mind, pushing his hand into his hip pocket and coming up with a photograph. 'Have you met this man – on the island here?' He handed me the photograph. It was a full-face picture, head and shoulders, of a big, bearded man wearing a seaman's peaked cap, a scarf round his neck and what looked like an anorak or some sort of dark jacket.

'What makes you think I might have met him?' I asked.

'Wade thought, if he was here, perhaps he'd have chartered a yacht from you, or he might have come to you about renting a villa.'

'We haven't any yachts for charter, only an old converted fishing boat,' I told him. 'As for villas, there are thousands here, and a lot of people doing what we do – care and maintenance.' The man in the photograph looked as though he had seen a lot of life, a very strong face with big teeth showing through the beard, eyes deeply wrinkled at the corners and lines across the forehead. There was something about the eyes. They were wide and staring, so that they seemed to be looking out at the world with hostility. 'What's his name?' I asked.

He didn't reply for a moment, then he gave a little shrug. 'Evans. Patrick Evans. Or Jones. Sometimes Jones – it varies. I thought he might be in Malta.' He shook his head. 'Wade said if he wasn't in Malta I'd probably find him here.'

'He's Welsh, is he?' I was still looking down at the photograph, puzzled by something in that hard stare that seemed vaguely familiar. Then, because of the silence, I looked up. 'A friend of yours?'

He seemed to have some difficulty answering that, his eyes slipping away from me. 'I've met him,' he muttered vaguely, picking up the charts and tucking the roll under his arm. 'Let me know, will you, if he turns up.' And he added, 'You can keep the photograph.'

I asked him where I could get in touch with him and he scribbled his address on a sheet of paper I tore out of our receipts book. It was in Fornells, a private address, not a hotel. And he had written his name – Gareth Lloyd Jones. 'Perhaps we could have a drink together sometime,' he suggested. Then he was walking out with an easy, almost casual wave of the hand, all the hesitancy gone as though relieved to get away from me and out into the sunshine.

I watched him drive off and then my gaze returned to the photograph. Soo called down that coffee was ready.

Weekdays coffee was all we had in the morning. Sunday was the only day we treated ourselves to an English breakfast. I went back upstairs, and when I showed her the photograph, she said without a moment's hesitation, 'I'm sure he didn't have a beard.'

I took it to the window, looking at it in the clear sunlight, trying to visualise the man clean-shaven. 'The eyes were different, too,' she said, joining me at the window, the bulge of her pregnancy showing through the looseness of her dressing gown.

'Who is he?'

'Es Grau, don't you remember?' And she added, 'You're not concentrating.'

'How the hell can I?' I gave her bottom a smack, caught hold of one buttock and pulled her close so that her stomach was hard against me. 'Any kicks yet?'

She thrust herself clear, turning quickly and pouring the coffee. 'He was in that little bar-restaurant where they haul the boats up. It was raining and we had a cup of coffee and a Quinta there after we'd looked at that villa out near S'Albufera. Now do you remember? He was with two or three Menorquins.'

She poured me my coffee and I stood sipping it, staring down at the photograph. I remembered the man now, but only vaguely. I had been more interested in the other two. One was Ismail Fuxá. I had never met him, but I had recognised him instantly from pictures in the local press. He was a member of the *Partido Socialista*, on the extreme left of the party and very active politically. My attention, however, had been focused on the little man sitting with his back to the window. I was almost certain he was the fellow I had chased one evening out near Binicalaf Nou. It had been dusk and I had stopped off to check one of the two villas we had under care in that neighbourhood. As I let myself in through the front door he had jumped out of a side window. He had had to run right past me and I had had a brief glimpse of his face looking scared. I went after him of course, but he had a motor bike parked down the dirt road and he'd got away from me.

When I returned to the villa and went into the big downstairs room I found he had sprayed URBANIZAR ES DESTRUIER right across one wall, and below that the letters SALV . . . I knew the rest of it by heart, so many villas had been sprayed with it – SALVEMO MENORCA. 'Yes,' I said. 'I remember now. But it was months ago, last autumn.' I was thinking of all that had happened since, the orchestrated build-up of hostility by the separatists. 'That was the first,' I added, gazing out at the limpid harbour water where a cruise ship showed white against the far shore.

'The first what?' Her back was turned as she filled her cup.

'The first of our villas to be daubed.'

'They've only sprayed two of them, and they're not ours anyway. We only look after them.' She turned, cup in hand, pushing her dog out of the way with a bare foot. It was a basenji so we called it Benjie and it slept on her bed, a pleasant little fellow all dressed in *café-au-lait* with a long, serious head, a perpetual frown, spindly legs and a curlycue of a tail. It was barkless and I could never understand the purpose of a dog that was a virtual mute. 'I've got something in mind,' she said. 'I want to talk to you about it.'

I knew what was coming then and turned my back on her, gazing out of the window again. 'Just look at it!'

'Look at what? You haven't been listening.'

'The morning,' I said. 'The sun on the water, everything crystal bright.' And I began to sing, '*Oh, what a bootiful mornin', Oh, what a bootiful day* . . . Remember that moonlit evening in the courtyard of your mother's house, the old gramophone?' I tried to grab her, thinking to take her mind off her obsession with property. But she evaded me, eyes gone black and suddenly wide, hands across her belly. 'Go on,' she said. 'Finish it, why don't you?'

'*I got a bootiful feelin', Everything's goin' ma way.*'

She came back to the window then, gazing out, but not seeing the sunshine or the golden gleam of the water. 'That's the feeling I've got,' she said, and she was looking straight at me. 'Miguel rang last night.' I could see it in her eyes. For weeks she had been on at me to take advantage of the rash of villas that had recently come on to the market. She put her cup down, then turned to face me again. 'It was just before you came in. I didn't tell you because we were already late for the Rawlings', and afterwards . . . Well, it wasn't the moment, was it?'

'What did Miguel want?' Miguel Gallardo was the contractor we used when there was maintenance work we couldn't handle ourselves. He was now building a villa out on Punta Codolar, a bare, bleak headland in the north of the island that was crisscrossed with the half-completed roads of a new *urbanización*.

'He needs help,' she said.

'Money?'

She nodded. 'It's all this build-up of trouble in the Med, of course – Libya in particular. The American he's building for has suddenly got cold feet and wants out. He's offering Miguel the whole place in lieu of what he owes him.' She reached out, her fingers gripping my arm as though she had hold of the villa already. 'I had a look at it with Petra when you were delivering that boat to Ajaccio, and now he says we can have it, as it stands, at cost. We pay Miguel's account, and that's that – it's ours.' She gave me the figure then, adding, 'It's a chance in a million, Mike.'

'Miguel to complete, of course.'

'Well, that's only fair.'

'It's barely half-completed, remember.' But it wasn't the cost of completion I was thinking about. It was the political tension building up locally. 'There's been windows broken, one villa set on fire, another smashed down by a runaway road roller . . .'

'That's just a passing phase.' I shook my head, but she went on quickly: 'It won't last, and when the panic is over, a lot of people will be cursing themselves for putting their villas on the market at knockdown prices. I'm thinking of the future.' The cups and plaques on the shelves behind her glimmered bright with memories of days gone. What future? She kept them so well polished I sometimes felt it was the crack shot, the Olympic sailor, the image she had of me, not myself, not the essential lazy, mediocre, ill-educated – oh hell, what deadly blows life deals to a man's self-confidence! Maybe she was right, polish the mirror-bright image, retain the front intact and forget the human freight behind. And now she wasn't thinking of us, only of the child. She had less than two months to go, and if this was another boy, and he lived . . . I hesitated, looking out to the bay. She had a good head for business and a highly developed sense for property, but politically – she was a fool politically. 'It's too lovely a day to argue,' I said, thinking of the smell of cut grass on the Bisley Ranges, the whiff of cordite in the hot air, gun oil and the targets shimmering.

'You're going sailing, is that it?' Her tone had sharpened.

A bit of a breeze was coming in, ruffling the water so that the surface of the harbour had darkened. She had always resented the sailing side of my life, my sudden absences. 'I'll take the dinghy, and if the wind holds I'll sail across to Bloody Island, see how the dig's going. You coming?' She enjoyed day sailing, for picnics and when the weather was fine.

'Petra's not there,' she said.

The phone rang and she answered it, speaking swiftly in Spanish. A long silence as she listened. Then she turned to me, her hand over the mouthpiece. 'It's Miguel. He's had a firm offer.'

The bell sounded from below and a voice called to me urgently from the chandlery. 'Tell him to take it then,' I said as I went down the stairs to find Ramón standing at the back of the workshop by the storeroom door, his teeth showing long and pointed as he smiled nervously. He had picked up Lennie, the Australian who did most of our repainting, but when they had arrived at the villa near Binicalaf Nou they had found the patio door ajar. It had been forced open and one of the bedrooms had been occupied. Both beds had been used, sheets and blankets grubby with dirt, a filthy pile of discarded clothes lying in a corner, and in the bathroom a tap left running, the basin overflowing, the floor awash. He had left Lennie clearing up the mess and had come back to pick up lime, cement and sand, all the materials they would need to replaster the kitchen ceiling immediately below.

We went through into the store, which was virtually a cave hacked out of the cliff that formed the back wall of the building. I don't know what it had been originally, probably a fisherman's boathouse, but it was bone dry and very secure, almost like having a private vault. As we went in Ramón said, 'No good, these people, señor. They make much dirt.' And he added, 'I not like.' His long face was tight-lipped and uneasy.

If only I had gone for a sail earlier . . . But it would probably have made no difference. There are days in one's life, moments even, when a whole series of small happenings come together in such a way that in retrospect one can say, that was the start of it. But only in retrospect. At the time I was just angry at the way Soo had acted. Instead of telling Miguel to take the offer, she had called out to me as she put the phone down, 'I've told him we'll match it.' She came halfway down the stairs then, clutching at the guard rope, her eyes bright, her mouth set in that funny way of hers that produced holes like dimples at the corners of her mouth, adding breathlessly, 'I'm sure we'll get it now. I'm sure we will.'

I was on my way out to the car with a cardboard box of the things Lennie would need and I stood there, staring up at her flushed, excited face, thinking how quickly one's life can be caught up in a web of material responsibilities so that there is no time left for the things one really wants to do. But it was no use arguing with her in that mood, her big, very white teeth almost clenched with determination, and in the end I went out, kicking the door to behind me.

My anger drained away as I headed out of Mahon on the San Clemente road, the sun a welcome change after weeks of cloud and blustery outbreaks of rain. The sudden warmth had brought the wild flowers out, the green of the fields a chequerboard of colour, yellow mainly, but here and there white splashes of narcissi. And there were kites hanging in the blue of the sky.

I passed the talayots by Binicalaf, my spirits lifting as they always did approaching this area of concentrated megalithic remains, the stone beehive-like mounds standing sharply outlined. The place where Lennie was working was on a track to the west of Cales Coves. It was about the nicest of the fifty or so villas we looked after. From the main bedroom you could just see the first of the coves, the cliffs beyond showing the gaping holes of several caves. He had cleared up most of the mess by the time I arrived, the sodden plaster stripped from the kitchen ceiling. It could have been worse, but it was unfortunate the squatters had picked on this particular villa, the owner being a man who argued over almost every item on his account. 'Where are the clothes they left behind?' I asked, wondering whether it was worth bringing the *Guardia* into it.

Lennie showed me a dirt-encrusted bundle of discarded clothing. He had been over it carefully, but had found nothing to indicate who the men were. 'Looks like they been digging. Two of them, I reck'n.' He thought perhaps the rains had flushed them out of one of the caves. Some of the old cave dwellings were still used and in summer there were women as well as men in them, kids too, often as not the whole family wandering about stark naked. 'It's like snakes out in the bush,' he muttered, holding up a filthy remnant of patched jeans. 'Always discarding their old skin. There's usually bits and pieces of worn-out rag below the cave entrances.'

In the circumstances there didn't seem much point in notifying the authorities. Lennie agreed. 'What the hell can they do? Anyway, look at it from their point of view, why should they bother? It's another foreign villa broken into, that's all. Who cares?' And then, as I was leaving, he suddenly said, 'That girl you're so keen on, mate –' and he grinned at me slyly. 'The archy-logical piece wot's digging over by the old hospital . . .' He paused there, his pale eyes narrowed, watching for my reaction.

He was referring to Petra, of course. The huge, hulking ruins of the old hospital were what had given Illa del Rei the nickname of Bloody Island. 'Well, go on,' I said. 'What about her?'

'Workmen up the road say they've seen her several times. I was asking them about these two bastards.' He tossed the bundle of rags into the back of my estate car. 'They couldn't tell me a damned thing, only that a girl in a Der Chevoh had been going into one of the caves. And this morning, just after Ramón and I got here, she come skidding to a halt wanting to know where she could find you. She was bright-eyed as a cricket, all steamed up about something.'

'Did she say what?'

He shook his head, the leathery skin of his face stretched in a grin. 'You want to watch it, mate. You go wandering around in them caves alone with a sheila like that and you'll get yourself thrown out of the house – straight into the drink, I wouldn't wonder.'

'Soo wouldn't even notice.' I couldn't help it, my voice suddenly giving vent to my anger. 'She's just bought a villa and now I've got to go over there and sort out the details.'

'Don't push your luck,' he said, suddenly serious. He looked then, as he often did, like an elderly tortoise. 'You go taking that girl on your next delivery run . . . Yeah, you thought I didn't hear, but I was right there in the back of the shop when she asked you. You do that and Soo'd notice all right.'

I caught hold of his shoulder then, shaking him. 'You let your sense of humour run away with you sometimes. This isn't the moment to have Soo getting upset.'

'Okay then, mum's the word.' And he gave that high-pitched, cackling laugh of his. Christ! I could have hit the man, he was so damned aggravating at times, and I was on a short fuse anyway. I had been going through a bad patch with Soo ever since she'd found she was pregnant again. She was worried, of course, and knowing how I felt about having a kid around the place, a boy I could teach to sail . . .

I was thinking about that as I drove north across the island to Punta Codolar, about Lennie, too, how tiresome he could be. Half Cockney, half Irish, claiming his name was McKay and with a passport to prove it, we knew no more of his background than when he had landed from the Barcelona ferry almost two years ago with nothing but the clothes he stood up in and an elderly squeezebox wrapped in a piece of sacking. I had found him playing for his supper at one of the quayside restaurants, a small terrier of a man with something appealing about him, and when I had said I needed an extra hand scrubbing the bottoms of the boats we were fitting out, he had simply said, 'Okay, mate.' And that was that. He had been with us ever since, and because he was a trained scuba diver he was soon indispensable, being able to handle yachts with underwater problems without their having to be lifted out of the water. It was just after Soo had lost the child and she had taken to him as she would have to any stray, regarding him virtually as one of the family.

While the distance between Port Mahon in the east and the old capital of Ciudadela in the west is at least fifty kilometres, driving across the island from south to north it is only about twenty. Even so it always seems longer, for the road is narrow and winding and you have to go through Alayór, which is the third largest town and the central hub of the island. I toyed with the idea of dropping off at the Flórez garage to see if I could get him to increase his offer for the *Santa Maria*. Juan Flórez, besides being *alcalde*, or mayor of the town, ran the largest garage outside of Mahon and was a very sharp dealer in almost anything anybody cared to sell that was worth a good percentage in commission. For the past few months he had been trying to persuade me to part with the old fishing boat I let out on charter. But the sun was shining, so I drove straight across the main Ciudadela-Mahon road and up through the old town to the Fornells road.

Here the country changes very noticeably, the earth suddenly becoming a dark red, and away to the left, Monte Toro, the highest point on Menorca, the only 'mountain' in fact, with its rocky peak capped by the white of the Sanctuary buildings and the army communications mast dominating the whole countryside, red soil giving way to gravel after a few kilometres, cultivated fields to pines and maquis, the scent of resin and rosemary filling the car.

It is the constant variety of the scene in such a small island that had attracted us in the first place, particularly Soo after living most of her life on an island that is about the same size, but solidly limestone with very little variation. Just short of Macaret, and in sight of the sea again, I turned left on to the road to Arenal d'en Castell, a beautiful, almost perfectly horseshoe-shaped bay of sand totally ruined by three concrete block hotels. Beyond the bay, on the eastern side, a rocky cape that had once been hard walking was now crisscrossed with half-finished roads so that one could drive over most of it. The few villas that had been built so far looked very lost in the wild expanse of heath and bare, jagged rock.

The villa Miguel Gallardo was now building stood right on the point, a little south and east of one he had completed two years before. There was a turning place nearby, but instead of swinging round it, I edged the car into the cul-de-sac beyond where it dipped steeply to the cliff edge.

A tramontana was beginning to blow and even before I had switched the engine off I could hear the break of the waves two hundred feet or so below. I sat there for a moment, looking out towards the coast of France, remembering how it had been two years ago when I had taken a boat over to Genoa and a tramontana had caught us, a full gale, straight off the Alps and as cold as hell. We had been lucky to get away with it, the boat leaking and one of the spreaders broken so that we could only sail on the port tack.

I put the handbrake hard on, turned the wheels into the rubble of rock at the roadside and got out of the car, the breeze ruffling my hair, the salt air filling my lungs. God! It felt good, and I stretched my arms. There were little puffs of cloud on the horizon, the scene very different from the quiet of the southern coast, no protection at all. The *urbanización*, when it was built, would be facing the open sea and the full brunt of the north winds, so why the hell buy a villa here? I tried to see it in summer, all white stucco and red tiles, cacti on the retaining wall, passion flowers and bougainvillaea, with trailers of morning-glory over a Moroccan-style façade. It would be cool in summer and a breathtaking view, the dreadful hotels of Arenal d'en Castell hidden by the headland and the rock coast stretching east all the way to the lighthouse of Favàritx on the dragon-toothed finger of land after which it was named.

The engine of Miguel's cement mixer started into life and I climbed back up the slope, making for the gaunt skeletal structure of the half-completed villa. He was waiting for me at the foot of a ladder lashed to the wooden scaffolding. '*Buenos dias.* You come to inspect, eh?' He was a thickset man with a long, doleful face and a big hooked nose. He was from Granada, from the Arab district of Albacein, and claimed kinship with both Moors and Jews, his family going back five centuries to Ferdinand and Isabella and the Inquisition that followed their conquest of the last Moorish stronghold in Europe. 'Iss your property now.' He said it hesitantly, seeking confirmation, the inflexion of his voice making it a question rather than a statement.

'Let's have a look at it,' I said.

I saw the sudden doubt in his eyes, his dark, unshaven features solemn and uneasy. 'Okay, señor.' The formality was a measure of his unease. He normally called me by my Christian name. 'But you have seen it before, also the plans.'

'I didn't know I was buying it then.'

'And now you are?' Again the question in his voice, the dark eyes watching me, his broad forehead creased in a frown.

'Let's have a look at it,' I said again. 'Starting at the top.'

He shrugged, motioning me to go ahead of him. The scaffolding shook as we climbed to the first storey, the heat-dried wooden poles lashed with ropes. Everything — boards, scaffolding, ladders — was coated with a dusting of cement that only half-concealed the age-old layers of splashed paint. A younger brother, Antoni, and a cousin whose name I could not remember, were rendering the southern face of the building.

'It will be a very beautiful villa,' Miguel said tentatively. 'When we have finished it, you will see, it will look — pretty good, eh?' He prided himself on his English.

We climbed to the top, and he stood there looking about him. He was one of a family of thirteen. Back in Granada his father had a tiny little jewellery shop in one of those alleys behind the Capila Real, mostly second-hand stuff, the window full of watches with paper tags on them. I think his real business was money-lending, the contents of the shop largely personal items that had been pawned. '*Buena vista*, eh?' And Miguel added, 'You can have a garden here. The roof is flat, you see. And the lookout . . . all that sea.' His tone had brightened, knowing I was a sailor.

'There is also a fine view of the water tanks on the top of those bloody hotels at Arenal d'en Castell.'

'You grow some vines, you never see them.'

'In tubs and trained over a trellis? Come off it, Miguel. The first puff of wind out of the north . . .'

He looked away uncomfortably, knowing how exposed the position was. 'It will be nice and cool in summer. It was good here when we make the foundations.'

We worked our way down to the ground floor, which was almost finished. He was using one of the rooms as an office and we went over the costings. I suggested certain adjustments, chiefly to the lighting, cut out the air-conditioning and one or two other luxuries I considered unnecessary, agreed a price for completion, and we shook hands on it.

There was never any need to have Miguel put anything into writing. His family had been small traders on the banks of the Darro and in the Plaza Bib-Rambla for generations. I had first met him when he was filling in as a guide to the Alhambra Palace and the Generalife. Then a few days later I had found him working on repairs to a building near his home, which was in the Cuesta Yesqueros, a stepped alley running steeply up the hillside opposite the old Puerta Monaita. I was staying at the Alhambra Palace Hotel at the time, waiting for an Italian to turn up who owed me quite a lot of money, and to this day I have no idea whether I was the cause of Miguel shifting to Menorca or not. He has never mentioned it, but I think it highly probable.

'Who was it made you the offer my wife agreed to match?' I asked him as he accompanied me back to the car. 'Or did you make that up?'

'No, of course I don't make up.' He glared at me angrily. 'You know me too long to think I play games like that.'

'Well then, who was it?'

'Somebody I don't trust so much.'

I got it out of him in the end. It was Flórez. And then, as

I was settling myself behind the wheel, he leaned forward, peering in over my shoulder at the back seat, his eyes narrowed and a frown on his face. 'A friend of yours?'

I turned to find I had tossed the photograph Lloyd Jones had left with me into the back and it was lying there face-up. 'You know him, do you?' I asked.

He shook his head, the frown deepening.

'It was probably taken some time ago,' I told him. 'He may not have a beard now.'

'No beard, eh?' I saw the dawn of recognition in his eyes and he nodded. '*Si. No barba.*' He looked at me then. 'Who is, plees?'

'You've seen him, have you?'

He glanced at the picture again, then nodded emphatically.

'When?'

'A month ago, maybe more. He come here and look over the work. Says he knows the owner and he want to see the progress we make in the construction of the villa as he is thinking he will make Señor Wilkins an offer.'

'Did he say how much he was prepared to offer?'

'No, he don't say.'

'What was his name? Do you remember?'

But he shook his head. He had been into Macaret that day to phone his suppliers and he had come back to find the man standing on the scaffold's upper staging staring eastward, out towards Faváritx. It was only when he had asked him what he was doing there that the man said anything about making an offer.

'And he didn't give his name?'

'No. I ask him, but he don't answer me. Instead, he speak of making Señor Wilkins an offer. I have not seen him since that day.'

He couldn't tell me anything else and I drove off after confirming that I'd get my lawyer to draw up something we could both sign. A bank of cloud was spreading across the sky, and as I approached the main Mahon-Fornells road the sun went in. The still beauty of the morning was gone and I gave up any thought of sailing. Instead, I headed westward through the pines to Fornells.

Ever since Lloyd Jones had given me the address where he was staying I had been puzzled as to why he had chosen the place. Fornells is a little fishing port almost halfway along the north coast. It has the second largest inlet, five of the best fish restaurants on the island and is the Menorquins' favourite place for Sunday lunch. Who had told him about it? I wondered. Since he wasn't staying at a hotel, and had clearly never been to Menorca before, Phil or Wade, somebody, must have told him about the private lodgings where he was staying in the Calle des Moli.

I kept to the main street through Fornells and asked my way of a waiter I knew who was leaning against the door of the restaurant that stands back from the harbour. The Calle des Moli proved to be a narrow little back street leading nowhere, except to the remains of a windmill and a bare hill topped by one of those stone round towers that dominate several of the island's headlands. The houses were small and stood shoulder-to-shoulder, their doors opening straight on to the street.

I left my car in the Plaza de Pedro M. Cardona. The address he had given me was near the top end, the door standing open and a little girl sitting on the step nursing a rag doll. The woman who answered my knock was big and florid. *'El señor Inglés!'* She shook her head. I had just missed him. He had been out all morning, had returned about half an hour ago and had then gone out again almost immediately, leaving his car parked in the street. She indicated the small red Fiat parked a few doors up.

I glanced at my watch and was surprised to find the morning had gone. It was already past noon and since she said she didn't provide meals for her visitors, and he had left his car, I presumed he was lunching at one of the restaurants in the port. I asked her how long he had been staying at her house and she said he had arrived the previous afternoon about five-thirty. No, he hadn't booked in advance. There was no necessity since it was early in the year for visitors.

I produced the photograph then, but she shook her head. She had never seen the man, and she didn't know how long her visitor would be staying, so I left her and drove back to the harbour where I found him at a table outside the better of the two waterfront restaurants. He was alone, bent over one of the charts I had sold him, which was neatly folded and propped against the carafe of wine in front of him. He looked up quickly at my greeting, then half rose to his feet. I pulled up a chair and sat down, enquiring whether he had had a rewarding morning.

He nodded vaguely, telling me that since I had last seen him he had driven round Villa Carlos, then on to the little inlet of St Esteve immediately to the south, had had a look at the tunnelled redoubt known as Marlborough's Fort, and finally, before coming back to Fornells for lunch, he had been all round the small fishing port of Es Grau to the north of Mahon. He spoke quickly, giving me a very precise inventory of his morning's tour as though he were making a report, and all the time he was staring past me, out towards the light at the end of the eastern arm of the harbour. There was a girl in a wet suit board-sailing across the entrance, a glistening, statuesque figure, the orange sail bright in the sun. But I don't think he saw her. I had a strange feeling he was talking for the sake of talking, as though he sensed what I had come to tell him and was putting it off.

The waiter appeared with a plate of four large mussels cooked with herbs and garlic. 'Will you join me?' The clouds were gone now and it was quite warm again sitting there in the sun, the town and the hill behind it sheltering us from the wind. I nodded and he said, '*Dos*,' holding up two fingers in case he had not made his meaning clear. After that he didn't say anything, the silence hanging heavy in the air as the waiter filled a glass for me. When he was gone I produced the photograph. 'When was that taken?' I asked him.

He shook his head. 'Several years ago, I imagine.'

'Is he a seaman? He certainly looks like one with that peaked cap.'

He didn't say anything.

'What's he do for a living then?'

He gave a little shrug, his head turned towards the harbour entrance again.

'But you do know him?'

'Of course.' He hesitated, then he added, 'We were at school together, you see.'

'You know him quite well then?'

'Well enough.' The words seemed forced out of him. 'He saved my life – not once, but twice.' His eyes were blank, his mind turned inwards.

'He hasn't got a beard now,' I said.

He turned his head then, a quick movement, his eyes staring straight at me, hard now and grey in the sunshine. 'You've seen him.' It wasn't a question. He knew, and suddenly he seemed a different man, no longer hesitant, his voice sharper, a note of authority in it. 'When? Recently? Within the last few days?'

'No. Several months ago.' And I told him about the three men Soo and I had seen that filthy wet day when we had gone into the bar-restaurant at Es Grau, and how Miguel had seen him more recently.

'Where?'

'On Punta Codolar.' And I told him about the villa Miguel was working on.

'Punta Codolar. Where's that? Show me.' He turned the chart towards me, but I pushed it away.

'It's only a few miles from here, the next headland to the east.'

'And he was at this villa. How long ago, did your builder friend say?'

'About a month.'

'He made an offer for it, for a half-finished villa?'

'So Miguel said.'

He opened the chart up, his stubby finger stabbing at the irregular shape of Punta Codolar. 'Why? Did he say why?' He didn't wait for me to answer, shaking his head – 'No. No of course not, he wouldn't tell you that. But the headland there is the western arm of Macaret and Port d'Addaia.' After that he didn't say anything. He seemed quite stunned, his eyes staring past me, seeing nothing.

'Better eat those while they're hot,' I said, indicating the *mejillones* in the little dish in front of him. 'They're very good, but it's important they should be piping hot.'

He nodded, picking up the small spoon and digging a mussel out of its shell, the movement quite automatic, his mind still far away. 'And you haven't seen him since the autumn?'

'No.'

'But the builder fellow saw him about a month ago. Has he seen him at all since then?'

'I don't think so. Miguel would have said if he had.'

'A month ago.' He repeated it slowly, chewing over a mussel, his eyes screwed up against the sun. 'And he was clean-shaven.' He gave a long sigh as though I had saddled him with some impossible burden. 'And when you and your wife saw him in that bar, who were the two men he was with – you said something about their being politically motivated. What exactly did you mean?'

I explained then about Ismail Fuxá, that he was supposed to be one of the leaders of the separatist movement.

'An activist?'

'I think so. But he keeps in the background.'

'And the other man?'

'I can't be certain,' I said, 'but he looked very much like a man I had surprised paint-spraying a slogan on the living-room wall of a villa we look after.' I started to explain how I'd only caught a glimpse of him, but he interrupted me.

35

'Where was this? Where's the villa he daubed?'

'Between Binicalaf and Binicalaf Nou.'

'Those names mean nothing to me.' He opened the chart out. 'Could you show me please.' I pointed to the position of the villa and he said, 'That's on the south side of the island, the opposite coast to Macaret. There's an inlet there.' He turned the map sideways so that he could read the name. 'Cales Coves. Do you know it?'

'Of course,' I said. 'I've sailed in there quite a few times. There are two inlets in fact, that's why Cales is plural. Coves refers to the caves.'

'I suppose you know just about all the inlets round Menorca.'

'Well, not quite all. There are over a hundred and fifty of them and not all are suitable for a deep-draught boat.' He enquired what sort of boat I had and when I said it was an old fishing boat, he asked me whether I hired it out to visitors.

'In the summer, yes,' I told him. 'The *Santa Maria* is not the ideal craft for charter work, but the sort of yacht I need to make that part of the business pay calls for far more money than we can afford. It's a risky game, a lot of competition.' He seemed more relaxed now, as though he had got used to the idea that the man he was trying to catch up with had been seen on the island. More mussels arrived and another carafe of wine, and he began asking me about other inlets to the south, particularly those closest to Mahon. Except for St Esteve he had only looked at the inlets to the north.

'How long have you been here?'

'Two days.'

The first day he had spent taking over his hire car and having a look at the peninsula that forms the northern arm of Port Mahon, the land that provided the view from our office window.

'What about the megalithic remains,' I asked him – 'the taulas, talayots and navetas?'

36

But he hadn't seen any of that, and I don't think he took it in when I told him the whole of Menorca was more or less an open-air archaeological museum. All he wanted me to talk about was the little ports and coves. For a man who hadn't got a boat, and who wasn't involved in sailing, it struck me as odd. I got to my feet, telling him I was going to phone my wife. 'I'll join you for lunch if I may, it's too late to go back home.'

When I got through to Soo she said she had Petra with her. 'She's waiting for the boat, and, Mike – she wants to take you into a cave over by Cales Coves.'

'I know,' I said. 'Lennie told me. Said she was very excited about something. Has she told you what it is?'

'No. She can't explain it, you've got to see it, she says.'

I offered to return to Binicalaf and meet her there after lunch, but she said Petra had to get back to camp to get herself organised for the evening. 'You haven't forgotten we asked her to the Red Cross do tonight, have you?' There was the sound of muffled voices, then Soo added, 'She says she'll try and explain it to us this evening.' And then she was asking me about my meeting with Miguel.

When I got back to the table Lloyd Jones had refilled my glass and was sitting with his head in his hands staring fixedly out to sea. He didn't look up as I sat down. The girl was still balanced on her sailboard, gliding effortlessly in towards the steps. Even then he didn't see her, while I was thinking how nice it would have been to have had her as a pupil when I was running my sailboard courses. 'Have you ordered?' I asked. The *mejillones* were merely an appetiser.

He shook his head. 'You know the place. Whatever you advise.' He didn't seem to care what he had, his mind far away, lost in his own thoughts.

I ordered *zarzuella* for us both, and because he didn't seem inclined to conversation, I began telling him a little about the megalithic remains and the hypostilic chamber

Petra Callis was excavating by the fallen dolmen on Bloody Island.

The food arrived almost immediately, and because *zarzuella* is roughly a stew of mixed fish in a piquant sauce, we were too busy dealing with the bones to do much talking. He wasn't interested in Bronze Age remains anyway, and as soon as he had finished he pushed his plate aside and spread the chart out again. He thought he would have a look at the other side of the island after lunch. Somebody had told him about the Xorai caves above Cala en Porter.

'They're strictly for the tourists,' I told him. 'Anyway, they're not open at this time of year. If you want to see caves, you'd much better look into Cales Coves.' And because the track down to the first inlet isn't easy to find I gave him instructions how to get there.

He thought about that, concentrating on the chart. And then suddenly he asked me which of all the inlets on Menorca I would choose if I had to land something secretly from a boat, something to be delivered to Mahon.

It was so unexpected that I stared at him, wondering what the hell he had in mind. 'Are we talking about contraband?'

He hesitated. 'Yes, I suppose we are.' And he added, 'If you were going to land something secretly –' His eyes were looking directly at me then. 'You ever run anything like that?'

I didn't say anything, suddenly wary. It was a long time ago, before I was married.

'If you had, I mean,' he said quickly, 'where would you have landed the stuff?' The tone of his voice had sharpened, so that it crossed my mind he could be a customs man attached to Interpol or something like that, his manner so abruptly changed to one of alertness, those grey eyes of his catching the sun again as hard as glass as they stared into mine. 'Well, where? I need to know.'

'Why?'

'That man you saw at Es Grau –' He stopped there. 'Well, where would you land it?'

By then I'd decided this was getting a little dangerous and I kept my mouth shut.

'I'm talking hypothetically, of course,' he went on. 'Let's say it's TV sets, something like that – something fairly heavy, fairly bulky ... What about Cales Coves? You mentioned cave dwellings.'

I shook my head. 'Those caves are in the cliffs, at least all those that look directly out on to the water, so you'd have to haul everything up. And then you wouldn't be able to get the stuff ashore – I don't think any of them have a landward entrance. They're just holes in the cliff face or up in the sides of the ravine that leads down into the twin coves.'

'So where would you land it?'

He went on questioning me like that, claiming it was all hypothetical and the motivation nothing but his curiosity. At least it made for conversation. He no longer sat in silence brooding over whatever it was that filled his mind, and as he questioned me about the sparsely inhabited north coast to the west of Fornells, he made entries on the chart against each of the coves I mentioned, his writing small and very neat. In the end he shook his head. 'It would have to be closer to Mahon, wouldn't it – a short drive on a good road.' His pen shifted eastward across the great headland opposite where we were sitting. 'What about Arenal d'en Castell?' And when I told him it was overlooked by three large hotels, he asked about the two big bays south of Favāritx.

'Too rocky,' I told him. 'But Addaia – you go in there, almost to the end, and there's a new quay not yet finished, the place still quite wild and more or less deserted.'

'Not overlooked?'

'Two or three fishermen's houses converted to summer homes, that's all.'

'I don't see any quay shown on the chart.' I marked the

position of it for him and he stared at it, finally nodding his head. 'I'll have a look at that after I've seen those cliff caves.' He called for the bill and got to his feet. 'That boat of yours. Has it got an echo-sounder?'

'Of course. VHF, too, a big chart table, bunks for six . . .'

'How much if I want to charter it – for a day, say?'

I told him it depended whether it was a bareboat charter or fully stocked and crewed.

'Just you and me.' And then he seemed to change his mind. 'Forget it. Just an idea.' He settled the bill, insisting I was his guest, and on the spur of the moment, as we were walking to the cars, I asked him whether he would care to join us at the Red Cross party that evening. 'It's run by a Menorquin friend of ours, Manuela Renato,' I told him. 'Usually it's at a dance hall and restaurant beyond Villa Carlos, but this year she's organised it in the Quarries just above where we live. Should be quite fun – barbecue, bonfire, dancing, fireworks, all in a huge great rock chamber that looks like something hacked out for the tomb of a pharaoh.'

Why I should have asked him, God knows. Curiosity, I suppose. The man was under pressure, I could see it in his eyes, something hanging over him. And the photograph. I tried to recall the scene in that bar, but Soo and I had been discussing the villa we had just looked over, and it was only when the three of them were putting on their coats and going out into the rain that I really took any notice of them.

We had reached my car and I stood there waiting for his answer, trying to figure out from the hard jut of his chin, the shape of that short neck and the solid head, the lines at the corners of eyes and mouth, what sort of a man he really was. What did he do for a living? Above all, why was he here?

'All right,' he said finally. 'I'll come.' He didn't thank me, his acceptance almost grudging, as though he felt he shouldn't be wasting his time on such frivolities.

40

'Good,' I said. 'That's settled then. Eight-thirty at our place.' And I got into my car, never dreaming that my casual invitation would be the catalyst to something that would get completely out of hand.

He wasn't looking at me as I backed away from the water's edge and drove off. He had turned his head towards the harbour entrance again and was standing there, quite still, staring towards the horizon with an intensity that left me with the odd feeling that he was expecting some visitation from the sea.

The road from Fornells enters the outskirts of Mahon at the opposite end to where we live, and instead of heading straight along the waterfront, past the *Aduana*, the Customs House, and the commercial wharf, I turned left and drove out on to the naval quay where the boats we had laid up out of the water were parked. I drove straight up to the elderly Hillyard we were working on and called up to Carp. The Danish owner, who had picked the boat up cheap in Palma the previous autumn, had phoned me just before Christmas and I had promised to have it ready in time for him to leave for a family cruise in the Greek islands at Easter. We had left it a little late, particularly as there was a new engine to be installed.

I called again as I started up the ladder and Carp's tonsured head popped out of the wheelhouse. He was his usual gloomy self as he showed me another frame with its fastenings gone, also at least three deck beams that needed replacement. 'Won't ever finish in time, will we?' he grumbled as he indicated one of the knees rotted where water had been seeping from the deck above. 'And the engine still to be fiddled in, all the rigging. I'll 'ave to take Rod off of the American boat for that.'

I told him that was impossible. He already had Luis varnishing the brightwork. With Rodriguez, that would make two of our locals, as well as himself, working on the one boat. 'Well,' he said, looking me straight in the face, 'd'you want 'er finished on time, or don't you?' And he added, 'Up to you. I didn't promise nothing.'

In the end I agreed, as he knew I would. And all the time we were talking I had the feeling there was something else on his mind. It wasn't until I was leaving that he suddenly blurted it out – 'That man outside the shop this morning – did you see him? A little red car. He was there just as I left. Did he come into the shop?'

I was on the ladder then, beginning to climb down, my face almost level with the deck. 'Yes. I sold him a couple of charts.'

'Did he say who he was?' I told him the man's name and he nodded. 'Thort so. He must have recognised me, but he didn't want to know me, did he, so I thort I was mistaken.' He leaned out towards me. 'If it wasn't for me that man would've died of cold. Well, not just me. There was four of us in the pilot boat, see, but it was me wot cut him down off the Woodbridge Haven buoy. Did he give you any sort of rank?'

'No,' I said, curious now and climbing back up the ladder.

'Mebbe he hasn't got one now. There was a lot of talk at the time.'

'About what?'

'Well, it was an arms run, wasn't it, and he was a Navy lieutenant.' And then he was telling me the whole story, how the Deben pilot at Felixstowe Ferry had seen something odd fixed to the Haven buoy and the four of them had gone out in the dawn to find a man fully clothed and tied to the side of the buoy with a mooring line. 'Poor bastard. We thort he were dead. Cold as buggery off the bar it was, the wind out of the north and beginning to whip up quite a sea. Then later, when he's out of hospital, he comes and buys us all a pint or two in the Ferryboat, so he knows bloody well I was one of those that rescued him. Funny!' he said. 'I mean, you'd think he'd come and say hullo, wouldn't you? I'd seen 'im before, too. When he

42

were a little runt of a fella living with a no-good couple and their son on an old 'ouseboat in a mud creek back of the Ferryboat, an' I wasn't the only one that recognised him. That's what started tongues wagging.'

'How do you mean?'

'Well, you bin there, when you was looking for a boat that spring. You know wot it's like there, an' a couple of kids, no proper man to control them. They broke into a yacht moored back of the Horse Sand and got at the drink locker. No harm done, but later they had a go at the RAF mess over at Bawdsey – for a lark they said. People remember that sort of thing.'

I didn't see what he was getting at. 'What's that got to do with arms-running?' I asked. 'You said something about arms-running.'

'That's right. But we didn't know about that at the time, did we? There was just a lot of rumours flying about on account of strangers poking around in the mud at the entrance to the King's Fleet. Then, after those terrorist attacks on police stations at Liverpool and Glasgow, and on that court in Clerkenwell, the papers were full of it. This Lieutenant Jones, he makes a statement, about how he'd been bird-watching an' had seen them unloading the arms at the King's Fleet, about half a mile inside the Deben mouth. It was an IRA gun run, you see, and they caught him watching 'em from the high bank of the river as they landed the stuff. That's how he come to be on the buoy. Didn't shoot him; instead, they threw him overboard out beyond the Deben bar, so he'd drown and it would look like an accident.'

He shook his head slightly, muttering to himself: 'Funny that – him not wanting to talk to me.' And then he brightened. 'Mebbe they sacked 'im. That'd account for it. There was a swarm of investorigaty journalists digging into his background, and some of the stories they ran . . .' He gave a little shrug and turned away. 'Well, better get on if we're ever goin' ter finish this job.' And without another word he went back to the wheelhouse and disappeared below.

Was that it? Was he now into some smuggling racket, having been forced to resign his commission? All those questions about coves and inlets ... I was wondering about him as I drove home along the waterfront, wondering whether I would be able to get anything out of him during the evening.

CHAPTER TWO

He was punctual, of course, the bell of the chandlery sounding virtually on the dot of 20.30. I called down to him to come up, and introducing him to Soo, I said, 'Is it Mr Lloyd Jones or do you have anything in the way of a rank?'

'Gareth Lloyd Jones will do,' he said, smiling and taking Soo's outstretched hand. Some sort of a spark must have passed between them even then, her cheeks suddenly flushed and a bright flash of excitement in those dark eyes of hers as she said, 'I think you'll enjoy this evening. Manuela and her friends have done a great job of the preparations.' But I didn't take note of it at the time, still thinking about the way he had parried my question. If my suspicions were correct I wasn't at all sure I wanted to be seen entertaining a man who might land himself in trouble.

Petra was usually late and that evening was no exception. She was a large-boned girl with a freckled face and wide mouth that always seemed to be full of teeth. But her real attraction was her vitality. She came thundering up the stairs, that broad grin on her face and breathless with apologies. 'Sorry. Found I'd ripped my pants dancing the other evening and had to change.' She saw Lloyd Jones and stopped. 'I'm Petra Callis.' She held out her hand.

'Gareth Lloyd Jones.' And then, as I was getting her a drink, I heard her say, 'Soo will have told you what I'm up to, digging about in megalithic holes. I live out there on Bloody Island, a leaky tent among the ruins.' She jerked her head towards the window. Then she asked with blatant curiosity, 'What's your line of country? Yachts, I suppose, or are you a villa man?'

'No, neither.'

But Petra wasn't the sort of girl to be put off like that. She opened her mouth wide and laughed. 'Well, come on – what do you do? Or is it something mysterious that we don't talk about?'

I glanced back over my shoulder to see Lloyd Jones staring at her, a shut look on his face, mouth half-open and his eyes wide as though in a state of shock at the blatantness of her curiosity. Then he smiled, a surprisingly charming smile as he forced himself to relax. 'Nothing mysterious about it. I'm a Navy officer.'

As I passed Petra her gin and tonic Soo was asking him what branch of the Navy. 'Exec,' he replied, and she picked that up immediately. 'So was my father. Came up through the lower deck.' A moment later I heard the word Ganges mentioned.

'HMS *Ganges*?' I asked. 'On Shotley Point just north of Harwich. Is that the school you were referring to this morning, the one you and Evans were at?' And when he nodded, I said, 'It's called Eurosport Village now, or was when I was last there. I know it quite well. There's a commercial range and I used to practise there before going on to Bisley for the Meeting.'

'These cups, they're for shooting then, are they?' He couldn't help noticing them. He was standing right next to the pinewood cabinet I had purchased to house them and Gloria, our help, was a determined silver polisher. We talked about Shotley for a moment, then Soo butted in again, asking him how it had been when he was being trained there. From that they progressed to Malta. It was her mother who was Maltese. Her father had been a naval officer posted to Malta back in the days when there was a C-in-C Med and an old frigate fitted out as the Commander-in-Chief's yacht for showing the flag and entertaining. He had been the Navigating Officer on board

46

and though she had been far too young to remember anything about it, she was always ready to talk of the parties
he had described on the open lamplit deck.

It was past nine before we finally left, and though it was
barely a mile away, by the time we had found a place to
park the car and had walked through the quarry, somebody
had already lit the bonfire. The effect was magic, the
flames lighting the great square stone buttresses, flickering
over the lofty limestone roof, shadows dancing on the
moonlit cliffs, so that the whole effect was like some wild
biblical scene. In the great rectangular cavern itself the
dirt base of it had been levelled off to provide a makeshift
dance floor round which chairs had been placed and trestle
tables bright with cloths and cutlery and bottles of wine.

The band began to play just as we found our table.
Manuela came over, and, while Soo was introducing Lloyd
Jones, Petra and I were momentarily on our own. 'You
wanted to talk to me,' I said.

'Did I?' Her eyes were on the movement of people
towards the dance floor, her foot tapping, her body moving
to the beat of the music.

'Now, what have you discovered?' I asked her. 'Another
of those hypostilic chambers or is it an underground
temple to the Earth Mother like that place in Malta?'

'The Hypogeum?' She shook her head. 'No, nothing like
that. Just a charcoal drawing. But it could be a lot older.
I've only seen part of it. I don't know whether it represents
a deer, a horse, a bison or a mammoth. I don't know what
it is. A woolly rhinoceros perhaps.' She gripped hold of
my arm. 'Come on, let's dance. I'll settle for a woolly
rhinoceros and tell you the rest while we're dancing.'

But she couldn't tell me much. 'You'll have to see it for
yourself. I think it's early man – cave-dwelling man – but
of course I don't know. Not yet.'

'Then why consult me? I don't know the difference
between the drawings of early man and a potholer's
graffiti.'

She hesitated, then said, 'Well, it's not just that I've unearthed what looks like a section of a cave painting, it's the fact that people have been digging in that cave.'

'Archaeologists, you mean?'

'No, no. People who haven't the slightest idea they've uncovered anything. And if they did know, I imagine they couldn't care less. The charcoal drawing was only uncovered because they had been clearing a roof fall, and part of the drawing has already been sliced away when they were shovelling the rubble clear. They've dug out a hole I think I could have wriggled through, but I wasn't going to risk that on my own, it looked too unsafe.' And she added, 'I could hear water slopping around, Mike, and there was a draught of air. I think they've opened up a way through to the sea. But why?' She stared up at me, her body close against mine. 'Do you think that's what they were up to, cutting a way through to the sea?'

'How do I know?' I said. 'I'd have to see it . . .'

'Exactly. That's why I want you to come over there with me. Now. Before they have time to block it up, or do whatever it is they plan to do with it. They may be working on it this minute, so if we went now . . .'

'What – right in the middle of the party? I can't leave Soo, and anyway –'

'Well, afterwards. As soon as the party is over.'

I shook my head. 'It's quite out of the question.' And I told her the sensible thing would be to wait for daylight and then go back in with the curator from the museum or somebody from the Mayor's Office, one of the planning officials. It crossed my mind that this might have some connection with the squatters who had been sleeping in the villa Lennie was repairing, but I didn't tell her that. 'Wait till the morning,' I said again, 'and take one of the local authority officials in with you.'

'No.' She stopped abruptly, standing back from me in the middle of that dancing throng staring me in the face. 'Tonight. Please.' And then in a rush: 'You know how things work here, or rather don't – not always. It could be days before any official bothered to come out. They're not interested in caves and digs. A few people are, Father Pepito for instance, but none of the officials I know, not really, and I want somebody to see it *now*, before the charcoal outline of that figure is totally destroyed or the roof collapses again. Please, Mike. It's important to me.'

'I'll think about it,' I said, and we went on dancing, which was a mistake with Soo in her condition. She had been watching us and she was furious, telling me I had humiliated her in front of everybody. That was after I had returned to our table and Lloyd Jones had taken Petra off to dance. It made no difference that we had only been dancing together because Petra had wanted to get me to visit the cave and see what it was she'd discovered.

'So you're going with her. When?'

'Oh, don't be so silly,' I said. 'She just wants to show me a bit of a charcoal wall painting, that's all. It won't take long.'

'When?' she repeated, and there was a hot flush on her cheeks.

'Tonight,' I told her. 'She wants me to go tonight.'

'I see.' Her tone was icy, and after that she wouldn't speak to me. In the end I went over to the bar and got myself a large Soberano to chase down the wine I had been drinking. A hand gripped my elbow and I turned to find Manuela's husband, Gonzalez, beside me. 'You come to our table for a moment if you please. The Alcalde wish to speak with you about the opening of the new *urbanización* near the lake at Albufera next month. Jorge has been asked to make the opening and he wish you to take part in it, okay?'

I was not altogether surprised that Jorge Martinez should ask me to take part in the official opening of a new *urbanización*. I was one of the founder members of an unofficial association of resident English businessmen and I had on occasions acted as spokesman when the bureaucrats in the *ayuntiamento* had proved to be more than usually difficult over a planning application so that I knew Jorge in his official capacity as Mayor at the Mahon town hall as well as socially. In any case, since I was involved in property it was important for me to keep in with him.

In the post-Franco era, the political structure of what had become a monarchical democracy had steadily developed. The Baleares islands became one of the seventeen autonomous regions with its own elected parliament. The centre of this local government was at Palma, Mallorca. Foreign policy, finance and defence was, of course, still administered from Madrid through a Provincial Governor appointed by the ruling party. There was also a Military Governor. But Palma was over a hundred sea miles from Mahon and the comparatively recent introduction of this regional democratic autonomy had increased the importance of the local town halls and their councils, and in particular the power of the mayors who were elected by those councils. At least that's how it seemed to me, and I mention it here because I cannot help thinking that this dissemination of power may have had a bearing on what happened later.

Jorge Martinez was a lawyer, a slim man with sharp features and a way of holding his long, narrow head that suggested a cobra about to strike. He was, in fact, a very formidable little man and quite a prominent member of the ruling party, the *Partido Socialista Obrero Español* or PSOE. He had only been Alcalde in Mahon a short time, but already he had his hands firmly on the local power reins, his political sense acute. He got up as I reached the table, shook me by the hand, holding my elbow at the same time, and waved me to an empty seat opposite him. His wife was there, a dark-eyed, vivacious woman, also another lawyer and Colonel Jiménez of the *Guardia Civil*. Gonzalez topped up my glass with more brandy.

The Alcalde not only wanted me to attend the opening, but would I make a speech? 'Five, ten minutes, what you like, Mr Steele.' And he smiled, his use of the English address rather than the Spanish *señor* quite deliberate. 'You are very much known in your community and you will comprehend that here in Menorca we have problems – political problems arising from all the villa people. Not those who come to end their lifes here, but the summer migration. It is a question of the environment. So you speak about that, hah?'

He stopped there, waiting for some acknowledgement, and when I made no comment he said brusquely, 'You speak about the regulations the developers are agreeing to. Also you say this *urbanización* is a good developing; it is small, villas not too close, the environment of Albufera acknowledged, and it is good for our island. It brings work, it brings money, some foreign currency. Okay? You speak first in Spanish, then in English, so very short speaking, but the political point made very clear.' And he added, 'I am informed you always have good co-operation with my officials at the *ayuntiamento*. So you agree, hah?'

He had that explosive way of asking a question and insisting on agreement at the same time. In any case, when you have had a few drinks, and the commitment is over two weeks away, it is easier to say yes than to think up some convincing excuse on the spur of the moment. *'Bueno, bueno.'* He smiled, a glint of gold teeth. 'So nice to talk with you, señor.' I was dismissed, and I left the table with the feeling that if I had declined his invitation he would have seen to it that next time I needed a permit for something from the Mahon town hall it would not be forthcoming. But a speech in Spanish – or did he mean the local Catalan, which is very different? In any case, my Spanish was a hybrid of the two, having been picked up quite haphazardly as occasion demanded.

Somebody had thrown a pile of furze on the fire, the band half-drowned in the crackle of the flames. Flórez passed, light on his feet, the young woman in his arms glittering with tinsel, the button eyes in his round face fixed on the table I had just left as though watching for an opportunity to ingratiate himself. I went back to the bar and stood there watching the shadows of the dancers moving against the limestone roofing and the far recesses of the great cavern. The dancers themselves were a flicker of fire-red images, the whole scene so lurid and theatrical that it seemed almost grotesque, the band thumping out a brazen cacophony of sound that ricocheted off the stone walls, the beat so magnified it almost split one's ears.

'Manuela has a good idea, no?' a voice shouted in my ear. It was the Commander of the Naval Base. 'Why does nobody think to use this place before? It is magnificent, eh?'

The music stopped abruptly, the dancers coming to a halt. Floodlights either side of the cavern entrance were switched on, spotlighting white-capped cooks and the charcoal fires with their steaming pans of soup and steaks sizzling and flaming on the coals. Lloyd Jones had stopped quite near us and I hailed him over. 'I'd like you to meet Fernando Perez,' I said. 'He's *Jefe* of the Navy here.' I introduced him as Lieutenant Lloyd Jones of the Royal Navy, adding, 'That's right, isn't it?'

I sensed a moment's hesitancy. 'In fact, I'm now a Lieutenant Commander.' He laughed, a little embarrassed. 'I've just been promoted.'

We offered him our congratulations and Perez asked him what he was doing in Menorca. 'You are on leave per'aps?' He had a good command of English, particularly sea terminology, having had a short exchange posting to an RN carrier, though quite why they sent him to an aircraft carrier when he was a gunnery officer I don't know.

'Yes, on leave,' Lloyd Jones said.

'You have a ship, or are you posting ashore, like me?' And Fernando Perez gave a deprecatory little smile.

'No, I'm very lucky,' Lloyd Jones replied. 'With the promotion I've been offered a ship.'

'And where is that?'

'I'll be joining at Gibraltar as soon as my leave is up.'

Fernando turned down the corners of his mouth. 'You are indeed fortunate. Except for the Americans, who have so many ships, like the Russians, all our navies are in the same boat, eh?' He smiled, looking pleased at having achieved a touch of humour in a foreign language. 'Myself, I do not have a ship since five, no six years now. Already I have been 'ere three, stuck on a little island where nothing ever happen.'

'But at least you have the biggest guns in the Mediterranean,' I said.

'That is true. But what use are they, those big guns? They belong to another age and we have so few ammunition . . . Well, you know yourself. We fire them once a year and everybody complain because windows are shaken all over Mahon, some broken.'

'Are these the guns out on the northern arm of the Mahon entrance?' Lloyd Jones asked.

'On La Mola, yes. If you wish I take you to look at them. It is a *Zona Militar*, a prohibited area, but there is nothing secret about those guns, they 'ave been there too long. Everybody know about them.'

They started talking then about the problems of island defence and after a while I left them to see that the girls were being looked after, Soo in particular. I didn't want her standing in the queue and maybe getting jostled. In any case, she was becoming a little self-conscious about her figure, I think because all our friends knew very well she had lost the first. But she was no longer at our table. She was at Manuela's. Petra, too, and they had already finished their soup and were tucking into steak and mashed potato, Gonzalez Renato sitting between them and everybody at the table flushed with wine and talking animatedly.

I went to get myself some food then and Miguel joined me in the line-up for the barbecue. He had his cousin with him, both of them in dark suits, their hair oiled and their faces so scrubbed and clean I hardly recognised them. They hadn't booked a table so I took them to mine. They had their wives with them, Miguel's a large, very vivacious woman with beautiful skin and eyes, Antoni's a small, youngish girl with plump breasts and enormous dark eyes that seemed to watch me all the time. I think she was nervous. I danced with her once. She moved most beautifully, very light on her feet, but she never said a word.

It was as I took her back to the table that I saw Soo dancing with Lloyd Jones. She shouldn't really have been dancing at all, but by then I'd had a lot to drink and I didn't care. Petra joined me and we danced together for the rest of the evening, and whenever I saw Soo she was with the Navy, looking flushed and happy, and talking hard.

At midnight the band stopped playing and Manuela lit the train that set the fireworks crackling. It was a short display and afterwards everybody began to drift off home. That was when Petra announced that I was going to drive her over to Cales Coves.

I should have refused, but the moon was high, the night so beautiful, and I was curious. I did make some effort to discourage her. 'It's almost midnight,' I said. 'Too late to go messing around in those caves in the dark. And you're not dressed for it.'

'That's soon remedied,' she said. 'Oh, come on. You promised.'

'I did no such thing,' I told her, but she had already turned to Soo, who was standing there with Lloyd Jones close beside her. 'Why don't you come, too – both of you?' And she added, 'It'll be fun, going there now. The moon's almost full. It'll be quite light. Anyway, it won't matter in the cave itself. If it were broad daylight we'd still need torches.'

I thought Soo would be furious, but instead, she seemed to accept it. Maybe the two of them had already talked about it when they had gone off together to the girls' latrine at the end of the meal. At any rate, she didn't say anything. She had hold of Lloyd Jones's arm and seemed in a much happier frame of mind, humming to herself as we walked down the grass-grown track to the road where I'd left the car.

There was no wind, the sky clear and the moon a white eye high in the sky as I turned the car off the Villa Carlos road on to the steep descent to Cala Figuera. 'Have you ever seen anything so beautiful!' Petra exclaimed. 'I love it when it's still, like this, nothing stirring on the water, and Mahon a white sprawl above it. Sometimes I wake up in the night and pull back the tent flap. It looks like an Arab town then, so white, and everything reflected in the water. It's so beautiful.'

'Malta is better,' Soo cut in. 'What do you think, Gareth? You've just come from there.' She was sitting in the back with him. 'The buildings are so much more impressive, so solid. You haven't seen Malta, have you, Petra? Compared with Valetta and Grand Harbour – well, you can't compare them, can you, Gareth? Mahon is just a little provincial port.'

'But still beautiful.' Petra's tone, though insistent, was quite relaxed. 'And from Bloody Island I can see the whole sweep of it.'

'I don't think beautiful is the right word for a port,' Lloyd Jones said. 'Not for Malta anyway.' Out of the corner of my eye I saw him turn to Soo. 'Impressive now. I think impressive is the word. Those old strongholds, the great castles of the Knights that withstood the Turks and the German bombs.' And he added, 'But Gozo – Gozo is different somehow. I took a boat out to Gozo. That really is beautiful.'

I looked at them in the mirror. They were sitting very close together and she nodded, smiling happily. I think it was her smile that prompted him to say, 'I've been thinking, you know, about this visit to Cales Coves.' He leant forward suddenly, speaking to Petra and myself. 'I saw the inlets this afternoon, but I was only there a short while.

55

It would be nice to see them by moonlight. And it's not far off my way back to Fornells, so I'll join you if I may.'

We had reached the end of the road and I turned the car on to the raw gravel of our new car park. We were facing the water then, close beside his little Fiat, and there was a yacht coming in under motor, her mains'l a white triangle in the moonlight as she moved steadily across the crouched outline of the hospital ruins.

'If Gareth is going,' Soo said suddenly, 'then I'm going too.'

'It's your bedtime,' I told her. 'Remember what the doctor said. You shouldn't have been dancing really.'

'Well, I'm not going to be left behind on my own, that's definite.' And then, as Lloyd Jones helped her out, she was asking Petra whether she could lend her anything. But she had come ashore with all the clothes she needed. 'You never know,' she said as she retrieved her holdall from under the trestle table in the chandlery. 'It can blow up pretty fast here and you only get caught out at a party once with a full gale blowing and nothing to change into. I've never forgotten it. I got soaked to the skin and so cold . . .' She went with Soo up the stairs and into the bedroom.

Lloyd Jones followed them with his eyes, and when the door was shut he seemed suddenly ill-at-ease, as though unhappy at being left alone with me. 'I'll get you something more suitable to wear,' I said and went into the back premises, where I found him a spare sweater of mine and an old pair of working pants.

We made a quick change right there in the chandlery. 'You knew I was a Naval officer.' He was staring at me. 'The moment I arrived here, you knew. Do you have a rank? you asked.' I didn't say anything, an awkward silence growing between us. Then he went on, 'When I arrived here this morning – yesterday morning now – there was a man here, a short man in overalls and sweater. He was coming out of the door there.'

'Carp,' I said. 'His name's Carpenter.'

'An employee of yours? English, isn't he?'

'Yes.'

'Where from?'

'A little place on the East Coast. Felixstowe Ferry.'

He nodded. 'Thought I recognised him.' He was standing quite still, staring at me. 'So you know the whole stupid story?'

'About your being found clinging to a buoy off the Deben entrance? Yes.' And I asked him why he had ducked his head inside his car to avoid speaking to Carp. 'He was one of the men who rescued you, wasn't he? In fact, he says it was he who cut you down.'

'Yes.' There was a long pause, and then he said, 'It sounds silly, you know, but it's not something I'm very proud of – Navy officer found half frozen to death and roped to a buoy off a North Sea estuary. The media had a lot of fun at my expense, and seeing the man coming out of your door – it was a hell of a shock. I just didn't want to be reminded of the episode.'

Soo's voice called to ask if we were ready. 'Well, take Benjie out for a pee, will you, and Petra says to remind you about torches.'

I slipped a sweater over my head. 'I see your point,' I told him, 'but it's no excuse for not even saying hullo. He was very hurt.'

He shrugged. 'I'm sorry.'

The little dog had been shut in the store where he had a box to sleep in when we were out, and after I had taken him down the road to do his stuff, I went into the store with him and searched out the spare torches I kept with our boat gear. By the time I had found them, and some spare batteries, Soo and the other two were waiting for me out on the road. 'You take Petra,' she said as I locked the door. 'I'll show Gareth the way. We'll meet you on the track down into the cove. Okay?' And she took hold of Lloyd Jones's arm, steering him across to his Fiat, as though afraid I might object.

'Well, she seems quite happy about it, now we're all going,' Petra said as we got into the car. 'But you'd better tell Gareth to stay with her while we're in the cave. It's one of those entrances that are halfway up the side of the ravine and the last part is a bit of a climb.'

It was just past twelve-thirty by the dashboard clock as I took the old Jag through San Clemente and out on the four-kilometre straight to the Binicalaf turn-off, the moon so bright we could see the talayot to the left of the road very clearly, a huge cairn of interlocking stone blocks. Shortly after that I turned left, past the Biniadris development and another talayot, Petra talking all the time about the cave drawings she had seen when studying in France. The one we were going to see now reminded her of Font-de-Gaume in the Dordogne, the entrance to it similarly placed, halfway up a cliff.

'When they'd opened up Font-de-Gaume they found a series of chambers with pictures of animals on the walls, chiefly reindeer and mammoth. And there was another cave, Rouffignac, much longer, and older I think. The drawings there were of rhinoceros and bison as well as mammoths, and the floor was pock-marked with the pits of hibernating bears, like small craters.' She laughed at the recollection, and then, suddenly urgent again: 'Most of those drawings were from way back in time, Mike, at least 17,000 years ago, and if the little bit of a drawing I'm going to show you is really that of a woolly rhinoceros, then it'll be at least as old as those Dordogne paintings.'

I remember the way she said that, the intensity, the excitement in her voice. She really did believe she had found something important. And then we were at the start of the track that wound down the cliff-edged ravine to the first cove.

'You turn left in about a hundred yards,' Petra said. 'After that we walk.'

I stopped at the turn-off, waiting for the others, and after that we were on sand and gravel – not a road, nor even a track, just a piece of cliff-top country, a sort of maquis. Judging by the litter and the worn patches of thyme people came here to picnic, fornicate, or simply park their cars and sleep in the sun. It was tired, worn-looking country, but as I pushed on, driving carefully round the worst of the potholes, I realised that we had moved on to some sort of a track. A sharp turning to the right, a cave entrance marked by a sprinkling of tattered rags, then we were dropping down very steeply. 'You'll be able to park at the bottom,' Petra assured me. 'There's just room to turn there. Do you know this place?'

'Once or twice I've stopped at the top,' I said. 'But only for a bite to eat or to relieve myself before going down to the cove.'

She nodded. 'If you'd got out and walked around you'd have found quite a few cave entrances. There's one that looks almost like a house. It's got a painted front door, a couple of windows, a stove pipe stuck out of the side and a vine trained over an arbour of wooden posts. I'm told the man it belongs to visits it regularly right through the winter.'

We reached the bottom, the narrow gravel track petering out into what looked like a watercourse. There was only just room to turn the two cars and park them with their back ends in the shrubbery. I thought we had reached the bottom of the ravine then, but Petra said no, we still had a hundred yards or so to go, then there was a soft patch, almost a stretch of bog to cross before climbing up to the cave entrance. 'It will take us about ten minutes.'

By then we were out of the cars, all four of us standing in a patch of moonlight. The bushes were higher here, their shadows very black, and no sign of the cliffs that edged the ravine. 'How did you find it?' Soo asked her.

'I don't know really – some sixth sense, I think. The first time I came to Cales Coves was about six months ago. I've always been fascinated by natural caves. Most of them are in limestone and water-worn like these. And after I had explored several of them, I made enquiries and managed to locate a fisherman who uses a cave down by the water, just by the rock ledge that leads round into the other cove. He keeps his nets and gear there and it was he who told me there were several caves above here on the far side of the ravine. He thought it probable that very few people knew about them. The cave openings are mostly hidden by vegetation. At any rate, he hadn't heard of anybody visiting them, and though he thought I was mad, he very kindly came with me that first time. There are about half a dozen of them up there at the base of the cliffs. I came here several times after that, and then yesterday I found somebody had been digging in one of them. That's where the wall drawing is.' She started to move off. 'Come on. I'll lead the way.'

But Soo wasn't at all happy at being left on her own, and it was only when Lloyd Jones agreed to stay with her that she accepted the situation. I hesitated, suddenly uneasy at leaving her there. But Petra had already bounded off into the bushes. 'I'll tell you about it on the way home,' I said and followed her along what seemed to be the ghost of a path. The ground became damper, the light of my torch showing the imprint of soft-soled shoes.

We came to water, a shallow flow over gravel, the bright green of aquatic plants, and at that point we could see the moon shining on the cliffs above us, a grey, very broken curtain of rock splattered with the black of cave entrances. Almost immediately the ground began to rise and we lost sight of them. We were moving across the steep side of the ravine, still following traces of a path. It reached a point where we could see the waters of the cove entrance black in shadow, then it doubled back on itself, steeper now as we moved out on to the detritus caused by weathering of the cliff face above. Once Petra stopped to point the torch I had lent her at skid marks on the surface of the scree. 'Looks as though a bed or a crate, something heavy, has been hauled up here. Did you notice the imprint of feet down in the bottom?'

She scrambled up the steep bend, following the path

across loose stone until it reached the base of the cliff where there were bushes growing, the entrance to the cave above screened by a dense thicket. Again there were indications of recent use, twigs snapped, small branches bent back, and in the black hole of the entrance itself the dry dust of the floor was scuffed by feet. 'That's not me,' she said, flashing her torch. 'I've only been into this cave once.' Again there were skid marks as though a box had been dragged along the ground. 'Watch the roof.' She went on ahead of me, the height of the cave gradually lessening until I had to stoop. The sides of it were very smooth. 'I'm not sure,' her voice echoed back at me, 'whether this has been scooped out by surface water making its way to the sea or by the sea itself.'

There were any number of caves around the coast, most of them well below sea level, some reached only by water-filled sumps or chimneys. Looking back at the moonlit half-circle of the entrance, I realised we were striking into the cliff at an oblique angle. We were also moving downwards. 'You've got to remember,' I said, 'that when the ice-caps and the glaciers melted at the end of the last ice age the level of the sea rose very considerably.'

'I know. The best of the caves are thirty to sixty feet down.'

'Is that what your diving friend says?'

'Bill Tanner? Yes. He says there's a marvellous one by Arenal d'en Castell, a sort of blue grotto, enormous. He's promised to take me down, sometime when I'm not fossicking around, as he calls it.'

I switched off my torch, looking back up the slope. The entrance was no longer visible, only the glimmer of moonlight on stone showing ghostly pale. The roof was getting very low, though at that point the walls had pulled back as though this were some sort of expansion chamber. Like the other caves in the Cales Coves area, the walls here were water-worn and the upper entrance high above sea level. It must have been formed at some period when the island's rainfall was very much greater than it was now. The pounding of the sea so far below could never have done it by air pressure alone.

'Here's the roof fall.' Petra's voice came to me distorted and booming. 'I'm just about there. But mind your head.' And then I heard her swear.

'What is it? Have you hurt yourself?' I snapped my torch on, swinging it to send the beam lancing ahead down the tunnel.

'No. Nothing like that.' She was crouched down, her torch on the left-hand wall. In front of her the cave appeared to have collapsed, loose rock piled almost to the roof, rubble everywhere.

'What is it then?' I scrambled down the slope.

'Look! It's gone. The bastards have put their bloody shovels right across it. They've scraped it clean away. Why did they have to enlarge the hole?' She was leaning forward, brushing at the rock face with her fingers, the fine limestone dust sifting on to the stone below and almost white in the torchlight. She sat back on her haunches, cursing softly under her breath. 'If only I'd sent you a message and come straight back here and waited. When do you think they did it?'

She turned her torch on the fallen roof and the gap that showed between the broken rock and the rubble below was about three feet wide and not more than two feet at the highest point. There was air coming through it. I could feel it cool on my face and there was a smell of the sea. 'I should have come back,' she said again. 'Knowing somebody had been working on this fall, I should have stayed here to explain to them how important that drawing was.'

I tried to tell her not to worry about it too much. 'This is quite an extensive roof fall. Get this rubble shifted and you may find more drawings as you expose the rest of the cave walls.' It wasn't the cave drawing that interested me, though I realised the loss of it meant a lot to her, it was the fact that a passage had been cleared through the roof fall. It wasn't only that I could smell salt water, I could hear it, the slop of wavelets on the rocks in the cove or against the base of the cliffs. 'I'm going through,' I said.

'No.' Her hand gripped my arm. 'It's dangerous.'

'Don't you want to know what's the other side, why they've been digging away at this roof fall?'

'Well, of course I do.' We were crouched together in what was clearly another expansion chamber, and as I circled it with my torch I saw that all the rubble they had cleared from the fall had been piled around the walls. Petra was straining at a large chunk of rock. 'Give me a hand, will you?' But when we had pulled it away, and she had cleared the rubble and dust that was piled behind it, exposing another foot or so of the limestone wall, there was nothing there, the surface completely bare. Her frustration and anger was something tangible. I could feel it as she shifted her body into the gap, kneeling now and working away at the rubble, dust rising in a cloud as she scooped the loose fragments of rock up in her hands and thrust them behind her.

'Leave it till tomorrow,' I said.

'No. I must know what's here.'

'In the morning you can come back again with the proper tools.'

'I must know,' she repeated, her voice urgent. 'If there are more drawings, then I'll have to stay here, make certain they don't start shovelling out more of this debris. If they come here again in the morning and begin enlarging the passage through this roof fall –'

'Listen!'

'What?'

'Just stay still for a moment.' She had been working so furiously, making such a clatter in the confined space, that I couldn't be certain I had really heard it. 'Listen!' I said again and she sat back on her haunches. Dust blew up into our faces, and in the sudden silence the slap of waves breaking seemed preternaturally loud.

'The wind's getting up,' she whispered. 'That's all.' And then, when I didn't say anything, all my senses concentrated on listening for that sound again, she asked, 'Did you hear something besides the wind and the sea?'

I nodded.

'What?'

'A voice. I thought I heard a voice.'

'Are you sure?'

'No. Of course I'm not sure.'

We stayed frozen for a while, listening. 'There's nothing,' she said. 'Just the wind. I can feel it on my face, much stronger now.'

I could feel it, too. It was as though a door had been opened and was letting in a draught. She bent forward again, working at a rock up-ended against the side of the cave. My torch, probing the hole through the roof fall, picked out a grey sliver of what proved to be bone. But when I showed it to her she brushed it aside. 'There are several bits of bone lying around. A sheep, or a goat maybe. Probably got trapped in here, or came seeking a dark den in which to die. It's drawings of animals, not their bones I'm looking for.' And when I again suggested that she leave it till it was daylight, she turned on me quite fiercely. 'Can't you understand? I must be sure there are no more drawings in danger of being destroyed.'

Five minutes later she was uncovering a mark on the wall that looked like discoloration. It was very faint, a faded ochre line sweeping upwards and stopping abruptly where the roof had fallen away. 'Could be the back of some animal.' Her voice was breathless with excitement. 'What do you think it is, Mike? The arch of the neck perhaps? A bull? At Lascaux there's a great bull right across the roof of the cave, and there are deer being hunted and plunging to their deaths over a cliff.'

She went on working at it, exposing more and more of the faded ochre line where it disappeared into the rubble. I was holding the torch for her and she was working so hard I could smell the warmth of her, dust clinging to her damp skin, her face a pale mask. Then I heard it again and I gripped her arm to silence her. 'Somebody called,' I said.

She turned, the piece of rock she had just prised loose still in her hand, her head on one side. Even her hair was covered with a grey film. 'I don't hear anything.' She brushed my hand away, thrusting the chunk of stone behind her.

'I'm going through,' I said.

She didn't seem to hear me, leaning forward again, brushing gently with her fingers at the section of wall she had just exposed.

I pushed her out of the way and crawled forward over the rubble, turning on my side. I was just starting to wriggle into the gap feet-first when, back up the slope of the cave, I saw a glimmer of light. It grew rapidly brighter, hardening into the beam of a torch, and a moment later Gareth Lloyd Jones was crouched beside us.

'Where's Soo?' I asked him. 'You said you'd stay with her.'

'Waiting in the car.' He was breathing hard. 'I came up to tell you.' He was kneeling now, his face close to mine as I lay with only my head and shoulders protruding from the hole. 'How far does it go, right through to the cliff face?' He thought I had already explored the continuation of the cave.

'I don't know,' I told him. 'I'm just going to find out.'

'But you've been here for a quarter of an hour or more.' Petra and I started to explain about the mark on the wall of the cave, both of us speaking at once, but he brushed our explanation aside. 'Have you heard something? Anybody moving about?'

'I thought I heard somebody call out,' I said. 'And before that there was something like the murmur of voices. It could have been the sea. Or it could have been squatters.' And I started to tell him about the villa near Binicalaf Nou.

'Voices,' he said. 'That's what you heard. There's somebody in there. I came up to warn you.' Instead of waiting
in the bush-shadowed dark of that track, he and Soo had
decided to drive down to the cove. They had left the car and
were walking down through the loose sand of the beach
towards the sea when they had seen a light on the cliff
face away to the left. 'We were just at the point where
somebody had made a little trough in the rock and put up
a notice to say the water in it was from a spring and good
to drink. You know where I mean?'

'Yes, of course. But where exactly was the light? In one
of the cave entrances?'

'Yes, and it wasn't there long. It wasn't very bright
either, more like a hurricane lamp, or even a candle. A
slightly yellowish light, and low down, only a little above
the sea.'

I asked him whether it could have been the riding light
of a ship, or perhaps the masthead light of a sailing boat,
but he said definitely not. With the moon so bright it
would have been impossible for them not to have seen a
vessel if there had been one there. 'Even with the cliff face
in shadow, the dark hole where we saw the light was
plainly visible. And then suddenly it wasn't there any
more.' He didn't know whether it had been snuffed out,
switched off, or whether somebody had moved it away
from the aperture. 'I was looking seaward at the time, so
was Soo. We both thought somebody must be signalling a
boat in through the entrance. But there was nothing
coming into the cove. Then, when I looked back at the
cave, it was gone. That's when I decided to come up here
and warn you. They're in one of the caves, but whether
it's this one . . .'

'Only one way to find out.' I started wriggling through
again, using my elbows, but he stopped me.

'No. If they knew we were here . . .' I could see his face
in the diffused light of our torches. It was shining with
sweat and his mouth was moving uncontrollably.

'What's the matter?'

'Nothing. It's just . . .' He reached out, gripping hold of my shoulder. 'Leave it till morning, man. Please. Then we can come back – with one or two of your employees, or the police. If you go in now –' He shook his head, his voice trembling.

Christ! The man was scared. 'They're only squatters,' I told him. 'Nothing to worry about. And if this is the cave they're in, then they'll have heard us. I'm going in,' I said again. 'Soon find out if there's anyone here or not.'

'What about your wife? And Petra here? If they know you're in the cave . . .' He stopped there, the rest of his words bitten back and his face set. 'All right,' he said. 'I'll come with you.'

'You don't have to.'

'Yes, I do. I'll come with you,' he said again, his voice quite obstinate now. He seemed suddenly to have made up his mind, and when I suggested he go back to the car and wait with Soo, he shook his head. 'If you're going to try and reach the cliff entrance, then I'm coming with you. It's my duty.' It seemed an odd way of putting it, but I didn't think about it then. I was already working my way in over the roof fall and he was coming after me headfirst.

The fall was only about ten metres through and then we were crouched low and moving down a steep incline, the breeze quite strong on our faces and our torches showing a low arched tunnel swinging away to the right. As soon as we rounded the bend we could see the cliff-face entrance, a pale rectangle of moonlight, and we could stand upright, for here, at the sea-worn end, the cave was much larger. There were camp beds ranged against the walls, four of them with sleeping bags, wooden packing cases for tables and seats and a paraffin stove that looked as though it had come out of some derelict fishing boat. The stove was for heating as well as cooking, and there were dishcloths, a couple of shirts too, hung on a line above the pipe that carried the fumes out to the cliff face. The whole place was equipped for living in, quite comfortably equipped, and propped against the wall was a heavy timber frame covered with plywood that had been tailored to fit the entrance. It had a little window and great iron bolts that slotted into sockets drilled in the rock so that even in a sou'westerly gale the place would be quite snug.

The noise of the sea was loud now, the dishcloths swaying in the wind. I went over to the entrance and leaned out. The cliff was sheer, a drop of about twenty feet or so to a narrow rock ledge that formed a sort of natural quay with deep water beyond, and the cave's entrance had been beautifully worked into scrolled pillars either side supporting a rather Greek-style portico. Inside, ledges had been carved out of both walls, a place for ornaments or household crockery. Whoever had originally fashioned the cave as a home must have been a real craftsman, a stonemason probably, everything so professionally done. 'All you need is a rope ladder,' Lloyd Jones said, peering down to the narrow ledge of rock below.

'And a yacht,' I added. 'Champagne cooling in the further recesses of the cave and a beautiful girl sunbathing down there in a bikini.' Or perhaps not in a bikini, just lying there on that ledge, nude in the moonlight.

He didn't laugh, and nor did I, for I found myself thinking of Petra, how well she would fit the picture in my mind. 'Nobody here,' I said.

'No.' He sounded relieved. 'But they've been here.' He had moved back from the entrance, his voice puzzled as he probed with his torch.

I was puzzled, too, the cave showing every sign of recent occupation and nobody there. The broken remains of an old cupboard full of cans of food. There were biscuits and cornflakes in a rusty cake tin, flour, rice, dried fruit, plastic containers with water, and those dishcloths and shirts hung up to dry.

'Where are the heads?' he asked.

'The heads?'

'It's all right throwing the slops out into the cove. But if I want to shit, where do I do it?' He swung his torch back up the way we had come. That was how we found the offshoot cave. It was quite narrow, the entrance draped with an old piece of sacking so covered with dust it was virtually the same colour as the surrounding wall, and when we pulled it aside, there it was, a chemical loo.

We were both of us standing there, peering down the narrow passage that continued on beyond the old oil drum with its wooden lid, when suddenly there was a cry and Petra was calling my name, her voice high and urgent, reverberating down the cave shaft – 'Mi-i-ke!' I was running then, crouched low. There was the sound of rocks dislodged, a man's voice cursing, and as I rounded the bend, the beam of my torch showed the soles of his canvas shoes disappearing over the rubble of the roof fall.

I must have been close behind him as I flung myself on to my belly, but by the time I had squirmed half through the gap, the tunnel beyond was empty. 'Two of them,' Petra said, her voice breathless. She was crouched against the wall. 'I thought it was you and Gareth, then my torch was knocked out of my hand and I was flung back, one of them cursing at me as they pushed past.'

'English or Spanish?' I was cursing too by then, my hands lacerated as I dragged my legs clear.

'I'm not sure.' She was on her knees, groping for her torch.

I glanced over my shoulder, struggling to my feet. 'Hurry!' He was right behind me and I was thinking of Soo, alone there in the car. Damn the man! Why hadn't he stayed with her? I ran, bent low, the beam of my torch following the curve of the cave until the gap of the entrance showed a pale oval. A moment later I was out into the cool of the night air, thrusting through the bushes to stand in the moonlight staring down the path where it ran steeply towards the cove.

There was nothing there.

I searched the hillside. Nothing moved. Then a car's engine started, down below, where we had parked, and a few moments later I saw it burst out on to the track where it crossed open country just before joining the road, its engine screaming. It was the red Fiat.

'My God!' Lloyd Jones, beside me now, had recognised it, too.

We went straight down the hillside then, moving as fast as we could in the tricky light, jumping from rock outcrop to rock outcrop, splashing through the water at the bottom. My car was still there, but no sign of Soo. Frantically I began searching the bushes, calling her name.

'They couldn't have taken her with them, surely.' He was standing there, staring helplessly about him.

'Well, she's not here. Nor is your car. Why the hell didn't you stay with her?'

'I'm sorry, but you were so long . . . She asked me to go –' He turned his head. 'What was that?'

It came again, high up the valley side from under the cliffs, and suddenly I knew what it was. 'Petra,' I said. 'It's Petra, and she's found her.'

We climbed back up the hillside, retracing our steps. 'Here,' she called, standing suddenly upright beside a patch of scrub. 'It's Soo. She's had a fall.'

I could hear her then, moaning with pain. Her body was lying twisted in a heap in the middle of a low clump of bushes, Petra bending down to her again, cradling her head as we reached the spot. 'I think she must have followed the path right up to the cave entrance, then lost her balance when they pushed past her.'

'Anything broken?' My torch showed her face badly bruised and shining with sweat. Her breath came in great gasps and she was moaning all the time.

'I've moved her limbs. They seem all right. But internally . . .'

'It's the baby then. If she's going to have it now . . .' I

70

turned on Lloyd Jones. 'Why the bloody hell didn't you stay with her, man? If she loses the child . . .'

Petra silenced me, gripping my arm, as Soo murmured quite coherently, 'It's not – Gareth's – fault. I asked him . . .' Her voice trailed away, her right hand moving to her swollen belly, a bubble of saliva at her mouth as she cried out with pain. Then she passed out.

'We've got to get her to hospital.' Petra's voice was sharp. 'As soon as possible.'

Soo only screamed once as we carried her down the slope to the car. I think she was unconscious most of the time. And she didn't cry out all the time I was driving back to Mahon. I drove like a maniac, Petra said afterwards, my face set and anger taking hold. Anger at Lloyd Jones for being the cause of her leaving the car and climbing the path to the cave alone, above all, anger at those two bastards who had brushed her from their path as they rushed down the hillside to drive off in that hire car.

I took her straight to the Residencia Sanitaria, which is just up from the Port Mahon Hotel. This is the emergency hospital, and the night Petra and I spent there is not one either of us is ever likely to forget. Fortunately they did have a bed available in the maternity ward. Two women were in labour at the time and the place was something of a mad house. There were nurses rushing about, a nun in attendance, no sign of a doctor. They got Soo to bed and I left Petra with her and phoned the *Guardia Civil.*

It was while I was telling them what had happened that Petra came down to say Soo was in labour. 'They've found a doctor. A very young man. I think he's scared. He's already lost one baby tonight. That's what one of the nurses told me.'

The time was 03.17, the words coming in a breathless rush. 'I'll go back now . . . No, don't come with me. There's nothing you can do. I'll let you know as soon as it comes.'

'It's not due for more than a month.' I remember I said that, standing there, helpless.

'What's it matter when it's due? She's having it now. I just hope to God . . .' She turned abruptly, not finishing the sentence, and hurried back up the stairs.

I remember getting rid of Gareth Lloyd Jones and then I was going over it all for the benefit of a young sergeant of the *Guardia*. Since it had happened in the country, not in Mahon, it was their responsibility. He made some notes, then offered his sympathies and said he would make a report. Perhaps it was a matter for the *Aduana*. At my insistence he agreed to inform Inspector Molina of the national police. I knew him slightly and I thought it might be something the plain-clothes boys should know about.

After the sergeant was gone I was alone there in that cold little reception area. Sometimes I paced up and down. Nobody came and time passed slowly. Dawn began to break in the street outside. Then suddenly Petra was there, her face very pale under the freckles, her eyes dark-edged with weariness and worry. 'She's all right,' she said slowly. 'I mean she's come through it. She's conscious.' The words seemed dragged out of her. 'The doctor thinks it's just that she's badly bruised inside. She'll be okay. That's what he hopes – when she's had some rest.'

'And the child?' I asked.

'For God's sake, Mike, what did you expect? She must have fallen right on top of it. It was a breech, didn't you know that from the scan? Round the wrong way, the poor little thing's head was right against the wall of the stomach. It hadn't a chance.'

'What was it, a boy or a girl?'

'A boy.'

I went up to her then, feeling tired and very depressed, wanting a drink and not knowing what the hell I was going to say to her. She was lying on her back, her eyes closed, the olive skin of her face looking sallow, a deathly pallor against the tumbled black of her hair. They had cleaned her up, of course, but her hair and skin were still damp, her features so drained that I thought for a moment she was dead.

I don't think I said anything, but she must have sensed my presence for her eyes opened. They stared straight up at me, great brown pools in a white face. Her lips moved. 'I'm – sorry.' The words came faintly, then she was gone, the eyelids closing down, consciousness slipping away.

I bent and kissed her. Her skin was hot as though she were in a fever, her breathing so shallow it was hardly noticeable. Petra touched my arm, motioning me with her head to leave. The nun was hovering and a sister had arrived and was talking to her. 'She'll sleep now. They've given her an injection.' Petra led me out.

I don't remember driving home. We drank the remains of a bottle of brandy as the sun came up, both of us sitting in the office, and all I could think about was Soo's eyes staring up at me, huge brown pools of sorrow in the whiteness of her face, her hair still dank where it lay unkempt on the pillow, and her words, those sad words of apology for a miscarriage she couldn't help.

And after that I fell asleep, my head on Petra's shoulder.

CHAPTER THREE

When I next saw Soo she had been moved to a smaller room and her face was to the wall. I don't know whether she was asleep or not, but when it happened on both the visits I made the following day, it was clear she didn't want to talk to me. Apart from the bruising, she was in a state of shock. Even so, the doctor, as well as the nurses, said she was making quite good progress and should be home in a few days.

By then the *Guardia* had recovered the stolen hire car. It had been found abandoned in Alayór, in one of the streets winding down from the church. They had also examined the cave, but had not been disposed to take the matter very seriously. Petra had been with them and she said they considered the two men who had been flushed out by our unexpected arrival to be cave squatters, and then, when they bumped into her at the roof fall and Soo outside, they had panicked and taken the car as a handy means of making their escape.

After the police had gone she had walked round to the second cove, past the sea-level caves. There was a small cottage at the far end, its cabbage patch clinging to the side of a steep ravine. The family there knew nothing about the two men. They hadn't even known the cave had been occupied. Remembering the light Lloyd Jones had seen, she had asked them if they had noticed any vessel entering the cove during the previous two nights. There had been one, they said, and they wouldn't have seen it but for the moonlight, for the boat was all dark, not a light anywhere, and it had looked like two ships rafted together. There had been an onshore breeze, quite strong at times, so the two vessels couldn't anchor and had left immediately. The only other boats they had seen during the past few days had been local fishing boats, mostly from Cala en Porter, which was the next cove to the west and one of the better tourist resorts with a big hotel and some plush villas.

This she told me when she came ashore the following day, hauling her inflatable out and parking it in our car park. She was on her way to Cales Coves, hoping to uncover some more of that cave drawing, and we were walking along the waterfront to where the Martires Atlante runs out past the Club Maritimo to the old fort that marks the entrance proper to Mahon harbour.

The sun was shining again, an easterly funnelling up the harbour, rattling the halyards of the yachts moored at the Club pontoon, and Petra, looking wildly attractive with her auburn hair blowing about her face, suddenly said, 'That Navy man, have you seen any more of him?' She was wearing faded denims, an orange shirt open almost to the navel, no bra and her feet were bare.

'No, not since that night,' I told her.

'Did you know he'd been seeing Soo? He's been to the hospital several times.'

I didn't say anything, sullen in the knowledge of what she was trying to tell me. Her face was in profile, a strong face, the nose fine-boned and straight, the teeth white in a mouth that wore no lipstick. 'Did Soo tell you that?'

'No. Gareth told me.' She stopped then and turned to me. 'He's in love with her, you know that?'

I half shook my head, shrugging it off. What do you say to a statement like that? And coming from a girl you're half in love with yourself. What the hell do you say? 'How do you know he's in love with her? How the bloody hell do you know?'

Soo, of course. Soo must have confided in her. Hurt and lonely, it seemed reasonable, two young women together

in the carbolic atmosphere of a hospital ward. But no –
'He told me himself.' And she added, 'You haven't seen
him, have you? He hasn't tracked you down – to say he's
sorry, offer his condolences, anything like that?'

'No.'

She nodded. 'Well, that's why. You don't go looking for
a man when you've fallen head-over-heels in love with his
wife. At least, I wouldn't think that's how they do it in
the Navy. Cuckolding a fellow, if only in thought – well,
not quite the thing, eh?' She gave me that wide grin of
hers and began to walk on again. 'No need to worry about
it, he says his leave will soon be over.'

'What about Soo?' I asked. 'How does she feel?'

She gave a little shrug. 'She likes him. I don't know how
much more she feels.' She glanced at me quickly, a flash
of something in her eyes and smiling now, quietly to
herself. 'I'm not exactly in her confidence.'

I caught hold of her arm. 'Let's go for a sail.'

'No.' And she added, still with that little smile, 'That's
your answer to every problem, isn't it? Let's go for a sail.'

'When did you see him?'

'This morning.'

'Where?'

'Bloody Island. At the dig.' She nodded towards the grey
sprawl of the hospital ruins looking quite distant now that
the harbour was full of whitecaps. 'He hired a boat and
came over to see me.'

'To say goodbye?'

She shook her head.

'Then why?'

'I think because he wanted you to know. He also said
he was sorry.'

'For leaving Soo on her own that night, or for falling in
love with her?'

'Both, I imagine.'

We had stopped again and I was staring seaward, out
beyond the fortress of St Felip to where the horizon lay, a

76

dark line in a blue sea flecked with white. So his leave would soon be up and he'd be off to Gib to take command of his ship. A Navy man, newly promoted and on his way up the service ladder. No wonder she found him attractive, feeling as she did about her father. I thought of the wretched little house, one of a line of Victorian dwellings in a back street in Southsea. It was all her father had to show for almost forty years in the Navy, his pay mostly spent on good living, and what savings he had achieved thrown away on speculative investments that had never produced the fortune they promised him. That lovely little courtyard full of music from the old record player, the mellow lime-stone house overlooking the sea between Sliema and St George's Bay, it had all seemed a long way away when we had last visited her parents. That was just after the loss of her first child, which I had thought might be some weakness inherited from her mother. But after that visit I was convinced that if it was an inherited weakness then it had to be from her father.

Still thinking about that, I glanced at Petra, standing Junoesque in the sunshine, the curve of a breast showing in the V of her orange shirt, the skin tawny brown with wind and salt, the patched denims filmed with the dust of the dig she was working on. No weakness there, and if she were to let up on the pill and have a child, she'd probably deliver it herself, no trouble at all, and get right on with the dig next day.

She turned her head and caught my gaze, the flicker of a smile back at the corners of her mouth. Something in her eyes made me wonder if she could read my thoughts. Were we that close already, and nothing said, just an acceptance that there were moments when the satisfaction of our needs . . .? 'You go for that sail. It'll do you good. I've got things to do.' She turned away then, a wave of the hand as she called over her shoulder, 'And don't fall in. It's blowing quite hard out there.'

I watched her as she crossed the road and disappeared

up the stone staircase leading to the upper road where she always parked her battered little Citroën. She moved with the grace of an athlete, taking the steps at a run, her hair catching the sun like a burnished helmet of bronze. She must have known I was watching her, but she didn't look back, and when she reached the top she didn't look down or wave, though I caught the flash of that helmet of hair for a moment above the ornate balustrade.

She was right about the wind. It would have been fine if she had come with me, but single-handed the Flying Dutchman I had picked up in lieu of an unpaid bill was quite a handful, more like board-sailing than cruising. I reefed, of course, before slipping from our pontoon and sailing out of the shelter of Cala Figuera, but the wind was funnelling down the length of the harbour approaches, and not much shelter to be had in the lee of the islands. It was very wet as I beat past Villa Carlos and out as far as the big island called Lazareto, and when I went about and freed the main for the run back, we were planing on the break of the waves and every now and then that powerful little dinghy took the bit between her teeth and tried to broach-to.

I was wet and tired by the time I got in. Instead of providing me with the opportunity of thinking things through, it had taken all my concentration just to keep the dinghy upright and avoid capsizing. Ramón was waiting for me with a whole string of queries, mostly about matters that Soo would normally have dealt with, and there was the mail. I hadn't dealt with the day's mail yet and I loathed typing letters. 'There is a telephone call.' He was hovering over me as I stripped and towelled myself down. 'About the *Santa Maria*.'

'You deal with it,' I said. 'You know the charter terms.'

'He don't want a charter.'

'You mean he wants to buy her . . .' I had been trying to sell the *Santa Maria* for over a year now.

But Ramón shook his head. 'He already have a boat.'

I paused in the act of stepping into a dry pair of trousers. 'Then what the hell does he want? Who is he?'

'Señor Flórez. He want you to phone him.'

Apparently Flórez was acting for the owner of a cata-maran lying at the commercial dock, in the area reserved for larger yachts and those on passage. 'He want to make some sort of exchange,' Ramón added.

A big cat had come in that morning. I had seen it running in under jib alone when I was talking to Petra, dark blue hulls with the paint flaking and a bad scrape along the port side. But she had still looked beautiful and very purposeful, a real thoroughbred.

I zipped up my trousers, pulled on a light sweater, Ramón still standing there and my mind in a whirl. The fishing boat wasn't worth much, not here in Menorca, and running it for charter was a lot of work with very little in it for us. It had never really paid its way. 'How big is this cat?'

Ramón shrugged. 'You phone Señor Flórez, then he tell you everything you want to know.'

But when I rang Flórez, all he said was, 'Come and see it for yourself.' He and the owner would be on board that evening. 'Then we talk about it, eh? I have a very good deal for you, Mr Steele.' And he had put the phone down, leaving me with all my questions unanswered and the deal not specified.

I would like to have driven over to the commercial dock right away. Looking through the yachting magazines, I had often thought what a perfect charter vehicle a big cat would be, and now I was being offered one, right here in Mahon. But the phone began ringing and I couldn't get away. There were two calls from England, as well as letters. Spring was in the air and people suddenly anxious to be sure their boats or their villas would be ready for the holidays.

I worked right through lunch, sending Ramón out to the restaurant at the corner for the fish-and-rice dish they often put up for us when Soo was too busy to cook anything for herself. It was shellfish this time, *arroz de marisco*, with *calamares* tentacles finely chopped to give it body. All the time I was eating, and afterwards, I kept thinking about that catamaran, wondering what it would be like, what condition it would be in, what accommodation it would have, the navigation equipment and the state of the sails, excitement building though I knew bloody well the Mediterranean was a graveyard of shattered dreams.

It was late afternoon before I finally caught up with the office work and then it was time to visit the hospital again. I didn't mention the catamaran to Soo, even though I found her sitting up in bed reading a Spanish novel she had been lent. She looked much better, the dark patches under her eyes almost gone, some of the old sparkle back and her face more animated. The doctor had said she would be fit to leave the following day. 'Eleven o'clock. Will that be all right? Can you come for me then?'

I said 'Of course', and then she talked for a bit, about the friends who had been to visit her, the gossip they had passed on, and particularly about the Renatos' Red Cross party in the Quarries. 'What will you say when you speak at the opening of that Albufera development? You never told me the Alcalde had asked you. Am I invited?'

'I imagine so.'

'But he didn't ask me, did he?'

'I'm sure he will. When they send out the official invitations.'

She was silent then and I feared she was going into one of her sulky moods. But after a moment she brightened and began asking questions about the business – how Lennie was getting on with the villa out at Binicalaf, whether the equipment for the extra bathroom in another of the villas in our care had been flown in yet, had I remembered about completing the forms for customs clearance, and the accounts to settle with two of our suppliers. 'You know, I'm really looking forward to being back. Lying here with nothing to do but read and listen to the radio and think.' And she added darkly, 'I've had all the time in the world to think these past few days.' And almost without a pause: 'Did Gareth come and see you before he left? No, of course – I remember. He said it was bad enough seeing me, feeling it was his fault I'd lost the child, and though I told him I might have lost it anyway, he still said he couldn't face you. You told him it was his fault. I have a distinct memory of that. *Why the hell didn't you stay with her?* you shouted at him, and accusing him like that . . .'

Her voice trailed away. Then suddenly she said, 'Did you know, he came up through the lower deck – *Ganges*, Dartmouth, the Fleet Board. Just like Papa. It makes a difference, doesn't it? You're more vulnerable then. Everything that bit harder. No admiral ever came up through the lower deck that I can remember. And it wasn't his fault. It wasn't anybody's fault.' Tears welled. I went to comfort her, but she pushed me away. 'I know what you think. And you're probably right. I'll never have a child now.'

I didn't know what to say. Life doesn't make sense. There was Petra who didn't want a child, but would almost certainly have no difficulty if she did find herself with a bun in the oven. And Soo's mother, she had had five, one every two years, regular as clockwork. Then, being a devout Catholic, she must have gone on strike. That was probably why Soo and her father had been so close.

It was almost dark by the time I left the hospital and cut down the little hairpinned gut that led to the waterfront. I could see the catamaran before I had even parked the car, a broad cabin top spanning the whole width of the twin hulls, her single mast standing very tall and overtopping the dock sheds. She was moored outside of a big yawl, and when I asked permission to cross over to the catamaran, an American in a blue jersey, half-glasses perched on his nose, poked his head out of the doghouse. 'Sure. But there's nobody on board. They're over at the café-bar across the road.'

I asked him where he was from and he said, 'Newport, Rhode Island, via Gibraltar and Ibiza.'

I swung my leg over his guardrails, crossed the foredeck to stand by the shrouds looking down on the long, slim line of the two hulls, their bows poking out from the broad foredeck platform, a safety net slung between them.

'Good trip,' he went on. 'We made it across the ditch in just over sixteen days, almost all of it under sail.'

A woman's head appeared in the hatch, grey-haired like the man. 'That cat belong to you?' she asked.

'I wish it did.' I jumped on to the cabin top, moving aft across the top of it to drop down into the cockpit. There was a swivel chair for the helmsman immediately aft of the wheel and a console full of dials – engine revs, speed through the water, true and apparent wind speeds, just about everything anybody could want, and though the door was locked, I could see through the glass panel that the whole arrangement was repeated in the saloon, which was broad and spacious, running across the ship with a semi-circular settle, a big folding table and steps leading down into the hulls on each side. Compared with the old *Santa Maria* the accommodation was so grand it was more like a house, and around the chart table, on the starb'd side, there was everything a navigator could wish for, radar, sat-nav and Decca, ship-to-shore radio telephone . . .

'Quite a machine, eh?' the American said.

I nodded, laughing ruefully. To own this sort of a vessel I'd have to sell both our villas. They were in our joint names, and even if Soo agreed and we succeeded in selling them on the present market, it would probably not be enough. The ship needed painting, of course, and the scrape along the outer curve of the port hull was deeper than I had thought. It looked as though some frames might be broken. But otherwise she seemed in remarkably good shape. There was even a big semi-inflatable moored alongside with wheel steering, spray screen and remote controls to the outboard engine.

I hauled myself back on to the American's deck. 'You came through Gib, you say. Did you see a Royal Navy frigate in the harbour there?'

'Not that I recall. It's a big place, all those high stone quays, and anyway we were round in the marina.' And he added, 'We saw some US Navy ships though. They were powering through the Straits as we came in from Cape St Vincent. Destroyers by the look of them. More watchdogs for the Sixth Fleet's carriers, I guess.'

I was back on the dock then, wondering why anyone should want an old fishing boat like the *Santa Maria* in place of that cat. I could see her name now. It was on the flat, sloping stern of each hull – *Thunderflash*. If I owned a machine like that . . . I turned back to the American. 'What made you think I was the owner?'

He smiled and gave a quick shrug. 'Something in the way you were moving about her. Thought maybe it was a delivery job.' There had been four of them on board, he told me, when they came in that morning. One he took to be the skipper, two were obviously crew, and there had also been a short, dark man dressed in a suit who looked and behaved like a passenger. They had had to clear immigration, as well as health and customs, so he presumed the boat had come from France or Italy, which could of course mean Corsica or Sardinia. The passenger had gone ashore immediately afterwards, the skipper about an hour later, while the others just sat around drinking wine and listening to the radio. The skipper had returned about half an hour before I had arrived with a man who was obviously Flórez and the four of them had then gone across to Anton's for a drink.

The café-bar was almost opposite the Estación Maritima, just back of the Customs House. Above it loomed the older part of Mahon, clouds scudding over a moon-dark sky. As always at this time of night, the bar was dark and very crowded. They were at a table at the far end, heads close together, coffee cups and glasses at their elbows, a bottle in the centre. They were talking in English and as I approached I heard one of them say, 'Fifteen minutes, and that's not driving fast.'

Flórez saw me then, and as he switched on a smile and got to his feet, the man sitting with his back to me raised his hand as though for silence. 'You want a drink with your coffee, Mr Steele?' Flórez called the order to the barman and pulled up a chair. 'Later we go over to the ship.' He didn't introduce me to any of the others, merely saying I was the man he had been talking about.

There was a short, awkward silence after I had sat down. I was between Flórez and the man I took to be the skipper. He wore an old reefer and his neck stuck out of the collar of it like a column running straight up into the long, narrow head. His face, what little I could see of it in that light, was weathered to a dark brown, a strong, flamboyantly handsome face with a powerful jaw line and a nose that hung straight and sharp over a narrow, tight-lipped mouth. It was an almost Gallic face, the eyes very bright, the brilliance of the whites under the thick head of black hair giving them a wide-eyed look that was almost a stare. A little black moustache, turned down over the corners of the mouth, seemed to split his features in two, dividing the jaw and the mouth from the sharp, pointed nose and staring eyes. If it hadn't been for the moustache, I think I might have recognised him at once.

'That fishing boat of yours . . .' he said. 'Señor Flórez took me to see it this morning. Just what I and my two friends here are looking for.' His two friends, seated across the table from me, nodded. One of them was small and sharp-featured, the other much larger, a big barrel of a chest, broad shoulders, his crumpled features reminding me of a boxer from Dublin I had picked up one time in Gib and delivered to Tangier. 'We got to earn a living.' He smiled an engaging, friendly smile. 'Nice place, Mahon.

84

Fishing good, too.' There was a softness in his voice, the accent faintly Irish.

'What he means is we're just about broke,' the man beside me went on. 'We need a fishing boat and somewhere ashore where we can live and store our gear. You happen to have what we want. I saw that villa you're building this afternoon. I also had a look at Port d'Addaia. If we had the villa we'd keep the boat there. Nice and handy. Well sheltered, too.' He wasn't looking at me now, his eyes on his coffee as though talking to himself and his hands flat on the table. They were big, fine-boned, very capable-looking hands. 'Now tell me something about this fishing boat of yours – speed, range, charts on board, sails, etc. I've read the details, of course, and one of your men showed me over her, but I'd like to hear about her from you, okay?'

My coffee came as I began to run through the inventory and the performance, and all the time I was thinking of that catamaran and trying to build up the value of the *Santa Maria*, knowing that the exchange was heavily weighted in my favour. To build a cat like that at the present time – good God, it would cost a fortune.

A glass had come with my coffee. He reached for the bottle and filled it for me. '*Salud!*' We drank, raising our glasses as though the deal were already completed.

'I saw you come in this morning,' I said. 'Where were you from?'

He stared at me, and there was something about the eyes . . . but then he had turned away. 'Fishing,' he said. 'We'd been fishing.'

'You had a passenger on board, so I naturally thought . . .'

'I tell you, we'd been fishing.' He looked at me again, his eyes coldly hostile. 'There was a friend of mine with us. We enjoy fishing. All of us.' He stared at me hard for a moment. 'Don't we?' he said to the other two, and they nodded. 'Okay.' He knocked back the rest of his drink and got almost violently to his feet. 'If you're interested in the deal, then we'll go over to *Thunderflash* and you can poke around down below. But –' and he leaned suddenly over me, prodding my chest with a hard index finger, 'don't go asking stupid questions, see. One of the reasons we're all here is because Flórez said you were discreet – when it was to your advantage. Right?'

I didn't say anything. Looking up at him and seeing those eyes staring down at me, I suddenly realised who he was. This was the man Gareth Lloyd Jones had been looking for. Evans. Patrick Evans. Slowly I got to my feet, the others too, and we all went out and across the road to the dock. The American was below as we clambered across his boat and dropped on to the deck of the catamaran. Evans unlocked the door, ushering me below in a way that left me in no doubt that he was the owner, and the moment I stepped down into that great saloon, with its breadth and comfort and the fabulous view for'ard, I was hooked. I had never been in this type of craft before. Even at the Boat Show in London, the last time I had been there, I hadn't seen anything like this, so immaculately designed, so perfectly suited to cruising in the Mediterranean.

He showed me round himself, double beds in each of the hulls with washbasin, loo and shower for'ard, hanging lockers aft and two single berths, the steps down from the saloon built over the port and starb'd engines, and all the time my mind racing, thinking what I could do with it, a different charter clientele entirely – San Tropez, Monte Carlo, Capri, the Aegean. We went back to the saloon and he produced a bottle of whisky. 'Well?' He was smiling. He knew from my comments, from the look on my face, that he'd be able to get what he wanted. And I? – with luck I would get what I wanted, what I'd always wanted – oh my God yes. We drank, smiling at each other, and then I nearly ruined it. 'I don't think I got your name.'

'Lloyd,' he said.

Not Evans or Jones, but the first part of Gareth's surname – Lloyd. 'Do you know a man named Gareth Lloyd Jones?'

His eyes snapped wide, suddenly wary, his face gone hard again and quite expressionless. 'He was here on leave,' I said, floundering slightly as I explained. 'He was looking for somebody — somebody rather like you. And I thought I saw you — in Es Grau, a bar there, three, four months ago. Were you here then?'

He glanced at Flórez, half rising to his feet, those powerful hands of his clenched so tight the knuckles showed white. But then he smiled at me and sat down again, forcing himself to relax. 'Yes,' he said. 'That's when I decided on Menorca. I was looking for somewhere to settle, you see.' He picked up his whisky, swallowed some of it, staring at me all the time, hostility gradually giving way to curiosity. 'How well do you know Gareth?' he asked me. And when I explained how we had met, he leaned back against the cushions of the settle. 'He's still here, is he?' he asked.

'No,' I said. 'He left yesterday.'

'How long was he here?'

'About five days, I think.'

'Did you see much of him?'

I shook my head. 'We had lunch together at Fornells, that's about all, and that same evening he came to the Red Cross barbecue with us. I think my wife saw more of him than I did.'

He sat there for a moment, quite still and apparently lost in thought, his eyes fixed on a shelf full of bottles at the end of the bar. 'That night,' he said slowly. 'He was with you, wasn't he? Flórez says there was some trouble. You flushed a couple of squatters out of a cave and they pinched his car. Right?'

I nodded, wondering at his interest.

'Did you see them? Would you be able to recognise them?' And he added quickly, 'I'm sorry about your wife. I believe she was hurt.'

'No, we didn't see them,' I said. And I told him briefly what had happened. But he didn't seem interested in the

87

details, only in the fact that Gareth Lloyd Jones had been there. 'You say he was looking for me?' he interrupted. 'Did he say why?'

'He said you were at school together, that you saved his life.' And because I wanted to get back to the business in hand and clarify the ownership details, I said, 'He also told me your name was Evans.'

I saw him hesitate. But it was only momentary. 'Lloyd Evans. It's a double name, see, like Gareth's.' And he added, 'Said we were at school together, did he?' He was smiling now, seemingly at ease again. 'HMS *Ganges*. That's what he was referring to.' He gave a little laugh. 'Yes, I suppose you could call it a school. It was a training establishment for naval ratings. It had a flagpole. Still there, I believe – a bloody great pole about a mile high, and some stupid sod of a PO makes him go up to the top almost his first day. A punishment, he called it, but it was straight bloody sadism. Christ! the poor little bastard had only just arrived, raw as a cucumber and scared out of his wits. I had to go up and talk him down. Practically carried him.'

He nodded his head, still smiling to himself. 'Got plenty of spunk, I'll say that for him. He was a town boy, East End of London, mother owned a greengrocer's, something like that. Don't reck'n he'd ever been up a mast before in his life. I remember watching, a squad of ten nozzers we were, and that bastard of a PO orders him over the futtock shrouds, wot we called the Devil's Elbow. It was all of a hundred feet up. Somehow he made it, and up the rope ladder. After that it was bare pole and he'd been told to touch the button at the top.' He looked at me quickly. 'Difficult for you to imagine what it's like. Most people never seen a mast that high except in the distance on one of the Tall Ships.'

I nodded, the picture of it clear in my mind. 'I've seen that mast,' I said. 'You don't have to tell me about the height of it.'

'Seen it?' He looked surprised, and when I explained, he

nodded. 'I heard it was turned into a sports centre. Best thing for it with all those messes and officers' quarters with polished wooden decks. And the ranges, of course. So you're into competition shooting, are you?' He was looking at me hard as though that somehow made a difference. 'Bisley?'

'Yes,' I said. 'Until a few years back.'

He nodded. 'I know somebody who practises at Shotley on the old ranges we used as kids. That's how I know about the commercial range facilities.'

'Who was that?' I asked him, but he was already back to the story of Gareth Lloyd Jones climbing that mast. 'Poor little bugger, he got himself to the top of the ladder and it was at that point he made the mistake of looking down. I know what it feels like, looking down from that height, because I was the cadet chosen to stand point, right on top of that fucking button. There's a lightning conductor there and that's all you've got to hang on to, standing to attention with the others manning the yard and some bloody admiral inspecting the school.' He leaned back, his eyes half-closed, and still that smile. 'Hadn't thought about it till now, but yes, I suppose he'd feel I'd saved his life.'

The way he had told it, such relish in the recollection, and now going on to explain how he had got Gareth down, talking to him all the time. 'You get pretty close to a boy when you've been through an experience like that together. It wasn't easy for either of us.' There was a flamboyance about the man. It was as though he had an urgent need for self-dramatisation. I think this is often the case with men who are preternaturally handsome, perhaps because their looks make things appear so easy at first, and then suddenly they begin to realise looks are not enough. 'Still in the Navy, is he?' And when I told him Lloyd Jones had just been promoted and had left Menorca to take command of a frigate waiting for him in Gibraltar, he nodded. 'Of course. He was cut out for it, real Navy material. But Lieutenant Commander, and a frigate of his own . . .' He swirled the whisky round in his glass. 'You sure he didn't say anything about why he was looking for me?' He raised his eyes, staring at me.

'I don't think I asked him,' I said. 'I presumed, when he said you were at school together, that you were close friends, is that right?'

'Yes, I suppose so. We're certainly close.' And he smiled as though at some private joke. He smiled a lot during that meeting on *Thunderflash*, but the smile never reached his eyes, and his face wasn't a smiling face. When he smiled it was a conscious stretching of the mouth that revealed teeth so white and even they might have been false. And it wasn't only his face that was hard. His body was hard, too. Even then I was conscious that he was a very fit, very tough man.

'You saved his life twice,' I said. But he wasn't to be drawn on that, his mind already back to the subject of the *Santa Maria* and the villa up on Punta Codolar. He wanted to start fishing right away. And he added with a thin, rather wry smile, 'Silly, isn't it? Here I am with this boat that's worth a small fortune, and I'm short of money and nowhere to live.' He wanted to make the exchange right away. 'Tomorrow. I'd like us to be free to shift our gear on to the fishing boat tomorrow. You're not using her for anything. I've looked her over and she's ready to go. So's *Thunderflash*. A quick clean round the ship after we've gone and you could have a charter party on board by the weekend. What do you say?'

What I said, of course, was that I'd have to talk it over with Soo and she wouldn't be out of hospital until next morning. 'Exchanging boats is one thing,' I told him. 'But that villa was my wife's idea. I don't know whether she'll agree.' For a moment I toyed with the thought that I might force through an exchange on a boat-for-boat basis, perhaps with a small cash addition, but he wasn't that much of a fool.

In the end he agreed to leave it over until I had had a chance to talk to Soo. 'Ring Señor Flórez here. He'll know where to find me. But I want that fishing boat by Saturday at the latest, tanked up with fuel and ready to go. That gives you two days, okay?' He got to his feet then, and when I asked him whether he needed anybody local to show him the best fishing grounds, he looked at me sharply and said, 'Don't bother. I know where I'm going.'

'What about charts then?'

'Not your problem. I got all the charts.' And he added, 'You ring Flórez, eh? Tomorrow, right after you pick up your wife from the hospital.'

I told him that might not be long enough to talk her into the deal, but in fact Soo proved much easier to persuade than I had expected. She was more interested in the man's friendship with Gareth Lloyd Jones at *Ganges* than in the future of the villa she had so recklessly acquired the day before she lost the child. 'But didn't you ask him?' she demanded almost angrily when I told her I had no idea what the relationship of the two men had been after the flagpole episode. 'I'm certain there was something between them, an intimacy – I don't think it was sexual. You don't think Gareth's in any sense gay, do you? I mean, he doesn't behave like one.'

'No,' I said. 'I don't think he is.' In fact, I hadn't given it a thought.

'Hero worship?' She was sprawled on the old couch we had picked up in Barcelona, her head turned to the window, staring at the sea. 'Was that why he was looking for this man?' Her smooth, darkish forehead was slightly puckered, her eyes half-closed, her body slim again, no lovely curve to her belly and the madonna look quite gone from her face so that it was now pinched, even a little haggard.

I think she was quite glad not to have to cope with the problems of overseeing the completion of that villa. At any rate, she accepted the situation. But later, much later, she was to insist that if I hadn't been so obsessed with my 'new toy' I would have known what was going on. She was, of course, much closer to the people of the island than I was. She had a lot of friends, not only in Mahon and Ciudadela, but out in the country among the farms, and she did pass on to me some of the talk she picked up about the growing popularity of the separatist movement. It was backed by the two communist parties, the *Partido Communista de España*, or PCE, and the *Partido Communista de los Pueblos de España*, or PCPE, and appeared to be gaining ground. *Menorca*, the *Diario Insular* or local paper, and even *La Ultima Hora* of Palma in Mallorca had carried the occasional article on the subject. But now I had no time any more to read the local newspapers. I was fully stretched getting *Thunderflash* ready for sea.

Once I had agreed the deal with Patrick Evans and checked the share ownership certificate, which showed him to be the sole owner, with sixty-four-sixty-fourths of the shares, I had pictures taken of the catamaran, some with the sails up, others of the saloon with the table laid, a vase of wild flowers and a large Balearic crayfish as the centrepiece. These I mailed off to a dozen of the most up-market agencies specialising in Mediterranean travel, together with a plan of the layout and full details. Three of them I actually phoned, and within a week two of these had expressed interest, and one of them, representing an American agency, had their representative fly in from Mallorca to inspect the boat and cable a report direct to Miami. Two days later I received a cable offering a two-week charter if I could pick up a party of eight Americans at Grand Harbour, Malta, on May 2. There was no quibble about the price, which would mean that in just one fortnight *Thunderflash* would earn more than the *Santa Maria* had made the whole of the previous season.

Moments like this make one feel on top of the world. I didn't stop to wonder why Evans had gone fishing instead of chartering the cat himself. I simply cabled acceptance, asking for twenty per cent deposit, and when this came through by return, I hardly thought of anything else, my energies concentrated on getting *Thunderflash* repainted and in perfect condition, the hulls white, not blue, and the boat in tip-top condition.

We finished her just three days before I was due to speak at the opening of the Albufera *urbanización*, and when I got back that night Soo was almost starry-eyed, not because *Thunderflash* was back in the water and moored right outside, but because she had received a note from Gareth Lloyd Jones in Gibraltar. 'He says he was piped aboard at fifteen thirty-two on Wednesday afternoon.' And she added, the letter clutched in her hand, 'It's there in the log – Captain piped on board HMS *Medusa*.' She looked up at me then. '*Medusa* was one of Nelson's ships, wasn't she?'

'Ask Carp,' I said. 'There's a *Medusa* buoy off Harwich. I sailed past it once on a navigational course.'

'But you were Army.'

'The outfit I was in, they expected you to be able to find your way at sea.'

'*It made me feel good* – that's all he says.' She folded the letter up. 'What a wonderfully exciting moment it must have been for him – the piercing whistle of the bo's'n's pipes, his salute to the quarterdeck, and thinking all the time that he'd made it, from *Ganges* and the lower deck right up to the command of a frigate.'

I went through to the office and checked the mail. Another charter – that made two lined up for the summer. Things were beginning to look real good. At least the boating fraternity weren't to be put off by the threat of bombs following the Libyan raid, or the fall in the dollar. Not even the information that another of our villas had been paint-sprayed could dampen my spirits. It was the usual slogan – URBANIZAR ES DESTRUIER SALVEMO MENORCA, and Miguel had written me a long letter of complaint in Spanish. I told Soo to deal with it, my mind still on *Thunderflash*.

The weather was set fair for the moment and next morning, standing at the open window in the blazing sun, drinking my coffee, I could hardly believe it, the twin hulls so beautiful, such a thoroughbred, lying there to her reflection, no wind that early in the morning, the surface of Mahon harbour absolutely still.

I called Soo to come and look at her. 'We'll take her out under engines as far as La Mola, wait for the wind there.' But she had promised to pick up one of the Renato girls at their vineyard farm beyond St Luis and picnic on the limestone rock ledges of Cala d'Alcaufar. Carp appeared with the semi-inflatable from the direction of the naval quay, the aluminium bows half-lifted out of the water as the big outboard thrust the tender close past the Club Maritimo, the metal masts of the yachts alongside the pontoon winking in the sun as they bobbed and swayed to the sharp-cut wake.

East Coasters tend to keep their emotions under control, but though he didn't show it, I sensed Carp's excitement as the two of us scrambled aboard and got the engines started and the anchor up. He had never skippered anything like this before and the fact that I had put him in charge of the boat had done wonders for his ego. He had bought himself one of those baseball-type hats with a long America's Cup peak and he couldn't stop talking as we motored out past Bloody Island, rounding the northern end of it, bare earth showing where Petra had trenched beyond the great stone capping slabs of the hypostilic chamber she had been excavating. The water was so still we could have nosed in for her to jump on board.

She would have loved it, but two days after Soo had left hospital I had had the unpleasant task of taking a telex out to her camp with the news that her father had been badly injured in a car crash. A vacant seat on a charter flight had enabled her to leave that same afternoon. We had not heard from her since, and now, sitting there at the wheel, driving the big catamaran close-hauled past the

La Mola fortifications, I missed her. It was such a perfect day for trials, the wind coming in from the south-east and building up through the afternoon, so that the B and G instruments showed us touching fifteen knots as we ran back into the harbour under full main and spinnaker, the spray flying, the sun shining, the wind hard on the side of my face. And the boat behaved perfectly. Nothing more to do to her, except a few replacements to the rigging, a little fine tuning.

'I've talked to Miguel on the phone,' was Soo's greeting as I came in, tired and elated. 'He'll have a word with you on Monday, after the Albufera ceremony.'

'What's his problem?' I asked, pouring myself the Balearic version of a horse's neck. 'We've paid him for the work to date.' I was thinking of the speech I had promised Jorge Martinez I would make. In the excitement of getting *Thunderflash* ready I had forgotten all about it.

'It isn't the money,' Soo said.

'What is it then?'

'It's the work. He's short of work.'

'What does he expect?' With the vandalism that was going on, builders were finding life difficult. 'He's lucky to have a villa to complete.'

'That's the trouble. Evans has told him to stop work. He and his two mates have moved into the ground floor and Miguel's been told to clear the site. Anything still to be done they'll do themselves. The agreement, you remember, was that we'd employ him to finish the building.'

'You may have told him that. I didn't.' I went over to the window, propping myself on the desk top and enjoying the ice-cold fizz of the brandy and ginger ale, my mouth still dry with salt. The lights were coming on, the old town showing white above the steps leading up to the Port Mahon Hotel and the Avenida Giron. 'He's got no claim on us at all.'

'He thinks he has.' And Soo added, 'A matter of honour, he said.'

'Oh, bugger that,' I told her. 'There's nothing in writing. I saw the lawyers early last week.' But in the end I agreed I would have a talk with him. 'It's not far from Albufera to Codolar Point. We could easily run over there either before or after the ceremony and see what Evans has to say about it, if he's in residence. Do you know if he is?'

'Miguel says not. He moved in with his two mates, did a quick do-it-yourself job making the lower half habitable, then brought the *Santa Maria* round into the bay at Arenal d'en Castell and the following morning they were gone.'

'When was that?'

'Last week. Friday, I think.'

'Then they should be back by now. Nobody stays out fishing off Menorca two weekends at a stretch.'

But they did. At any rate, there was no sign of them on the Monday morning when I drove out to the point just before the opening ceremony. This was due to start at twelve-thirty followed by a buffet lunch in the hospitality pavilion on the Addaia–Arenal approach road. The villa was deserted, some of the windows covered with sheets of plastic, the scaffolding still there and the whole place a mess of builders' rubble. People I spoke to on the approach road to the development said they had seen no sign of anybody there for more than a week.

The site for the ceremony was a newly completed villa standing on a rise a little back from the road and close to the entrance to the Albufera development. A white tape had been stretched across this road and a little crowd was already gathered on the villa's terraces and by the shrubbery that covered the hillside. The sun was shining and there was a magnificent view across Arenal to the Fornells peninsula. There was a guard of honour provided by the military, also a band, which began to play just after Soo and I had taken our seats. The Renatos were there and several other friends, the atmosphere that of a provincial function almost anywhere, except for that view and the ever-present Menorcan wind.

The Mayor arrived, only eight minutes late, accompanied by a *Guardia* motor-cycle escort. His car drove straight up to the tape and Jorge Martinez jumped out. Waving and smiling, he came running up the steps, his body slim in a sky-blue suit, his face dark in shadow and full of vitality. 'You speak after Señor Alvarez,' he said to me as he shook hands. Mario Alvarez was the construction engineer for the project. 'First in English, then in Spanish – just a few words. Okay? I speak last.'

I nodded and he took his place, sitting quickly down and signalling for the band to stop. In the sudden silence the voices of the children playing hide-and-seek among the shrubs seemed startlingly loud, and I could hear the gulls calling as they planed above the cliffs.

Alvarez spoke for perhaps five minutes, a very flowery speech, both in his reference to the project and to the Alcalde, who looked pleased. So did the workmen, who were also complimented, the faces of all those present wreathed in smiles suitable to the occasion. Then it was my turn, and since I made a point of referring to the activities of the separatists, the smiles disappeared. Jorge Martinez understood English better than he spoke it. He was not amused, but a reference to the involvement of the PCE and PCPE had him nodding his head vigorously. He was a right-wing socialist and detested the communists. And when, after I had repeated my remarks in Spanish, I sat down, he was smiling again and nodding as he clapped his hands, and everybody did the same, apparently happy at what I had said.

Abruptly, he jumped to his feet, and just as abruptly, the clapping ceased and everybody fell silent, except the children. As always, he spoke very fast, not reading his speech, but talking as though straight from the heart. His line was that Menorca was a small island with few natural resources. But it had the sea and it was warm. Tourism and the foreigners who purchased villas such as this one, bringing much-needed foreign currency – hard currency so that the life of the people could be improved and made less hard . . .

It was as he was saying this, his arms outflung as though embracing the island and all its people, his face lit by that broad political smile of his and his voice carrying conviction across the little gathering to the rock outcrops of the cliff line beyond, it was then that a sound cracked like a whip over the proceedings. His head jerked forward, the smile still there, a rictus in a spreading welter of blood and grey matter, his whole body toppling forward, a staggering, headlong fall that took him down the flight of six steps that led from the upper terrace where he had been standing.

I remember my eyes recording with a sort of instant paralysis of horror the neat round hole in the back of his head as he fell sprawling forward. Then his body hit the lower terrace and rolled over, the eyes seeming to hang loose in that dreadful, bloody mash-up of a face. Manuela let out a stifled cry, Soo was retching, her face white and her eyes closed. From shocked silence, the little crowd was suddenly in an uproar of noise, women, and some men, screaming, soldiers moving forward as their officer shouted an order, the *Guardia* abandoning their motor bikes, drawing their pistols and looking about them in bewilderment.

Somebody shouted for a doctor. But there was no doctor, no need of one anyway. Jorge Martinez was patently very dead, killed instantly by a single bullet, and no sign of the killer who must have been an expert marksman. The soldiers were running now, up over the terraces and round the back of the villa, sealing it off. But though the shot had obviously come from behind us, perhaps from one of the villa windows, the gunman could equally have fired from the shrubbery on the hill above.

The minutes passed in a seemingly aimless search, the official guests and the little crowd of local people all beginning to talk as the initial shock wore off. A small boy was brought to the *Guardia* corporal, his little face white and creased with tears, his mouth hanging loose, his eyes large. Word spread in a sea of whispering – the child had seen the gunman as he went into the bushes behind the villa. No, he wasn't playing with his friend. We could hear the child's voice now, high and very frightened. He had gone to have a pee and had found the man lying there with a gun. The kid had been right there when he had fired, only feet away, and then the killer had scrambled to his feet and disappeared up the slope.

Soldiers and bandsmen fanned out, climbing the slope behind us, and Alvarez in a shaken voice asked us all to go down to the pavilion where there would be some wine and something to eat. Would we go now please, then the authorities could take any statements they might need. He glanced down at the body of the Mayor. A soldier was covering it with a plastic sheet encrusted with cement. Alvarez made the sign of the cross and turned abruptly, walking stiffly erect down to the road. I watched Gonzalez Renato stand for a moment, head bowed over the body, then go to his car. Most of the guests did the same, and watching them pay their respects to the inert bundle that only a moment before had been so full of vitality, I had the feeling they were not thinking about Jorge Martinez, but about themselves, and wondering what would happen now. Politically he was the nearest to a strong man the island had known since the end of the French occupation in 1802. Now he was dead and nobody to replace him, nobody who had the charisma and the public appeal to guide a volatile, insular and basically peasant people into an increasingly uncertain future.

We were held in the hospitality pavilion most of the afternoon. Plain-clothes police arrived, noting down names and addresses, interviewing those nearest to the murdered man and anyone who might have had a glimpse of the gunman. The food disappeared almost at a gulp, the wine too, the babble of voices on a high pitch as speculation reached the verge of hysteria. Who had done it – the extreme right, the extreme left, Eta? Or was it a delayed reaction to events in Africa? *Salvemo Menorca*. For myself, and the scattering of other ex-pats attending the ceremony, it was not a pleasant experience. We might not be directly responsible, but you could see it in their eyes – we were to blame.

There was something quite primitive in the way some of them looked at us, as though we had the Evil Eye. And the *Guardia* in particular reacted in a similar manner, their manner of questioning increasingly hostile. It was almost as though they had convinced themselves that one of us, one of the *extranjeros*, must know who had done it and be connected with it in some way. You could see it from their point of view. This was an island. To kill like that, in cold blood, it had to be somebody from outside – a terrorist, some representative of a foreign organisation, not one of their own people. It was a gut reaction. They were looking for a scapegoat, but the fact remained that all of us who were being questioned, all except the children and a mother who had gone looking for her little boy, we were all of us gathered there in full view, so that in the end they had to let us go.

Soo and I didn't talk much on the drive back. It was late afternoon, the air full of the clean smell of pines and everywhere the fields massed with colour, the predominantly golden carpet of flowers patched with the startling white of wild narcissi, the sun blazing out of a blue sky. What a lovely day for a killing! What the hell was wrong with Man that he couldn't enjoy the beauty of the world around him? Politics. Always politics. I felt almost physically sick. There was so much here in Menorca that I loved – the sea, the sun, the peace. And now it was shattered. Martinez had been much more than just the Alcalde of Mahon. He had been a power throughout the island.

That evening several of us met in a restaurant near the square in Villa Carlos. But though we talked late into the night we achieved nothing except a fragile sense of solidarity. There were men there who had been in the island many years, but though they tried to kid themselves they were now Menorquins, they knew in their heart of hearts they were still foreigners. We were all of us *extranjeros.*

I was not in a happy frame of mind when I finally returned home. Soo, thank God, was already in bed and asleep. I undressed in the dark, a breeze blowing the curtains. Lying there, eyes closed, my mind went over and over the events of the day, the talk at that crowded restaurant table. Too much brandy, too much coffee. And then the phone rang.

I thought it might be America. Sometimes Americans forget the time difference. I rolled over, reaching blindly for the receiver, but Soo was before me. 'Yes?' She switched on the light. And then, after a moment: 'For you.' She passed it across to me and turned over, away from the light, as a man's voice spoke in my ear: 'Wade here. We've just got the news. You were there, I gather.'

I came awake then, wondering who the hell he was. 'Who is it? Who's speaking?'

'Wade,' he repeated. 'Commander Wade.'

I remembered then. 'Where are you speaking from?'

'London,' he said. 'Where did you think?' He had a quiet, crisp, well-educated voice. 'Did you see him?'

'Who?'

'The man who shot Martinez, of course. Did you recognise him?'

'I didn't see him. How should I? Nobody saw him, not to recognise him.' And I asked him, 'What's it got to do with you, anyway?'

But he ignored that. 'We have a picture here. It's just come in. It shows you seated right beside the Mayor. You must have seen what happened.'

'Of course I did. But the shot came from the villa behind and I was looking at Jorge Martinez, we all were, watching him as he pitched forward down the steps on to the terrace below. The police have full information, they took statements –'

'Yes, yes, we've got a telex copy of your statement here.'

'Then why the hell are you phoning me? It's after one in the morning.'

'I'm well aware of the time.' His tone was slightly weary and I guessed he had been at some Navy office most of the evening.

'What are you, Intelligence?' I asked. But all he said was, 'This is an open line, so let's keep to the point. I'm phoning you because Lloyd Jones reported you'd been very helpful in locating a *friend* of his.' His emphasis on the word friend made it clear he didn't want the man's name mentioned. 'I understand you have now exchanged an unfinished villa and an old fishing boat for his catamaran. Where is he, do you know?' And when I said I had no idea, that he was away fishing somewhere, he asked when I had last seen him.

'Almost two weeks ago.' And I added, 'What business is it of yours? Anyway, you have my statement. You've just said so.'

'Yes, but there's nothing in it about your dealings with this friend of Lloyd Jones. We need to know where he is now, and where he was at the time the Mayor was shot . . . Hullo, hullo! Are you still there?' His voice had sharpened.

'Yes, I'm still here.'

'You didn't answer.'

'Why should I?' I was fully awake now and wondering what his real purpose was. 'I've no intention of acting for your organisation.'

'What organisation?'

'Intelligence,' I said. 'I want no part of it and I'm going to hang up now.'

'No. Don't do that. Not for the moment.' He said it as though he were giving an order on his own quarterdeck.

'I'm sorry,' I said. 'Goodbye.'

'Ahmed Bey. Remember? And the Mattarella brothers.'

'What do you mean?' The receiver was back at my ear, a quite involuntary movement.

'Kenitra,' he said. 'On the coast of Morocco.' And he added, 'You see, I've had a few enquiries made about you. I don't think I need say any more. Now answer my questions please.' There was a coldness in his voice that hadn't been there before, a certainty that I would do what he asked. 'Have you seen our friend since you handed the *Santa Maria* over to him ten days ago?'

'No,' I said.

'Have you asked the police where he is?'

'Why should I? A man out fishing . . .'

'You think he's fishing?' He didn't wait for an answer. 'So you don't know where he is now or where he's been?'

'No.'

'Well, kindly find out.'

'I'm busy,' I said. 'I have clients . . .'

'Just find out for me. Understand? I'll ring you tomorrow night.'

I opened my mouth to tell him I wouldn't be in, that there was no point, but instead I heard myself say, 'When?'

'Eighteen hundred hours.'

I started to say I would be out then, but the line went suddenly dead.

I lay back, my eyes closed. Ahmed Bey! Jesus! that was more than ten years back. The Jedida-Marseilles run.

'What did he want?' Soo was propped up on one elbow, her large, dark eyes staring at me. 'Who was he?'

'A client, talking about boats.'

'At this time of night?'

'Go to sleep,' I said. I needed to think.

'He said his name was Commander something or other. Was it about Gareth?'

God almighty! She was still thinking of Lloyd Jones. 'No, of course not.' But I could see she didn't believe me.

'Why did he ring then? It's almost half past one. Was it

about this man who persuaded you to part with the villa? You shouldn't have done it, Mike. A lovely villa like that, the *Santa Maria* too, and all you've got for it is that bloody catamaran. What did he say? What did he want?' She was leaning forward, fingers gripped urgently on my arm. 'Is it to do with – what happened today?'

'Yesterday,' I said. Already it was yesterday and Wade in London, the man who had told Lloyd Jones to contact me . . . No, ordered more likely. Ordered him to check with me in the hope of discovering Evans's whereabouts . . . Wade was concerned enough about what had happened here in Menorca to ring me in the middle of the night.

'Patrick. That's what Gareth called him.' She let go of my arm, slumping back on the pillow. 'What's he been up to now?'

'Now?' My mind shifted from my talk with Wade to Lloyd Jones sitting across from me at that table on the Fornells waterfront. Had he told her more than he had told me? 'What do you know about Patrick Evans?' She shook her head quickly, her eyes sliding away from me. 'What did he tell you?' I was leaning over, shaking her, but all she did was stare at me blankly. 'Nothing – only that he'd saved his life.'

'I know that. Anything else?'

She hesitated, and then she said, 'They're related.'

'In what way?'

'Just related, that's all. He was explaining why he was so anxious to find the man. A message, I think it was the man's mother. She had asked Gareth to take a message.'

She didn't know what the message was. She thought it might be something to do with a cottage they owned in a place called Gwenogle. 'I remember the name because it sounded so odd, and yet the way Gareth said it . . .' She was smiling to herself. 'I think maybe he was born in that little Welsh hill village.'

'Who – Gareth or Patrick Evans?'

'Patrick. They're both of them Welsh, of course.' She reached out and switched off the bedside light. I closed my eyes and in the silent darkness I saw Ahmed Bey's face as I had seen it that last time, the bullets slamming his thickset body backwards into the wake of the Italian boat ranging alongside. That was the last trip. They dumped us in an inflatable, no food, no water, the west coast of Africa more than twenty miles away and all desert when we reached it. We were lucky to get out of it alive.

How the hell did Wade know about that? We'd never been caught by the authorities. Was there some sort of a file on me at Naval Intelligence? And then I began thinking about Patrick Evans. There had to be some connection – first Lloyd Jones searching for him with out-of-date pictures, then the man himself, and now Wade.

It was in the very middle of the night, still half awake, my mind drowsily running over the possibilities, my imagination working overtime, that I suddenly had an ugly thought. If Wade knew what I'd been up to as a kid, there might be others, Evans, for instance. In which case . . .

The feeling was so strong, so frightening, I nearly got up there and then in the middle of the night. I didn't sleep after that, waiting for the dawn, certain now that Evans would have retained a key to the catamaran.

At first light I slid out of bed and dressed in the office across the stairhead. I was just searching my pockets for the car keys when Soo emerged, a pale shadow in her cream nightdress, her face still flushed with sleep. She didn't ask me what I was up to or where I was going. She simply said, 'I'll make you some coffee.'

I could have hugged her then, all the love we'd felt for each other surging back in that moment. She knew. That intuitive sense between those who have shared several years of their lives, the sense that at times is pure telepathy, had communicated my fears to her. She knew where I was going, and why. The terrible thought that was in my mind was in hers.

She brought me my coffee, then stood by the window to drink her own. She didn't say anything. There was no need. The sun shining through the thin nightie limned the dark outline of her body, her face, her breasts, the long legs, all in silhouette. She looked infinitely desirable.

I drank the coffee quickly, urgent to be gone, to set my mind at rest, alternatively to . . . But the alternative didn't bear thinking about. If a search of the boat confirmed my fear, what would I do about it – where would I take it? Out to sea? Come back with it here and take the dinghy?

I put down the cup and walked over to her. I didn't put my arms round her, and she just lifted her face to me, our kiss without passion, gentle and understanding. After all, we had both been there, we had both heard the crack of the gun, no silencer, had seen the poor devil's face explode in a red mash as he had fallen. 'I may be some time,' I said, and she nodded, still not saying anything, but I knew she would be here, waiting for me when I returned.

CHAPTER FOUR

The sun was just rising as I drove round the end of Cala Figuera and on to the Levante, the harbour water still as glass, not a breath of wind, and as yet hardly anyone about. At the harbour end I turned right, then right again on to the approach road to the naval barracks. The naval quay is a large open space used occasionally as a parade ground. Yachts are allowed to be lifted out and laid up there, and there was still quite a line of them not yet in the water. The cat was lying stern-on just next to an old wooden yawl, the paint of her starb'd hull a-glint with the sun's reflected light as the wash of a harbour tug brought ripples slapping against the concrete walls. Beyond her, the city shone red and warm against a blue sky.

The tug hooted as I jumped on board. Aft, by the wheel with its swivel chair, I stood for a moment looking the vessel over, trying to sense whether anybody had been on board during the night. No footmarks and the lock on the saloon door had not been tampered with. But that didn't mean anything. He had given me two ignition keys, but only one for the saloon door. Some fool had dropped the other overboard, he had said.

I must have stood there for several minutes, thinking it over, trying to put myself in his shoes. But then the trouble was I was jumping to too many conclusions, and in the end I said to hell with it, opened the boat up and went below into that big saloon with its repeat bank of instruments, large chart area and semi-circular banquette behind the table on the port side. There were some overalls bundled up on the ledge below the low sweep of windows. They hadn't been there last time I had been on board, nor the long-peaked cap. That would be Carp's, probably the overalls, too. There was a cardboard box full of paint tins and brushes, and the steps to the left that normally led down into the port hull had been folded back so that he could get at the engine. A steel tool box stood open on the floor nearby.

I had brought a couple of torches with me, for this was a bilge-and-hidden-cranny search. A rummage, in fact, and however long it took, I had to be sure the ship was clean.

I started on the starb'd hull, cupboards, lockers, drawers, mattresses, then finally the bilges, remembering the one time I had experienced a customs rummage. It was in Juan-les-Pins where I had run for shelter, six *officiers de douane* turning the whole ship inside out, body searching myself and my crew. I think they would have liked to beat us up, but I was Morocco-registered, flying the Moroccan flag, and there were political reasons why, having found nothing, they should respect that flag.

It took me a good half-hour to go through that one hull, despite the floor being well supplied with inspection covers, each with a brass ring for ease of lifting. All I found in the bilges was a pair of glasses in a slipcase, some dirty overalls and a couple of bottles of Mistra, a Maltese wine, that looked as though they had been there some time.

The saloon didn't take long. If he had hidden it somewhere it was unlikely he would have chosen such an obvious place, unless of course he was willing to take his time and unscrew the panels housing the electrics. And the port hull was as clean as the other, odds and ends of equipment, a half-empty bottle of Gordon's in the bilges, nothing else, and both engine compartments I could see at a glance were clear.

I returned to the saloon, sat on the helmsman's swivel chair and tried to think what I would have done in his place. He had had the boat for some time, that much had been clear at our meeting. If I had known the boat as well as that, where would I have hidden it? Fuel or freshwater tanks were the obvious places for small packets, but there was no way he could have introduced such a large object into any of the tanks without dismantling them. Sails? But I had checked the sail bags. They were in the bows, in lockers for'ard of the loos on both sides that held chain, anchors, rope, paint. My eyes, roving round the saloon, fastened on the up-ended steps of the port hull, the exposed top of the port diesel engine. Engines! It was always engines that caused trouble.

I went over to it, bending down again and directing my torch below the shock-absorbent bedding bolts and aft along the line of the drive shaft to the propeller, sure that he or his engineer would have known every detail of the compartment. There was an area below the prop shaft that the beam of my torch could not reach. There was nothing for it but to strip down and wriggle in there. I got thoroughly dirty, of course, and it proved to be wasted effort, though the slope of the bilge underneath the shaft was fully long enough and deep enough. I came out of that painful exercise cursing, the room for manœuvre in that restricted space so limited that I damn nearly got myself stuck. Nobody, I was certain, would have attempted to hide anything in such an awkward place, not if he were in a hurry.

I stood there, naked except for my pants that were now streaked black with oil. I was staring at the steps down into the starb'd hull that concealed the other engine. And then there was the panelling. I was already scratched and bleeding in a couple of places, but I knew if I didn't check out that other cavity I would never be really certain. I lifted the steps. The compartment was exactly the same as the other, just room for me to wriggle my way headfirst between the outboard side of the hull and the cold metal of the engine. The torch was dimming, but rather than go back for the other, I squirmed further in, feeling down below the shaft with my outstretched hand.

That's how I found it — a hard, chunky package wrapped in plastic.

It took some ingenuity and some juggling to extract it from the confined space, working my way backwards at the same time. But when I was finally out, standing in the sunlight streaming through the saloon windows, and the thing in my hand, there was no doubt what it was. The only question was the type and where it had come from.

I turned quickly to the open cockpit door, feeling suddenly furtive as I slammed it shut and bolted it. Christ almighty! If somebody saw me holding this . . . My hands were trembling as I unwrapped the package. It had been zipped into one of those plastic travelling cases for suits, rolled into a tight bundle, then taped. I had to get a carving knife from the galley to rip it open.

By then I hadn't much doubt, the shape of the telescope and the folding butt apparent through the stiff red plastic. It was that most common of guns, a 7.62 mm Kalashnikov. But not the ordinary assault rifle. What I unwrapped from the plastic was the sniper's version of the AK-47. In addition to telescopic sights it had a double strut folding metal butt. The struts were in the folded position. Automatically, almost without thinking, I unfolded them, bringing the rifle to my shoulder and sighting through the for'ard window of the saloon at a gull on a mooring buoy out by the naval jetty. It felt snug and workmanlike, and I could imagine how it had been to the killer, the back of Jorge's head there in the magnified field of vision, dead-centred on the cross wires.

I glanced at the maker's stamp on the side of it, Czechoslovakian, not Russian. Then I checked the firing mechanism. The safety catch was on and it was set at single shot. I sniffed the muzzle. It still smelt faintly of gun smoke, so did the inside of the plastic, and when I took the magazine off I found one round was missing.

My worst fears confirmed I stood there in a sort of daze,

appalled at the evil of the man. To kill for political reasons, yes, maybe that could be justified by somebody deeply committed to a cause – that was a matter between him and whatever god he accepted. But Evans could have no possible commitment to a Menorquin, or even a Spanish political faction. To kill in cold blood as a mercenary, and then to plant the weapon on somebody else, on a man he didn't know, had only just met . . .!

I felt the chill of it in my guts. Man might be a rogue species; Petra certainly thought so and had discussed it with me in one of her more serious moments. But this – this was quite abnormal, quite outside of my experience. Once, and once only, I had undertaken an arms run. Explosives, detonators, some land mines, Kalashnikovs and Birettas – we had landed them in a deserted cove just south of Finisterre, handing the whole cargo over to Basque separatists. At least the Eta boys who took delivery had had a cause. But this . . .

I sat down in one of the chairs that stood by the saloon table, wondering what to do now. Go to the *Guardia*? Tell the plain-clothes detectives of the national police who had been put on to the case? But I could see the expression of disbelief on the face of the *Inspector Jefe*. I had met him once, a small, very dark man with eyes too close together and a sharp, suspicious face. They would be looking for somebody they could pin the atrocity on and I had a feeling I would do just as well as anyone else, so long as it was a foreigner and local politics not involved. The fact that I had been standing beside Martinez didn't mean I couldn't have organised the whole thing. And now, with the killer's weapon in my hand, what the hell was I to do with it? Dump it at sea, I suppose. Take it out in the dinghy and dump it, somewhere out beyond Bloody Island, and hope nobody would have their binoculars trained on me at the time.

Carp arrived just as I put the kettle on. I heard his motor bike splutter to a stop on the quay and I called out to him to ask if he would like a cup of tea. By then I had cleaned myself up and dressed, everything more or less normal, except for the rolled-up bedding on the settle by the cockpit door. I told him I had spilled some oil on it and was taking it ashore to be cleaned.

He wasn't surprised to find me on board at that hour. The boat was due to leave for Malta in a few days' time and everything was in the last-minute-rush stage. We sat around for ten minutes or so, drinking our tea and talking over all the things that still had to be done.

It was when I was in the car and actually driving back along the waterfront, the gun in the back, that the idea came to me. I eased up on the accelerator, my mind racing as I glanced in the rear mirror. It was such a neat counter-thrust, but was I sure? Was I absolutely certain it was Evans who had planted that thing on board? But who else? And even if it was one of the others, then it didn't make any difference. I eased into the parking space just past the commercial wharf, swung the wheel over, making a U-turn that headed me back, past the turning to Cala Rata and Mesquida, past the connecting road to the main Mahon–Ciudadela Highway and out along the Fornells road. A quarter of an hour later I had reached the crossroads and had turned right on to the side road heading to Port d'Addaia and Arenal d'en Castell, the sun higher now and the air warm as it blew in through the open sunshine roof.

The headland running out to Punta Codolar was brown against the blue of sea and sky. It was just after nine and everything bright and fresh. Bougainvillaea flashed purple on the wall of a villa. A beautiful morning, one of those days it was good to be alive. I should have been singing at the top of my voice. Instead, all I could think about was that bloody rifle and whether I would find Evans back from his voyage in the *Santa Maria*. What the hell did I do if he, or one of his mates, was in residence?

The villa rose slowly above the flat, scrub-clad rock of the headland like the rusty hulk of a ship coming up over the horizon. There were still vestiges of Miguel's scaffolding clinging to the breeze-block sides and as I drove up to it I thought how ugly it looked in its half-finished state, its upper windows gaping squares that looked like the gun embrasures of a coastal defence blockhouse.

I parked the car and got out, standing for a moment, staring up at it, thinking about what I would say if there was somebody there. I could have left something behind. Any excuse would do. But there was no vehicle anywhere around and it looked empty enough. I went up to the door and hammered on it. Nobody answered. I tried it, but it was locked, or more probably bolted from the inside, for when I went round to the back, I found a hasp had been screwed on to the rear door frame and there was a brand new padlock to secure it.

The villa, isolated there on the very point of the headland, was several hundred metres from any other building. Looking round, I counted seven villas within sight, all of them only just visible, and all of them apparently deserted, no sign of any movement of either people or vehicles. The garage window was the one I finally chose, bunching an old dinghy sail I had in the car against one of the four panes and slamming my elbow into it until the glass cracked. Only one piece fell on the floor and that I cleared up later; the rest I was able to pull out by hand, leaving a neat empty square through which it was easy to reach the latch. There was always a chance that the absence of that one pane might go unnoticed for a time.

It took me several minutes to find what I wanted, a loose section of flooring where the electrician had been at work. It was in the kitchen and I prised it up with two of the knives lying among a pile of unwashed plates in the sink. Underneath, between the concrete base and the wood floor, grey plastic-coated wires followed the copper piping that carried water to the kitchen taps and the water heater above the draining board. I took the wrapping off the gun, wiped it over carefully with my handkerchief, then thrust it as far into the cavity as I could and hammered the shortened section of floorboard back into place with my feet.

Looking at it, I felt a certain sense of satisfaction. There was nothing to indicate that it had been tampered with, but police officers searching the building would certainly want to see underneath. I left by the way I had come, gathering up the little pile of broken glass and latching the window after me. It was only when I was driving back to Mahon that I began to wonder where Evans and his two men were now, how long it would be before they returned to the villa.

Back at Cala Figuera I found two plain-clothes detectives waiting for me, their car parked outside the chandlery. They were in the office, an inspector and his assistant, both of them drinking coffee while Soo, her dressing gown over her nightie, sat across the desk from them, looking pale and angry. 'I keep telling them where we were sitting we couldn't possibly have had anything to do with it. They came just after you left. They wanted to talk to you, but I didn't know where you'd gone, how to get in touch with you, so they started asking me questions, then this man –' she jerked her head at the inspector – 'said they must search the house and they have been over everywhere, including the store.' All this she said in a rush, the words tumbling over themselves. 'Now they're waiting for you, so I gave them some coffee.' And she added, 'They want to search the boat, too. They seem to think we're hiding something.'

By then they were on their feet, their behaviour very correct. 'Some questions please. Then we go to this cata-maran you have acquired.' The inspector was the taller of the two, a dark, hook-nosed man, his Spanish markedly Catalan. 'You have been down to this catamaran this morning?'

'*Si*.' And I told him why. 'It is due in Malta shortly to pick up some American tourists.'

'So you are getting it ready.' He nodded. 'You go with it, or you stay here – which?'

I hesitated. It hadn't occurred to me until then. 'I'm not sure,' I said. 'Señor Carpenter may take her with just one other man, but if the weather is bad –' I left it at that and he began questioning me about where I had been, what I had done after we had been allowed to leave the Albufera hospitality pavilion the previous afternoon.

'I've already told him,' Soo said.

He understood English, even if he did not speak it, for he said, '*Si, si*, but, señor, I wish to hear it from you.'

So we went over it all again, an interrogation that took about quarter of an hour. Then suddenly he seemed to get bored with it. 'Now we go and inspect your ship please.' He called it a *barco*, so avoiding the word catamaran. 'You want to come, señora?' He turned politely to Soo.

She smiled. 'Not unless you insist.'

'No, of course not. I do not insist.' He bowed politely as she took her cue and left the office. 'May I use your telephone please?' He lifted the receiver and when he got through he spoke to somebody who was obviously his superior, reporting that he had discovered nothing new and telling him that they were on their way now to search the boat. '*Si, Jefe.* Señor Steele will be accompanying us.'

It took them a good hour to search the boat, and when they had finished, having failed to find what they were looking for, they settled themselves at the saloon table, the inspector taking out a notebook and beginning to scribble a report. Knowing from the phone call he had made in the office that they would stay here until their chief, an *inspector jefe*, arrived, I asked them whether they would like a drink. The inspector hesitated, then declined somewhat reluctantly. I told him I had work to do and would he excuse me, but he shook his head, becoming suddenly quite excited and making it very clear that I was to stay here on board.

'For how long?' I asked him.

'As long as is necessary.'

'And if I go ashore now?'

'I shall be forced to stop you.' He used the word *detención*.

I went up on deck then and gave Carp a hand. He needed to go up the mast to reeve a new spinnaker halyard and wanted somebody else besides Luis on the winch. It was while we were hoisting him up in the bo's'n's chair that the *Inspector Jefe* arrived. As soon as Carp was at the top, we made the hoist fast and I went aft to welcome him.

'Garcia Menendez.' He gave a little bow as we shook hands, his manner polite, but at the same time assertive, his sharp eyes, almost black in the sunlight, staring at me full of alert curiosity. 'Inspector Molina, is he still here? . . . Good. Then we go inside where there are no distractions.' He made a gesture with his hand that seemed to embrace the sunshine, the water, all the movement of Mahon harbour at noon on a fine spring day. He had an engineer with him. He did not introduce him to me, but he did ask my permission before telling him to go ahead with a search of the engine compartments.

We went below and I offered him a drink. He shook his head, taking the inspector's place on the banquette and waving me to a position opposite him. The engineer was already slipping into a pair of white overalls. I watched him as he folded back the steps to the starb'd hull accommodation and probed the interior of the engine compartment with his torch. I felt slightly sick, knowing that somebody must have told them where to look. 'Some questions please,' the *Jefe* said. 'Matters that have arisen in the course of our investigation. First, the ownership of this yacht which arrive here from Marseilles. There is a passenger on board. You know him?'

'No.' And I explained about the deal Evans and I had agreed on, all the time conscious of the engineer working his way into the afterpart of the engine compartment. Like

116

so many engineers he was not a small man and I could hear him grunting with the effort of squeezing his way to a point where he could check the whole length of the prop shaft and the bilge cavity below it. There was no doubt about it – they had been told exactly where to look. If I hadn't got there before them . . . 'I would like to see the documents please.' Menendez's words, sharp and official, cut across my thoughts. 'The documents of exchange,' he added. 'You have exchanged a fishing boat and an uncompleted villa on Punta Codolar, you say, for this big catamaran yacht. Who is your lawyer?'

'Martin Lopez.'

'Ah *si*. And he has the documents I suppose?'

'He is drawing them up,' I told him. 'It was all done in rather a hurry.'

'The ship's papers then. I would like to see the Certificate of Registry. Or are they also being prepared by your lawyer?'

That was when I realised how complete the trap had been, how cleverly prepared, for I couldn't produce the ship's papers, and all I could tell him was that I had seen them, but Evans had told me he had had to lodge them with the Banca Español as security for a small overdraft he had requested after opening an account with them. 'He is arranging for a copy to be sent to my lawyer.'

'I have already spoken to Señor Lopez and he does not have it. He has sent it to England for the boat to be registered in your name.'

The engineer had emerged from the engine compartment, his overalls no longer white. He was breathing heavily and reported he had found nothing. 'Then it is in the *other* engine,' Menendez said. The engineer nodded and crossed to the port side of the saloon beyond the chart table and lifted the steps that covered that engine. Menendez watched me, waiting for some sign of panic. 'Also,' he said, speaking slowly, 'there is some problem about the exchange document.'

'What problem?' I asked him. It was the first I'd heard that there was any difficulty over the paperwork and from what he was saying it was obvious he had known every detail of the arrangement between Evans and myself before coming on board and asking me questions. But then in a place like Mahon, where everyone of importance knew everyone else, I suppose it is inevitable, particularly as I was an *extranjero*. 'That's the first I've heard that there's any difficulty over the papers,' I told him. 'Did you gather what the trouble was?'

'Only that Señor Lopez was unable to contact this man Evans.'

'He is away fishing. That's why he wanted the *Santa Maria* in a hurry, so that he could earn some money fishing.'

The *Jefe* nodded. 'Of course. He is a *pescador*.' And then looking straight at me – 'Do you think he is a good one?' The thick lips under the hooked nose gave me a little crooked smile.

'I've no idea.'

'But you let him go off with your boat, the *Santa Maria*, and with no proper security. You are a businessman, Señor Steele. Does it surprise you that I find that a little strange?' He stared at me a moment, then switched his gaze to the torch-lit cavity of the open engine compartment, waiting for his engineer to report that he had found what they were looking for. 'It is a question of dates,' he added, his eyes still fixed on the starb'd side, the fingers of his right hand tapping impatiently at the table top. 'The precise date when you take over this boat.'

I sat there, feeling numb, the trap springing shut, and seeing the way they had planned it, the devilish simplicity of it. He was watching me again now, pulling out a packet of cigarettes. He offered me one, and when I said I only smoked a pipe, he laughed, and then in the act of lighting his own, quite casually, he said, 'The *Cruz Rojo*. You remember? And after, when the fireworks are over, where do you go then?' And when I didn't say anything, wondering what his question was leading up to, he went on, 'It was the night of the gala Manuela Renato arrange in the Quarries above Figuera. We were both there. Remember?'

I nodded, wondering what Petra had said, or Soo, talking to the sisters, babbling under anaesthetic? Had they dreamed up a scenario in which I was involved in running contraband into the island?

'No,' he said. 'You don't forget because in the early hours of the morning your wife gives birth prematurely and your baby is dead.'

'Have you found the men?' I asked him. 'The two men who pushed her down the slope in their haste to get out of that cave?'

He shook his head. 'No. I don't think we ever will. They are not Menorquin and we think they almost certainly leave the island very soon after.' And he added, 'Unless they go to the mainland of Spain, it is very difficult for us to trace their movements. Even in Barcelona, if they take the ferry, it is simple for them to disappear across the French border. No,' he said again, 'we do not know anything about them. What we do know, however, is that the night before there is a boat in Cales Coves and it is tied up against the rocks below the cave you were in that night. We have a description of that boat, a description that is indicative of a single mast and two hulls. We have checked with the harbour authorities and there is no boat of such description in either Mahon or Ciudadela, not in Fornells either – only this one.'

'So,' I said. 'What is the significance of that?' But I knew bloody well what was in his mind.

He was smiling now. 'Did you know there is a landward exit from that cave?' And when I explained we had been solely concerned with the two men who had rushed out from that passage, he nodded. 'Of course. And it is unfortunate about the father of Señorita Callis, that she is not here to answer some questions.'

'You're checking, I suppose, that her father really does exist, that his car accident did happen?'

'Of course. It takes time, and meanwhile you are here to answer all our questions. Let us suppose,' he said, his eyes almost closed. 'It is just a thought, eh? Suppose it is this yacht that is in Cales Coves the night before she take you to that cave. What do you think it might be doing there?'

'Sheltering, I suppose.'

'Why? Why Cales Coves and not Mahon or Ciudadela?'

'If they'd had a longish passage, from Mallorca or Corsica —'

'Or Tunis,' he said softly. 'Somewhere along the shores of North Africa.'

'If there'd been a passage like that,' I told him, 'with poor weather conditions you can get awfully tired, even in a stable boat like this. Then you just put in to the first shelter you find, head down and lights out.'

He nodded, still with that little smile. 'Of course. I understand. But no navigation lights when coming in. Also there is a light in that cave mouth for a full hour before the boat appear. That is what attracted the attention of this witness we interview.' He paused, watching me. 'The boat has no lights all the time it was tied up under the cliffs, and there is no light any longer in the cave mouth. But there is the occasional flash of torches. There was a moon, you see, and some cloud in the sky.' He sat back, suddenly relaxed. 'Well now, you are a businessman, Señor Steele, you have a position in Menorca, Spanish friends. But it was not always like that, eh? Before you come to Menorca, before your marriage. So, what does the description I have given you of what our witness saw suggest to you?'

If I said it suggested smuggling, he would think I was involved. If I said it didn't suggest a damn thing, he'd know I was lying and be even more suspicious.

'You don't say anything?'

I shrugged, stretching my face into a smile. 'Your guess is as good as mine.'

'You have been to Bisley?' The question took me by surprise. But of course, somebody would have told him about the cups. The inspector might have taken a note of them and reported. 'You are a good shot I think.' He was smiling again, the eyes bright like a bird that has seen a particularly succulent snail.

I nodded. 'Why? What's that got to do with it?'

He sat there, smiling still, and not answering, everything so quiet I could hear the distant chime of the cathedral clock. 'Look, for God's sake! I was there, right beside Jorge Martinez, sitting in front of a whole crowd of people. However good a shot I was at Bisley, there's no way I could have done it.'

'No. But there is somebody else. Antonio Barriago. You know him? A Spaniard who live in Algiers.'

Barriago! We stared at each other. Had he been the passenger that American yachtsman had said was on *Thunderflash* when she arrived in Mahon? Had Evans sailed the boat from a North African port, merely calling in at Marseilles on the way? 'What about him?' I asked. Barriago had been in the final shoot-off for the Oporto Cup, which was almost the last event I had taken part in.

'You don't know him?' It was put subtly, an invitation to deny all knowledge.

'No, I don't *know* him,' I said. 'I've shot against him. That was three years ago and I haven't seen him since. Why?' And when he didn't say anything, just sat there staring at me, I asked him why he was searching the boat.

For a moment I thought he wasn't going to tell me that, but in the end he gave a little shrug and said, 'Suppose it is Barriago who kill the Alcalde. And suppose – just suppose, Señor Steele – he has been on board this boat –'

But I stopped him there. 'I tell you, I haven't seen the man for three years.'

'All right then. Suppose he is on board when Señor Evans

is the owner of it.' He nodded at the engineer's protruding feet. 'That is why we are searching your boat. It has been in your possession since more than two weeks before the Alcalde is killed and we have been advised where is the most safe place for him to have hidden it.'

'Who advised you?' I asked him.

But he had turned away, watching the engineer again as he began to wriggle backwards. 'Now I think we know whether you are involved or not. '*Bueno?*' he asked.

The engineer grunted something unintelligible, and when he finally emerged, switching off his torch and standing there, wiping his hands and face on a bit of cotton waste, Menendez repeated his question, his voice sharp and urgent – '*Bueno y bueno, qué has encontrado?*'

'*Nada.*' The engineer pulled up the steps, slamming the engine compartment shut. It was clear he had had enough of clambering round in the confined space of the yacht's engines.

Menendez turned to the inspector, checking the details of their earlier search. Then he gave a little shrug. '*Eh bueno*, it seems this boat is now clean.' He was staring at me, a hard look in his eyes as he emphasised the word *now*.

'Barriago,' I said. 'Why do you think he killed Jorge Martinez?'

'You do not know?' Still that hard stare as he waited for an answer. 'A man answering his description, but with a different name, took an Aviaco flight out of here for Mallorca less than two hours after the shooting. At Palma he changed planes and flew on to Tunisia. The police in Tunis are endeavouring to trace him for us.'

I told him I didn't see what this had to do with me, but all he said was, 'He is a crack shot –' He used the words *tirador experto* – 'and you knew him. That is all. Nothing more.' He reached for an ashtray and stubbed out his cigarette. '*Eh bueno*,' he said again and got to his feet, the others following him. 'When you wish to make a statement . . .' Those sharp little eyes were fixed on mine. 'A full statement, then you come to my office. Okay?' He was suddenly smiling again.

'You really think I had something to do with Martinez's death?'

He shrugged. 'That is between you and your conscience. When you are ready to talk . . .' He said this over his shoulder as he went up the steps to the cockpit, his two officers behind him. 'The truth, that is all I am interested in.' He was standing like a cut-out against the blueness of the sky, his hair very black in the sunlight.

'I wonder you don't ask for my passport?' It was a silly thing to say, but he could have arrested me if he had been sure enough to charge me with anything.

He turned as he reached the quay. 'I already have your passport,' he said. 'It was the main reason I sent my officers to search your premises. In fact, your wife was kind enough to give it to them.' He raised his hand, a little gesture of farewell. '*Adiós*.' His driver was holding the car door open and he stepped in and was driven off. The other two lingered for a moment, staring at the boat as though trying to remember everything about her. Then they, too, drove away and I was left alone with Carp, his craggy features more puckered than usual. He didn't speak Spanish, but he understood enough to know I was in trouble. 'Come the next few days reck'n you'll find out who your real friends are,' he said, his Suffolk accent broader than ever. That was all and he turned away. 'That spi rope's rove, but Luis an' I gotter coil down the port anchor warp. Be for'ard if you want me.' And then, as he crossed the coachroof, heading for the port bow, he said over his shoulder, 'I'll be ready whenever you say – just in case you're coming too.'

I went back into the saloon then, standing there alone and trying to think things out. Antonio Barriago. That was three years back, the thousand-yard range and the two of us lying side by side shooting it out, a crowd gathered

123

behind us, the smell of gun oil and cordite hanging on the still air and the targets shimmering in the haze. And afterwards, in one of the messes – I couldn't remember which – the two of us professing our friendship and promising to meet again. We never had, and the next I heard of him he was a mercenary captured by SWAPO on the Zaire border.

That was all I knew about him. He might well be Basque and a member of Eta, but why risk a terrorist attack so far from the political centre of Spain? In any case, a mercenary was hardly likely to be a committed political activist.

Either his departure from Menorca so soon after the shooting was purely coincidental, or else, if he really had killed Martinez, then he had been hired to do the job. In which case, hired by whom, and for what purpose? Did the Chief Inspector really think I had hired him? In that case, he must think I had a reason. What? What possible reason could I have for wanting Jorge Martinez killed? And Wade, where did he fit in? Or Lloyd Jones, or Evans? If the police were tapping my phone . . .

I got myself a glass of iced coffee from the ship's fridge and sat there thinking about it, conscious all the time of Carp and Luis moving about the deck. I should be up there with them, helping prepare the boat for sea, not sitting alone at the saloon table wondering what the hell to do. Ring the lawyer, check about the exchange documents, contact some of the people who might know where Evans was. But what I was really thinking about was Soo giving them my passport. She might at least have told me. And Wade phoning me again this evening.

I finished my coffee, then drove back to the office. Soo was out. She had left a note to say she would be back around four. I phoned Martin Lopez, catching him just as he was going to lunch. He confirmed that the catamaran's certificate of registration had been sent to England for alteration. And yes, there had been a little problem with the exchange contracts, nothing serious, just a matter of dating it. Evans had signed it all right, but he had dated it the previous month. Intentionally? No, just a mistake, it happened quite often.

Like hell it did! Not if you knew the purpose behind it. For a moment I was tempted to take him into my confidence, tell him about the Kalashnikov. But that meant telling him what I had done with it, and anyway a lawyer who handled the affairs of some of the most prominent people in Menorca would hardly relish the thought that he might be acting for a foreigner who had got himself involved in the murder of a politician so universally popular as Jorge Martinez. I kept my mouth shut, and in doing so made myself not only accessory to an act of terrorism, but also to all that followed.

How was I, yachtsman, charterer, small-time businessman, an escapee if you like into the lotus life of the Mediterranean, to know, or even to understand, the machinations of those far removed from the little Balearic island of Menorca? There was Wade, of course, and Gareth Lloyd Jones, Patrick Evans with his two toughies and a lovely catamaran with which to tempt me. I should have known. At any rate, I should have guessed. But that is hindsight. God almighty! I couldn't possibly have known, not then, sitting at my desk with a gin and tonic and staring out of the open window, not a breath of air stirring, the water mirror-calm and the shimmering hulk of the hospital riding to its upside-down reflection like one of those great floating batteries the French and Spanish navies had used against Gibraltar at the end of the eighteenth century.

If only Petra were still here. I could have talked it over with her – practical, matter-of-fact, and that bouncing, vital body of hers. I had a sudden picture of her lying naked on top of me, that last time, the day after Soo had lost the baby. If only she'd been out there in that tent on the far side of the island. No breeze at all and the air outside almost as hot as midsummer.

I got suddenly to my feet, finished my drink and drove

round to a little restaurant I often used near the Club Maritimo. I had *gazpacho* and *gambas plancha* with half a bottle of Campo Viejo, sitting there in the darkened interior, shocked to find myself eating alone as though I were some sort of pariah. In the old days I'd done that quite often. I'd had to. But since I had come to Menorca . . . since then, of course, there'd always been Soo and the host of friends we had made – people we knew, anyway. Never the need to be alone.

Back in the office I began ringing round to discover whether Evans had put in anywhere. I think if I had phoned Flórez he might have told me right away. But Flórez was the last person I wanted to contact in the circumstances. It took me three calls before I thought of Félipe Lopescado who ran a little *taberna* on the Ciudadela waterfront. '*La* Santa Maria? *Si – un señor Inglés.*' He even knew the name. 'Pat Eevanz.' The boat had come in to the *puerto* at Ciudadela late the night before last. There had been three men on board and they had come ashore for a drink about ten-thirty. '*Si*, at the Taberna Félipe.'

'Is the boat still there?' I asked him.

'*Si.*'

'Was it there yesterday?'

'*Si*, all day.' And he assured me the men were still on board, all three of them.

'Do you know where they were at midday yesterday?' I had to ask him straight out like that, there was no alternative.

'They were here in the *taberna.*'

'For how long?'

'About three hours. You have eat here, señor. You and the señora. You know how long it takes.'

'They had lunch at your place then, all three of them?'

'*Si.* They have *mejillones.* The mussels are fresh in that morning, very good, very beeg. Then the *capitán* have *rabo de toro* and there is one *pollo* and one *escalope.* Also my *taberna* Rioja and some Quinta with the coffee.'

'And the captain's name?'

'I tell you, he is Pat Eevanz.'

I had him describe the man then, but it was Patrick Evans all right, and after leaving the *taberna*, Evans, with one of the others, had taken a taxi into the *centro*, while the third man returned on board. Félipe couldn't tell me when Evans had returned, but he assured me the man had been there this morning, because he'd seen him talking to the harbour master on the quay, and the *Santa Maria* was still anchored in the same position. He thought it likely that their catch had been off-loaded at some other port. Certainly, no fish had been landed from the vessel in Ciudadela.

I was left wondering when Evans had planted that gun in the starb'd engine compartment, even whether he had.

I cleared my desk, then drove out to the airport just south of the San Clemente road. I thought Alejándro Suárez, the assistant manager and one of the few islanders who really enjoyed sailing, might be able to produce somebody on the airport staff, or at the Aviaco desk, who had actually spoken to Tony Barriago, somebody who could give me an idea of the man's state of mind. It would have taken him no more than half an hour at the outside to clock in at the airport, which would mean perhaps half an hour of waiting before actually boarding the plane. Plenty of time for his nerves to become ragged.

But Alex said the police had already interrogated everyone who might have spoken to him and the only person who had been able to recall him was the Aviaco woman who had dealt with his ticket. She remembered him because he had come back afterwards to enquire whether the plane had arrived yet, and when she said it was due in almost immediately, he had thanked her and turned away, apparently quite satisfied. He had appeared relaxed, not in the least nervous or upset. 'Do they think he is the killer of Don Martinez?'

'Possibly.' We were standing in the airport lounge, which

was packed with people. The PA system suddenly broke into life, the hubbub rising to a crescendo as friends and relatives said their goodbyes to passengers on a Barcelona flight.

'Pardon. I have to go now. If there is anything else . . .' Alex smiled at me apologetically and went through into the departure area where, in addition to immigration and customs officials, security officers were screening the passengers before embarkation. Would Tony Barriago have been sweating as he went through the last stage before boarding the plane? But the security officer on duty now might not be the same as yesterday, and anyway, it was such an obvious line of enquiry that the police would have covered it already.

The crowd in the main lounge had thinned to a few people sitting at tables drinking coffee or wine and waiting for another flight. I wandered out into the long passageway that led to the arrivals area. This was what Tony would have done, mingled with the crowd from an incoming flight, even taken a stroll outside, anything rather than sit in the main lounge, boxed in and too conspicuous until it had filled up. I had a word with Maria at the stand that sold magazines and postcards, and then it occurred to me that he might have had a taxi waiting for him outside, just in case.

I went out and began checking with the drivers. A British charter flight was due in and there was quite a line of taxis waiting. It was about the ninth or tenth I spoke to, a fat man with a Panama hat perched on his head, who said he'd been there the previous afternoon when the *Guardia* drove up to the airport, and yes, he had seen a taxi waiting in the car park opposite. He had noticed it because normally taxis waited in the line. They did not park with the private cars. And when the police arrived, a short, hook-nosed man, who had presumably hired the taxi, went across and spoke with the driver. He had stayed there talking to him for several minutes, right up until the time his flight was called. Then he had hurried back into the airport.

'And the taxi?' I asked him.

'He come out of the car park and join us in the taxi line.'

'He had paid him off then?'

'Yes, the man pay him before going back into the airport.'

'Did the taxi leave the car park immediately?'

'No, he wait there until the plane take off. Then he join us.'

I asked him the driver's name then and he said 'Gonzalez.' He did not know his other name, but he thought he came from Villa Carlos.

I thanked him and went back to my car, convinced now that Menendez had been right. The description fitted and Tony Barriago had got away with it. At the time he flew out to Palma, and then on to Tunis, the police had had no idea who they were looking for.

Soo had returned by the time I got back. She had been to see Manuela Renato's sister, Maria, who was married to Hernando Pons, the most successful of the local property developers. 'They're very worried,' she said. 'Jorge's death leaves a vacuum and they're now getting together with their friends to fill it. The problem is they don't have any one man in mind, so that already there is a danger they'll split up into factions, each advancing their own candidate. The effect may well be that a man nobody wants will be elected.'

'Who?' I asked.

'Maria couldn't say. Flórez perhaps since he has a garage in Mahon as well as in Alayór, and of course business friends in both towns. Even Ismail Fuxá's name was mentioned. Those were the two worst possibilities, of course, but it shows what a problem this thing has created, and what she was saying to me was that it was time to be out of property in Menorca, at least until things have settled down. I saw Carmen, too. She was in one of her tense moods, a little scared I thought, and she had that wicked little woman, Mercedes, with her. Mercedes said we should leave now, go back to England, or wherever it was we came from, that it was all our fault – Thatcher, Reagan, bombs, new development . . . She was quite rude.' And Soo added, as though it were all part of the gossip she'd picked up, 'They took your passport, by the way.'

'Menendez said you gave it to them.'

'They asked where it was, so I told them.' And she added, a little defensively, 'They'd have found it anyway.'

'Possibly.'

She flared up at that. 'Not possibly – inevitably. You can't pin the loss of your passport on me. They'd have turned the whole place inside out if I hadn't told them.'

I went through into the kitchen, got some ice and mixed a strong dry martini. Damned if I was going to have a row with her over it, but just to give it to them without argument or even any sort of protest . . . 'Do you want one?' I asked her.

She nodded, standing by the window with Benjie in her arms.

I took down two glasses, and when I had poured the drinks, we stood there, not saying anything, just drinking in silence. And all the time I was conscious of her staring at me, her dark eyes big and round, the question she dared not ask on the tip of her tongue. In the end all she said was, 'Your passport wouldn't be any use; they'll be watching the airport, the ferry terminal –'

'They know who did it,' I told her.

'Who?'

'A Spaniard. He left immediately afterwards – by plane.'

'Then why –'

'I knew him, at Bisley.'

She turned to glance at the cups, then gulped down the rest of her martini, her eyes very wide and fixed on me. 'The weapon then? Where is it?' Her face had a pallid, frightened look.

I gave a little shrug. The closeness that had once been

between us was gone now and I was no longer willing to share my thoughts and actions with her the way I had. It wasn't that I didn't trust her. It was just that the links that had bound us close were no longer strong enough, so that I felt instinctively it was best for her not to know what I had done with the gun, or even that I had found it hidden on board.

'So you'll be taking the boat yourself.' She was still staring at me, holding herself very stiff, her small body almost quivering with tension.

I hadn't made up my mind, and the way she said it I knew what she must be thinking. But I wouldn't be running away from anything, only giving myself time and room for manœuvre. The boat was just about ready, and in Malta I could probably produce some reasonable excuse for being without a passport.

'I'm right, aren't I? You'll go with the boat to Malta.' She had put the dog down, holding her glass tight with both hands and gazing out across the water.

'Perhaps,' I murmured. I can remember the way I said it, flatly, without feeling, and looking back on it now, I realised it wasn't fear of arrest that was driving me to get away on my own for a time. Even if Menendez did decide to accuse me of smuggling arms, the knowledge that I was completely innocent made me certain Martin Lopez would be able to sort the whole thing out, given time. No, it was Soo. If she had slept with the man, had an affair with him, that was something I could have lived with. But love, a real passion – that is something that strikes at the heart of a man. It leaves him nothing – nothing to strive for, no purpose. Both pride and practicality dictated a break.

'Are any of the people you knew still there? Have you kept in touch?'

I shook my head. 'Mintoff and the new man will have made it impossible for them.'

'There's my mother's relatives.'

'Your mother hasn't been back since your father retired.'
I took her glass and refilled it, then mixed some more and went back to the window. Flurries of an onshore breeze were darkening the water. This was the view I had looked out on ever since we had married and settled down to build a business on this island.

'Gareth might be useful.' She said it tentatively.

'How do you mean?'

'In addition to showing the flag in the Balearics and one or two of the Italian islands, he thought it possible Malta would be included in his orders. He asked if I had any messages.'

'Did he say when he was leaving Gib?'

'No. His letter was written the day after he went on board. There was no mention of his having received orders, only that he looked forward to seeing us again when *Medusa* visited Mahon.'

'Wade may know his movements.' I stood there, sipping my martini, staring out of the window and thinking about the future. Malta was over six hundred miles away and even if we averaged ten knots, which was just possible with a favourable wind, it would take us the better part of three days.

We didn't say much after that, our thoughts locked in on ourselves, and as the shadows lengthened and six o'clock approached, I asked her to leave me so that I could talk to Wade on my own. I remember I shut the door behind her and in doing so it seemed as though I was shutting myself out from the past.

Wade was late. Only a few minutes, but expecting him to come through prompt at 18.00, waiting, it seemed an age. The sound of the phone when it came was startlingly loud, his voice even more upper-class English, more clipped than when he had phoned me in the early hours. 'Wade here. Did you locate him?'

'Yes.' And I told him where Evans was and how he had been having a meal in the Taberna Félipe on the Ciudadela waterfront at the time of the shooting. 'He couldn't have done it,' I said.

'Of course not.' And he added, 'Yesterday the Spanish police asked Interpol to locate an Italian from Naples who was booked out of Menorca on two consecutive flights, the first to Mallorca, the second to Barcelona. The name on his passport, which was forged of course, was given as Alfredo Geronimo. In fact, they now discover he is Spanish and his real name is Antonio Barriago. I believe you know him.'

'I've met him,' I said cautiously. 'Three years ago.'

'You fired together in the finals for the Oporto Cup. Had you met him before that?'

'Once,' I said. 'When I was shooting in Spain.'

'He wasn't one of the men with you when Ahmed Bey was killed?'

'No.'

'Or on the Italian boat?'

'Not as far as I know.'

'The police in Mahon seem to think the connection is a lot closer than just competition shooting. They've asked both Interpol and the Yard people over here for all the information they have on you, a dossier in fact. You and Barriago.'

'And Evans?' I asked. 'What about Evans?'

'I don't think so.'

'He's involved,' I said. 'I'm sure of it.'

'Why? You say he was at Ciudadela.' His voice was sharper now. 'What makes you think he's involved?'

But I was already regretting my attempt to involve Evans so directly. 'I just feel it,' I answered rather lamely, wondering how my words would be interpreted when they searched the villa and found the gun. 'Lloyd Jones,' I said. 'Where does he fit in? He came out here with a picture of Evans in his pocket.' I was remembering what Carp had told me, that odd incident on the East Coast of England. 'He said he was on leave, a holiday before taking up his new appointment. But his sole object seemed to be to find Evans. Why?' There was no answer. 'Are you still there?'

'Yes.' And then he said, 'They were at HMS *Ganges* together, almost the last batch of youngsters to go through before the school was closed.'

'I know that. But they are related in some way.'

'Who told you that?'

'My wife.' And I added, 'Is it true? Are they related?'

I thought he wasn't going to answer that, but then he said, 'They both have the same father. No reason you shouldn't know that.'

'But why send him to me?' I asked. 'He said it was at your suggestion he was contacting me.'

'Not my suggestion. Philip Turner's. He put us on to you.' And he added, with something near to a smile in his voice, 'When we checked your background, it was obvious you were just the man we were looking for. Malta, Menorca, Gibraltar, you know them all – all the Western Med, that is.'

He was covering himself. Phones are funny things, very revealing. You pick up nuances of expression, the hint of hidden meanings. I had the sudden sense of a void opening up, certain he had let something slip, that he hadn't meant to be so specific. 'I'll be in Malta a week from now,' I said.

'Malta. Why?' And when I told him I had a charter fixed for the catamaran, he said, 'I know that, but you can send somebody else. There are things I want to know and you're the man who can tell me. The new mayor, for instance. Who is it going to be? Who are they going to elect?'

'I've no idea.'

'Well, find out for me, will you?' And when I told him I wouldn't have time, that I needed to get away tomorrow night, he said, 'What's the hurry? Has something happened I don't know about?' I told him then how the police had searched the office and my home, then rummaged the boat. 'Are you under house arrest?'

'No, but they took my passport.'

'Under surveillance?'

'I don't think so.'

'But they suspect you?'

'How can they?' I said. 'I was sitting there in full view when it happened.'

'Yes, but the gun. I take it they haven't found it yet.' And he added, 'You see, they don't know how Barriago came by it. He couldn't have entered Menorca with the thing tucked under his arm. And what did he do with it afterwards? Do you know?'

'Of course not.'

He didn't say anything then, and I wondered whether he believed me.

'Has Lloyd Jones left Gib yet?' I asked him.

'I can't answer that.' And when I persisted, he said he was not privy to the detailed movements of ships. That was when I asked him what department of the Navy he was. He hesitated before answering. 'Planning. Forward Planning.'

'Then perhaps you can tell me if *Medusa* will be putting in to Malta.'

'I think she may.'

'Before or after she visits Mahon?'

'Before probably.' And then he asked me what my ETA Grand Harbour would be. 'You're leaving tomorrow, you say?'

'No, not tomorrow.' I couldn't do that. I couldn't just sail out of the port here and head straight for Malta. 'It'll have to be the early hours of the following day,' I said. Carp could motor the catamaran round to Es Grau, or Port d'Addaia, one of the smaller inlets, then we could slip out when everyone was asleep.

'And your ETA?' he asked again.

'Five days from now,' I said. 'If we're lucky and the weather holds.'

'I see.' He seemed to be thinking something out. Then to my surprise he said, 'Well, good luck!' He said it in quite a cheerful, friendly voice, and with that he rang off.

II

MALTA INCIDENT

CHAPTER ONE

The weather, in fact, did not hold. Carp had the boat ready
for sea well before noon, he and Luis motoring her across
to the commercial quay where they took on fuel and water,
cleared customs and immigration, and loaded the fresh
stores Soo had ordered, also the last-minute purchases.
They were away by 14.30. By then it was blowing force
four from just north of east, the wind funnelling up the
harbour so that they were motor-sailing with jib and main
hard in.

I was there to see them off. I had spent most of the
morning talking to people on the phone, chiefly the
foreign element, those who had established themselves in
business and were permanently resident. Some of them,
of course, like myself, had not involved themselves in the
political life of the island. But even they were beginning
to get worried. Those with Spanish connections were more
deeply concerned and Fuxá's name constantly cropped up.
Others were mentioned, of course – one of the leading
PSOE figures, in particular – but it was Ismail Fuxá who
really scared them. Most regarded his separatist, anti-
foreign movement as having grown alarmingly in recent
months, some even thought he might have enough support
in council to get himself elected as the new alcalde.

Only one of them was willing to talk about it openly and
at length. That was Freddie McManus, a retired property
developer who had once stood as Conservative candidate
for some Scottish constituency. He pointed out to me that
however the 1978 constitution might try to safeguard the
powers of the central government, the establishment of the
Balearics as one of the seventeen independent provinces

meant in practice that the potential power of the locally elected alcaldes was greatly increased. 'It's a charter for the emergence of little Gauleiters. All that's required is a dominant personality. And if the man has a cause, then he's even more dangerous.' And he had gone on to point out to me that to islanders stuck out on the eastern fringe of a small group in the Western Mediterranean, Madrid was a long way away. Also, and he had emphasised this very strongly, the power of the alcalde was rooted in the history of Spain, when in 1485 Queen Isabella struck at the nobility through the *Ordenancas Reales* with a court of two alcaldes to administer justice in every town of thirty or more inhabitants. 'Given a weak governor in Palma,' he said, 'anything could happen if that man Fuxá became Jorge Martinez's successor.'

None of the others I talked to were as forthcoming as that and quite a few were unwilling to discuss the political situation with me at all, some making it clear in the nicest possible way that they wanted to distance themselves from me, others quite blunt about it. There was, of course, an element of guilt involved. An island the size of Malta with a third of its wildest rock coast blanketed by villa and hotel development is not a pretty sight and most of us were getting our living from the *urbanizacións* in one form or another. It wasn't as bad as Benidorm or Tenerife, but to those with a conservationist conscience it still left a nasty taste in the mouth, bearing in mind how unspoilt Menorca had been before.

I must have contacted between twenty and thirty people that morning, all men who had as much to lose as I had if the political stability of the island was destroyed, and by the time I drove round to the commercial quay to check that Carp was cleared and ready to sail, my mind was made up. Tongues were wagging, and if I stayed, I might well find myself the scapegoat for what had happened. I was lucky to be free at the moment. If I hadn't got up at first light the previous day and searched the ship I would undoubtedly be under interrogation at *Guardia* head-quarters, perhaps even flown off to mainland Spain. I had talked it over with Carp late that night. He knew what to do and the deterioration in the weather would make it all the more convincing that he had to put back into the nearest shelter to clear a warp wrapped round one of the prop shafts or deal with some water in the fuel tank. The probability was that nobody would bother to report the cat in Addaia, but if they did, then he had any number of good excuses.

The *Policia Municipal* building looks right down on to the commercial quay, so that I was not surprised when a police car with two officers in it drew up on the quayside. We were just taking the last of the fresh stores on board and they parked there, watching us. If I had not come ashore when Luis uncleated the stern warp preparatory to letting go, they would have been on the radio immediately for a harbour launch, which would have stopped us before we had even reached Bloody Island.

I watched from the quay as Luis coiled down the stern warp, then ran for'ard to hoist the jib. The mains'l was already set and flapping on a loose sheet as the engines took her out into the open waters of the harbour and Carp turned her into the wind, heading east to clear the old grassed-over fort on Figuera Point at the entrance to the harbour proper. She looked a lovely sight once the sails had been hauled in tight, a rather hazy sun glinting on the new paint of the hull and transforming the twin bow waves into silver glitters of spray.

I turned then, thinking as I walked back to my car that I might catch up with them before they cleared the point. But then the police car cruised up alongside. 'You are not going with them?' It was Inspector Molina, and he was smiling at me. 'Such a nice boat. It must be very tempting. And Malta. Your wife comes from Malta.'

He was still smiling as I said, 'Yes, I would have enjoyed the trip. But you have my passport.'

'Ah *si*, and you are a law-abiding citizen of our island.'
And he added, 'They can see your boat is preparing to sail
from up there.' He nodded in the direction of the citadel
with the slip road snaking up like a staircase with two
hairpin bends in it. 'I just come to make sure.'

It was on the tip of my tongue then to tell him he would
have been better employed searching the *Santa Maria* and
the villa on Punta Codolar, but I checked myself. Sooner
or later it was surely inevitable they would find the gun
where I had hidden it. '*Adiós.*' They drove off and I went
back to the office to ring Lopescado at the Taberna Félipe
in Ciudadela. The *Santa Maria* had left.

'When?'

But he didn't know. Sometime during the night, he said,
for it had been there the previous evening. In fact, all three
of them had come ashore about eight o'clock. They had
sat around outside and had a few drinks, then they had
gone into the fish bar for a meal. They had left about
ten-thirty and gone straight back to the ship.

'All of them?' I asked.

'Yes, all of them, and the boat is still there when I go to
bed, with a light shining in the wheelhouse aft as well as
a riding light at the forestay.'

'Did you gather where they were going? Did they clear
customs, anything like that?'

'No, I never saw any official go on board, not then, nor
any time earlier during the evening. But then I was very
busy last night, a beeg party from Banyos, a German
party . . .' He hesitated, then said, 'Once, when I am serving the next table, I hear your name mentioned. It was
something about the *policia*. They were arguing about
why some information had not been acted on. The last I
hear they think you will try to leave Mahon sometime
today. No, you will *have* to leave. Those were his words.'

'Whose words?' I asked. 'Was it Evans who said that?'

'*Si.* The boss man with the Guevara moustache. Pat
Eevanz.'

He couldn't tell me anything more and when I put the phone down I sat there at the desk for a moment, gazing out towards La Mola and the Mahon entrance four miles away and wondering where the *Santa Maria* was now, what Evans was up to. I could just see *Thunderflash*, her white hulls and sails outlined against the hazy shape of Lazareto Island. Once they were clear of Punta del Esperó, the easternmost tip of La Mola, they would have a beam wind and a fast run to Cape Faváritx, then only five miles and all downhill to Macaret at the entrance to Port d'Addaia. Perhaps I should have arranged for them to put into Es Grau, but the entrance was very narrow and overlooked by almost every house in the little fishing village. In any case, I hadn't known then that Evans had sailed, and even if he did intend to spend the night at the villa on Punta Codolar he would probably anchor the *Santa Maria* in Arenal d'en Castell. It would be very sheltered there in an easterly blow. A picture flashed through my mind then of him opening a can of beer, or sitting down to a quick meal, at the table in that kitchen with the gun he thought was still on board the catamaran right there under the floorboards at his feet.

Soo came in then with the news that the council had been in session at the *ayuntamiento* most of the day. Nothing had been decided and there was talk of a local election.

I finished my packing and took her to the Atlante, the restaurant a few doors away, for an early meal. Sitting there, drinking *vino verde* as an aperitif, we discussed the possible choices that a newly elected council would have. But even we, whose interests were identical, could not agree – I favoured Gonzalez Renato, while Soo wanted Antonio Alvarez to be the next alcalde, chiefly I think because he would support a progressive building and development policy.

It was just as the waiter was serving our marinated sardines that the door opened and a small man in a brightly coloured short-sleeved shirt, and wearing a red floppy hat pulled down over his ears, looked in. He said something to Manuel, the patron, glanced quickly across at us, nodded and then left. 'Who was that?' I asked the waiter, conscious suddenly that I had seen the man lounging against one of the bollards when I'd come back from seeing Carp and Luis off in *Thunderflash*.

The waiter hesitated, looking at Manuel and repeating the question. Manuel in his turn looked uneasy, as though reluctant to be drawn into giving me any information about the man. *'Vigilancia?'* I asked him, and after a moment's hesitation, he nodded. The *Cuerpo de Vigilancia* were plain-clothes security police and like the *Guardia Civil* they were paramilitary and came under the direct control of the Provincial Governor. The fact that they had me under surveillance was confirmation, if I needed any, that I should get out while the going was good. Also it suggested that the killing of Martinez was regarded by the authorities as something more than just an isolated terrorist incident.

I suppose I had fallen silent after the door had closed on the man and Manuel had confirmed he was one of the *Vigilancia*. Certainly my mind was concentrated on the future, on what life held in store for me – for both of us. 'Eat up,' Soo said, 'these sardines are delicious.' And then, almost in the same breath, 'What will you do when you get there? How long will you stay? Have you decided yet?'

It was a strange meal, both of us trying to look ahead, and at one stage, when we were sitting over our coffee and a large Soberano, I had the distinct impression that she was flying something close to a flag of seduction. Soo was odd that way, always had been. I think it was the Maltese in her. She was so volatile in her emotions, one minute cold as ice, the next minute . . . I remember we sat there like a couple of lovers, gazing into each other's eyes and actually holding hands across the table, clinking our brandy glasses.

God almighty! Why can't people be more sensible, more consistent? And why the hell was I so set on a son? What would a son do for me? You change its nappies, see it through all those infantile diseases, watch it teething and grow up, and the next thing it's borrowing the parental bed to poke a girl or getting high on drugs, or worse still, standing for cap'n in place of Dad, waiting for the old sod to drop dead.

I ordered more coffee, and another brandy for us both, and we sat there, not saying anything, each alone with our own thoughts. I touched her hand again, the fingers answering to the pressure of mine, her grip almost urgent. Did she want me to stay? Was that the message she was trying to convey? And the slight flutter of her nerves. Was she scared? I hadn't thought about it until that moment, my mind so concentrated on my own predicament. Now I tried to see it from her point of view, alone here, her husband slipping away on a yacht bound for Malta and the police suspecting him of complicity in a political murder.

Political? It had to be political. Martinez had no other interests. He hadn't been in business, he hadn't fiddled his taxes. He hadn't slept with other men's wives. No breath of scandal had ever touched him. But political enemies – he had those all right, and of course decisions had been made that did affect the business community. 'It'll be all right,' I said, holding her hand tight. 'Once I'm away they'll forget all about me and concentrate on other leads. A week and they'll know for sure that I had nothing to do with it. They'll get the date when I took *Thunderflash* over and then they will begin to enquire into Evans's movements.'

Her hand tightened on mine as she slowly nodded her head. 'But suppose –' she hesitated – 'suppose the police are in on it? Suppose it's political and they're covering up.'

'Then there'd be a single name emerging as the new alcalde.'

She sat there for a moment, her head still bent and not saying anything, the almost black hair gleaming in the lights, which had just been switched on. 'Fuxá,' she murmured. 'I keep hearing the name Fuxá. Ismail Fuxá.'

'He makes a lot of noise,' I said. 'But the separatist element is only a small minority. The people know very well an island like this could never make it on its own.'

We talked about it for a moment, then I paid the bill and we left, hand-in-hand, and the man in the red floppy hat watched us from his post by the bollard just a few yards from the Atlante. Maybe it was the brandy, but I felt warm and very close to Soo at that moment, and my mind, dreaming in the softness of the evening, the faint lap of wavelets the only sound, turned to thoughts of a ménage à trois, wondering whether I was macho enough to keep both a wife and mistress satisfied. Petra with child! Petra on Bloody Island, a kid running around the dig, our son, Soo here in the house with her basenji, running the office. She and Petra, they liked each other. They were so different it might work. Soo cared about marriage. The Navy and Malta, she'd been very conventionally brought up. But Petra – I had never discussed it with her, of course, but I was quite sure she didn't give a damn.

It might work, but as I climbed the stairs my mind returned to normal and I knew it was only a dream.

I got my holdall and my oilskins and dumped them in the boot of the car. 'What about your minder?' Soo said. 'The guy in the floppy hat.'

'You drive,' I said, still buoyed by the drink. 'I'll ride in the boot till we're clear of the town.' I crawled in, holding the lid of it slightly open. I had done it more or less as a lark, and Soo, who was always very quick to respond to a mood, was giggling as she said, 'You look like something out of *Alice* crouched in there.' She was still giggling to herself as she got in and started the engine.

We went about a hundred yards and then she slowed to a stop and I heard her say, 'Am I permitted to drive out to see my friends? I'm supposed to be playing bridge tonight.'

And a male voice answered her in Spanish, 'Of course, señora. You do not take your husband?'

'No. He's looking after Benjie.'

'Benjie? I do not understand.'

'The dog – *el perro*.'

'*Ah si, el perro.*' And then they were both laughing as though Soo was out on a cuckolding run. I nearly burst out laughing myself, thinking of Gareth Lloyd Jones safely tucked away in a frigate under the massive bulk of the Rock.

She drove fast after that, following the curves of the waterfront, and I watched the road astern through the slit under the boot lid. Nothing followed us, the cars along the Levante all parked, their owners still occupied with whatever it was they had come to the harbour for. By the Aduana I glimpsed the lights of a vehicle snaking down the Abundancia from the centre of town, but when it reached the Customs House it turned away from us.

By then we had reached the point where the Andén de Poniente runs into the Passo de la Alameda and the road to Fornells. I banged on the lid and after a while Soo stopped. 'I thought perhaps you'd gone to sleep.' She was still in a giggly mood. 'You could have got out back by the Maritimo. There was nobody following us. I was watching in the mirror.' And she added, 'Are you sure you haven't got delusions of grandeur? I'm beginning to wonder if it's all an excuse to go for a sail in that damned cat.'

I didn't answer that, simply got in beside her and we drove on. Now that I was on my way and committed to leaving Spanish soil without clearance, I was in a more sombre mood.

'You're sure this journey of yours is absolutely necessary?' She said it lightly, still joking, but there was an undercurrent of concern in it that matched my own mood. I said nothing and we drove on in silence.

It was 22.57 when we turned north on to the Macaret road, 23.07 when we started down into Port d'Addaia. Soon we could see the water of the inlet, the islands at the entrance dark shapes, no moon, no stars. *Thunderflash* was already there, riding to her anchor just off the new quay, the semi-inflatable ready alongside. I flashed our lights, then switched them off and got my gear out of the boot.

The tender was on its way almost immediately, so there was only a brief moment of privacy to say goodbye. Perhaps that was as well. I don't know what Soo was thinking as I kissed her, but my own thoughts were already on the voyage ahead and what it would be like to be back in Malta, this time without a passport. She didn't cling to me. In fact, she showed remarkably little emotion. Perhaps she was thinking of Lloyd Jones, wondering if his frigate would put into Mahon while I was away.

It was Luis driving the tender and he cut the engine just right, sliding in to the concrete edge of the quay and throwing the painter to me as the little launch floated to a stop. 'Good trip?' I asked.

'*Si, bueno.* We take five hours, speed reach sixteen knots. No motor.' A flash of teeth in the dark face grinning up at me. He had enjoyed himself and I was glad. 'Beeg sea, but everything very steady.'

'What's the forecast?' I asked him.

'Do'know. Carp attending it now. But we have nearly twenty knots, a levanter from Mahon to this place.'

I tossed my gear into the stern, gave Soo a final hug and jumped in. It might be blowing force five outside, but here, at the upper end of the long Macaret inlet, all was quiet, the water barely ruffled. By the time I got myself and my gear on board, Soo was already climbing the hill out of Addaia, the beam of the car's headlights altering as she took the sharp bends.

Carp came up out of the saloon. He looked pleased with himself. The ship had behaved itself – he called it a ship – and there had been no problems, the helm very easy on all points of sailing. 'We have a fast run to Malta – with luck.' He gave a gap-toothed smile. 'Wind twenty to twenty-five knots, backing north-east, possibly north, viz good.'

'A tramontana then?'

He nodded. 'But no rain. There's a high to the west of us moving south. Seas two to three metres, so it could be bouncy.'

I glanced back at the quay and the loom of the land behind it. It was quite dark now, no sign of Soo. So this was it – the moment of departure. We hauled the tender up on to the stern, fixed the lashings, then went below. 'Had any sleep on the way over?' It was unlikely for they would have been too busy in the rising wind and sea.

Carp shook his head. 'Would you like some coffee?' he asked. 'Something to eat?'

'No thanks. We'll get our heads down for a couple of hours. We need to be away about two, then we'll be well clear of the island and in international waters by first light.'

I had the double bed in the port hull and had just drifted off when I felt a shake of the shoulder and opened my eyes to see Carp's face leaning over me. 'We got company.'

'Coastal patrol?' I had come fully awake in a flash, the duvet thrown back and my feet already feeling for the locker top beside the bunk.

'No. Nothing official.'

'Who then?' I was thrusting my bare feet into my sea-boots.

But Carp was already climbing the steps that led up to the saloon. 'Come and see for yourself.'

He was standing in the open, beside the helmsman's seat, looking aft when I joined him, the rattle of a chain sounding loud in the quiet of the anchorage. No lights anywhere now, the houses all asleep, clouds low overhead. And there, a dim shape and barely fifty metres astern of us, was a fishing boat. 'The *Santa Maria*?' I asked him.

He nodded. 'Thought you'd want to know.' And he

added, 'I was asleep on the settee just inside the saloon door when I was woken by the thump of a diesel close alongside. You reck'n they've come in for shelter?'

I didn't say anything and we stood there watching as the chain was stopped with a clunk and they began to lower the dinghy, the *Santa Maria* gradually swinging bows-to-wind so that we lost sight of all that side of the vessel. Luis started to come up just as the dinghy came out from under the *Santa Maria*'s stern and I told him to go back. 'Two of us,' I said. 'They must only see two of us.' Carp nodded, the night glasses trained on the dinghy, which had swung towards us, one man in the stern handling the outboard, the other amidships, his head tucked into his shoulders as the spray began to fly. 'Who is it?' I asked.

'The gaffer, I reck'n.' He passed me the glasses. 'You have a look. I only seen the fellow once.'

It was Evans all right. I recognised the strong, column-like neck, the way it held his head. 'I'll be in the port hull, right for'ard in the loo.' And I added, 'If he wants to know where I am, as far as you know I'm at home.'

Carp nodded. 'I'll see he doesn't bother you.' He gave me that gap-toothed smile. 'Reminds me of the days when we used to slip over to Holland and come back into the Deben, crossing the bar at night and dumping a couple of bags full of de Kuyper's Geneva bottles with a float attached like we were laying lobster pots.'

I nodded and ducked below, sending Luis up on deck while I went to the double bunk I'd been using on the port side to make certain there was nothing lying around to indicate I was on board. Soon I caught the sound of the outboard approaching, then a voice hailing us. The engine died with a splutter and after a moment I heard the sound of Evans's voice – 'Wrapped around the prop, eh? Which one?' Then feet on the steps down into the saloon and a voice much nearer: 'Well, it's fortunate I found you. When we swapped boats I discovered I was missing a packet containing a spare aerial and masthead bracket picked up

with other radio gear duty-free in Gib on the way out.
Stuffed it all in the bilges and conveniently forgot about
it. You know how it is.'

I heard a non-committal grunt from Carp and Evans's
voice went on, 'Tell me, did customs, police, anybody
search the ship before you left yesterday?'

'No, not yesterday,' Carp replied. 'Day before we had an
Inspector Mallyno on board with 'is sidekick. The Heffy
too.'

'The Heffy?'

'Ah. The Chief Inspector of police. Inspector Heffy.'
Carp invariably got awkward names or words slightly
wrong. He'd call a transistor a transactor or a tachometer
a taxmaster, and always that slight sibilance as the breath
whistled through those two broken teeth of his. 'They was
on board quite a while talking with the boss.'

'Mike Steele?'

'Ah, the boss.'

'What were they talking about?'

'Oh, this and that, I reck'n.'

A pause then. Finally Evans came right out with it.
'Well, did they search the ship or not?'

'How would I know?'

'You said you were there.'

'I was up the mast, wasn't I?'

'How the hell would I know you were up the mast?
I wasn't there.' Evans's tone was one of exasperation
at Carp's odd turn of phrase. I couldn't hear anything
after that. He must have turned away. Then a moment
later, his voice sounding much louder, as though he had
moved to the entrance to the starb'd hull, 'And what about
the starb'd engine compartment? Did they look in there, too?'

'They may have done. That where you hid it?' I heard
the steps being folded back. 'Well, there you are, mate.
You can see for yourself. There's nothing there.'

'Right at the back.'

There was the sound of movement, then Carp's voice

again, much sharper. 'No you don't. You're not pushing in among those pipes an' leads.'

Evans started to argue, then the stepped lid slammed down and Carp said, 'You lost anything, you talk to the boss. I don't want that engine conking out again. Not halfway to Malta I don't. And anyways, if we find it, we'll know whose it is and see you get it back.'

A pause, then Evans said, 'Okay, so long as you don't show it to anybody. I don't want it to get around that I slipped anything in under the noses of the customs people, not when we're trying to set ourselves up in the fishing here. All right?' And then, his voice fading as he turned away, 'Where's your boss now? Do you know?'

I didn't hear the answer, the murmur of their voices lost as they went back into the saloon. I came out of the loo then and moved aft as far as the turn of the steps over the engine. I could hear Evans's voice then, sharp and hard as he said, 'Felixstowe Ferry! What the hell are you talking about?' And Carp answering, 'Well, ever since you came down to the Navy quay to take over the *Santa Maria* I bin wondering. Thort I recognised you, see. But red hair – that's wot fixed me.'

'Red hair? What do you mean?'

'Moira. That's wot I mean. Red Moira.' And Carp went on, his accent broader and talking fast: 'Just before you get to the Ferryboat there's a dyke runs off to the left alongside a little tidal creek full of old clung-bungs used as houseboats. There was one, I remember, belonged to some bit actor feller – was on TV once in a while, then he'd be full of drink an' happy as a lark for a week. After that, broke again and morose as if he'd had sight of Black Shuck himself. Used to wander alone along towards the King's Fleet. Same name as yours.'

'So what?' Evans's voice was harsh. 'It's a common enough name.'

'Well, he's dead now. Shacked up with this Irish broad. Red Moira she was known as all along the beach. Lived in an old boat called the *Betty-Ann* that lay there in the mud, with a rickety old bit of flotsam planking the only way of getting on board. They had a son. Used to call 'im Pat.'

'You've got me mixed up with somebody else.'

'Mebbe. But then this Navy fellow came looking for you, and the odd thing is that when he was a kid he was sent to stay with the Evanses. I'd see the two of you out swimming together, larking about, all over the place you were until you broke into a cabin cruiser, downed some drink and got pissed as farts. It was the other one fell into the 'oggin, I remember, and Billie had to go after 'im with the pilot boat, the tide fair sluicing and the poor little bugger carried right out towards the shingle banks.'

Evans said something about it being time they were in bed and the sound of their voices faded as the two of them went out into the night. Shortly afterwards the outboard started up, the sound of it gradually dying away as Carp called down to me that I could come out now. He was grinning. 'Couldn't get away fast enough, could he? I reck'n it was him all right.'

'The boy you knew as a kid?' He nodded, and I said, 'I thought you said he had red hair.'

'That's right. Real Tishan. But you can dye it, can't you? Dye it black and it alters the whole look of a man. And that funny moustache. That's why I couldn't be sure, not at first. But the way he said it was 'is bedtime ... You know there was a moment when I thort he was going to call up his mate and have a go at searching that engine compartment without permission. That's why I started telling him about Felixstowe Ferry. Pat Evans. That was the boy's name. Same name, you see. And both of them sent off to *Ganges*. It was the nearest place, outside of the Borstal over by Hollesley, to instil some discipline into the young rascals.'

He rubbed his hands on his denims. 'Quite a dag up on deck, real wet, like a mist had come down. Care for some coffee?' And before I could reply, he went on, 'Had the nerve to ask me if we'd got any liquor on board. He'd run out, he said. What he was after, of course, was to start a drinking session, so as he'd get my tongue loosened up and mebbe learn something I wouldn't have told him otherwise. I said we needed what little we'd got on board for the voyage over.' He shook his head, rubbing his hands over the greying bristles of his chin. 'Don't ever change their spots, do they? Well, wot about you? Shall I brew some coffee?'

He didn't feel like turning in and nor did I. We'd lost a precious half hour's sleep and already it was 01.37. 'Coffee and a small glass of something warming,' I said. 'Then we'll get under way.'

'Didn't like my reminding him he'd been at Felixstowe Ferry when he was a kid, did he?' He grinned as he turned away towards the galley at the after end of the port hull. 'It'll be instant, I'm afraid.' I heard the clink of metal, the sound of water running, then the plop of the butane burner igniting. 'Funny about that hair of his,' he called out. 'Makes you wonder what goes on in a man's mind, don't it?'

'How d'you mean?' I asked.

'Well, how long's he had it dyed, that's what I mean. Can't be just to conceal his identity, otherwise he'd've changed his name, wouldn't he? You see, we didn't reck'n they were married – Tim Evans and Red Moira. She was just a living-in girlfriend on a houseboat, that was our reck'ning. Partic'ly as she was pretty free with her favours. Well, not free if you know wot I mean. She charged – when she felt like it, or when she was short of cash.'

The kettle began whistling, and when he returned with the coffee, he said, 'They claimed they was married. Mr and Mrs Evans.' He laughed. 'But if they wasn't, then that makes son Patrick a bastard. Reck'n that's why he dyed his hair – not wanting to be tarred with his mother's red brush?' He was opening a locker beside the table. 'Soberano or a real genuine malt that Lennie scrounged from one of the yacht skippers at the Maritimo.'

He pulled out the bottle and poured two stubby glasses full of the golden liquor. It was Macallan twelve-year-old, a mellow dream after the sweeter, more fiery taste of Spanish brandy. 'Little better than a whore,' he went on. 'And a tongue on her that could lash an East Coast barge skipper into silence. An' she used it, too, whenever she was drunk, which was pretty often. No wonder the poor devil committed suicide. To be shacked up with a whore who's been sleeping around with other men is one thing, but a red-headed Irish bitch with a tongue as coarse as a barge-load of grit . . .' He shrugged. 'Ah well, he's dead now, so who cares?'

Knowing the area, even the little mud creek back of the Ferryboat Inn with the dyke-top path running north to join the Deben riverbank, remembering the old houseboats I had seen there that cold, bleak spring day, their slimy bottoms sunk deep in the tide-exposed mud, I could picture what it must have been like for a boy to grow up in a home and a family atmosphere like that. And the father committing suicide. 'How did he do it?' I asked.

'Drowned 'isself,' Carp answered. 'Wot else? It's easy enough to do at the Ferry with the shingle beach dropping almost sheer and a sluicing ebb tide that runs over five knots at springs. He was missing two days before anybody took Moira's whimpers seriously. He'd done it before, gone off on 'is own without her knowing where. Very unpredictable man. Once he slept out at Minsmere in the woods there two whole days. Bird-watching at the Reserve there is wot he said, but we all reck'ned it was because he'd 'ad enough of it. They found 'is body out by the Haven buoy . . . That's right, the same buoy that young lieutenant was found clinging to. It was a yacht outward bound for Dutchland wot found 'im. Helluva way to start a cruise, fishing a body out of the water that's been dead – well, it must have been close on a week by then.'

A horn blared from the direction of the quay and I poked my head out of the saloon door, thinking perhaps Soo had come back for some reason. There was a car parked there, its headlights at high beam and directed straight at the *Santa Maria*. The wheelhouse light came on and a moment later the dinghy slid away from her side, the outboard sounding as harsh as a chainsaw in the stillness.

We watched from the doorway as the dinghy swung alongside the quay where the driver was waiting to receive the box or large carton that was handed up to him. The car drove off and the dinghy returned to the *Santa Maria*. The lights went out, everything still again, only the wind moaning in the trees and undergrowth of the protecting peninsula to the east of us.

'Some more coffee?' Luis had emerged and was holding the pot up in invitation. We had it with the rest of our Macallan at the chart table, checking the position at which we would finally turn on to our course for Malta. It was a straight run on a course of 155° that passed some thirty miles south of Sardinia. 'Six hundred miles,' Carp said. 'We should make it without motoring in a little over three days.'

'If the wind holds,' I said. 'Which it seldom does.'

It took us only a few minutes to get ready for sea, then we hoisted the main, holding the cat head-to-wind and pulling the anchor warp in by hand until it was up and down. I didn't start the engines, not even one of them, sailing the anchor out and hauling in on the main sheet until, with the wind abeam, we were headed to pass east of the island that lay across the inlet's narrows like a cork in a bottle and separated Macaret harbour from the upper reaches of the inlet, which was Port d'Addaia. We passed within less than a cable's length of the *Santa Maria*, slipping through the water quite silently, only a slight chuckle at the bows. Nobody stirred, no lights came on, and in a moment the bulk of the island hid her from view.

Carp and Luis hoisted the jib, and as we hardened in on

the sheet, *Thunderflash* picked up her skirts and began to move. Off Macaret itself we began to feel the weight of the wind, the speed indicator moving towards seven knots. There was movement, too, as we got the wind coming in through the entrance. 'Everything stowed?' I asked Luis, and when he nodded I told him to go below and check again. 'It will be rough when we come out of the lee of Illa Gran.'

Carp suddenly hailed me from for'ard. 'There's a boat coming in.'

'Where?'

But he was already pointing, his arm indicating a position straight over the bows. By then the speed indicator was flickering on ten and a second later I saw it, a dark shape, with no lights. It was only the white of her bow wave that had enabled Carp to pick it out. 'Bloody fool!' he said as he landed on the teak grid beside my swivel chair.

'What is it?' I asked him. 'Coastal patrol?'

'Don't reck'n so. Bugger's coming in without a single light showing. Could be Navy. An exercise. Otherwise . . .'

I was thinking of the *Santa Maria*, lying at the head of the inlet, and the car that had met Evans on the quay. I was certain it was Evans who had taken that box or case ashore. 'We'll know soon enough,' I said. Already we could hear the thump of her diesel, and at that moment she was picked out for an instant by the headlights of a car on a bend ashore. There were barely a dozen metres between us as she went thundering past, and caught like that in the sweep of the car's lights, the dark silhouette of three men showed in the wheelhouse. She was a motor yacht of the fifties vintage or even earlier. 'Saving her batteries,' Carp said. 'Either that or she's bringing in a nice little present for somebody on the quiet.'

I didn't say anything, certain now that this clandestine arrival had something to do with the presence of the *Santa Maria* in the inner anchorage. But I had no time to dwell on that, for almost immediately we opened up the gap between the promontory of Macar Real and Illa Gran, the starb'd hull beginning to lift as the wind, funnelling through the gap, hit us. I had my work cut out then to keep her on course for the entrance.

A few minutes more and we were out into the open, the sea short and very steep with a lot of white water. I was steering 040°, the speed risen to almost eighteen knots, and every wave that broke sent the spray flying, droplets of water that were hard as shotgun pellets driven against my face by an apparent windspeed that must have been well over forty knots. I called to Carp to get his oilskins on and take the helm while I went below to get a fix on the Faváritx light.

It took us only twenty minutes or so to run our distance off Menorca, the bows smashing through the waves, spray bursting almost as high as the radar scanner at the cross-trees and the twin hulls slamming their way through the water at a speed that made it seem hard as concrete, the shocks of impact jarring every bone in our bodies. At 02.27 we went about on to the port tack, setting course for Malta, and with the wind tending to back in the gusts, the motion was easier, though we were still close-hauled. We changed down to the number two jib, took a couple of rolls in the main and went into two-hour watches.

From my bunk I had periodic glimpses of the moon through the perspex hatch and when dawn broke I went up into the saloon on the chance of getting a last sight of Menorca and so fix our position. But there was no sign of any land, the catamaran now on a broad reach, driving fast and comfortably across a wilderness of broken water.

It was a long day merging into night, intermittent sun and cloud. I was able to get a noon fix that was close to the sat-nav position and showed we had been clocking up an average of nine and a half miles per hour over the ground during the ten hours we had been at sea. The movement was very different to anything I had known before. A monohull does not bash into the seas, it accommodates itself to the rise and swoop of the waves. A multihull is much more uncompromising, and with no let-up in the wind, we were all of us very tired by the time night fell, the sun going down in a ball of fire and an odd-looking rainbow curling across a black rain cloud to the south.

We had two days of force five to seven from between NNE and NNW and there were times when I thought for a moment she was going to start flying a hull. On the third day, the wind backed into the west so that we were able to shake out our reefs and for almost four and a half hours we had a spinnaker run. After that the wind fell light and we started to motor. From white, breaking waves the sea smoothed out till it took on an oily, almost viscous surface, only the low swell from the north to remind us of the hard weather that had been pushing us south-eastward down the Med at such a spanking speed. A pod of dolphins joined us and we spent over two hours watching them as they cavorted round the bows. Carp tried to take a picture of their underwater shapes, lying flat on the safety net that stretched between the twin hulls at the bows. He came back aft soaking wet, one of the dolphins having slapped its tail on the surface and showered him with spray. 'I swear he did it o'purpose, because he rolled over on his side and looked me straight in the face, an' he was grinning! Not sure 'e didn't wink 'is eye at me. Talk about a sense of fun . . .'

As suddenly as they had arrived, the dolphins disappeared. The sun was shining out of a blue sky as they left us, the spray thrown up by their speed and the arching curve of their sleek bodies glittered silver in the bright light. A noon sight put us within fifty miles of Sicily and by evening we could see the mountains standing pale in the sunset, wisps of cloud clinging to their tops.

It had been a lazy day, hot and sleepy-making, a welcome

contrast. I had spent part of it trying to explain to Carp how to calculate his position from sights taken with the sextant. He was a good inshore pilot, but he had never had occasion to learn navigation, had never handled a sextant before. We had sat-nav and Decca on board, everything as automatic as could be, which is fine so long as your batteries hold out and no electrical faults develop in the hardware. The joy of a sextant is that there's virtually nothing to go wrong, unless you're fool enough to drop the thing overboard or forget to bring your azimuth tables with you.

That day I also began to think about our landfall. If we went straight into Grand Harbour, then it was unlikely I'd get ashore without being observed. The alternative, which was to slip into one of the smaller bolt holes like Marsax-lokk in the south of the island, or even drop off at the smaller island of Gozo, involved a risk that Carp could be in real trouble with the authorities if I were picked up by the police for having no papers and entering Malta illegally. In any case, when it came to leaving the island, I would have to do it secretly.

I didn't discuss the matter with Carp. It was something I had to make up my own mind about and in the end I decided to brazen it out and tell the authorities I had inadvertently lost my passport overboard, a very easy thing to do at night if one was stupid enough to leave it in one's anorak.

By late afternoon a heat haze was developing and we took in the clothes and bedding we had hung out to air. At six Luis relieved Carp at the helm and for the first time in three days the two of us were able to relax over an evening drink before putting the stew back on the stove. Two questions had clarified in my mind during the night watches, both concerning Gareth Lloyd Jones. First and foremost was the exact relationship between him and Evans, but all Carp said was, 'If he's bringing his ship into Mahon, then you'll be able to ask 'im yourself.'

'How long were the two boys together on that house-boat?' I asked.

'Not more'n three weeks, a month or so. If it'd been longer reck'n they'd've bin in real trouble, they was getting that wild. And Tim Evans accusing that Moira of all sorts of unnatural practices, accusing her publicly, right in front of everybody in the Ferryboat.' He knocked back the rest of his whisky and poured himself another, staring down at his glass, lost in his recollections.

'What do you mean – unnatural practices?' I was intrigued by his extraordinary choice of words.

'Well, can't say I know exactly wot the women were clacking about, but the fact is that the boy Gareth was just about the age for it and he was there on the boat with Moira an' nobody else for – oh, I forget now, but Tim Evans was away quite a while. Filming was wot Moira said. But I heard later he was so desperate for money he shipped as cook on a deep-sea trawler sailing out of Yarmouth for that Russian place, Novy Zembla.'

'And he accused her of taking the boy into her bed – is that what you're saying?'

'Well, I was in the pub there, wasn't I? Heard 'im say it myself. Shoutin' at 'er, he was.'

'So what was the boy's position? Why was it unnatural?'

Carp shrugged. 'There was rumours, you see.'

I waited, and when he didn't say anything further, I asked him what sort of rumours.

'That they was half-brothers. That's wot some people said.' He gave a little shrug. 'Place like the Ferry, tongues wag, partic'larly over people as strange as Tim and Moira.'

'Which of them was supposed to be the common parent?' I asked.

'Oh, the bloke of course. Moira was much too fly to get caught more than once. Least that's my reck'ning. But that boy, he had hair as red as hers, an' freckles, too. He was her kid, no doubt o'that. An' older than Gareth. A year at least. The local paper gave their ages as thirteen and fourteen.' And he went on to say that as he remembered it Gareth was the son of a couple named Lloyd Jones who ran a newsagent's somewhere in the East End of London. Seems it happened when Tim Evans was working at a municipal theatre in the Mile End Road. It was then, at the theatre, that he met up with Moira. She was barmaid there, so rumour had it.

'You mean Tim Evans was having it off with both women at the same time?'

'Oh, I don't know about that. Story was that this Lloyd Jones fellow had to go into hospital for an operation and his wife was left running the newsagent's on her own. By then Tim Evans was out of a job, so she got him into the shop to help her. That's how he paid for 'is lodgings.'

'By giving her a son?'

He grinned. 'All I said was he helped her in the shop. As far as we was concerned it was the red-haired lad as was illegit.'

Luis called down to us that he had just picked up the loom of a light almost dead over the bows. After about a quarter of an hour, when the white beam of it finally lifted above the horizon, we were able to identify it positively as the lighthouse on the highest point of the island of Gozo, which is 595 feet above sea level and has a range of twenty-four miles.

With no vessel in sight, I stopped both engines and we lay to, so that for the first time in three days we could have our drinks and our evening meal together in the saloon. By then I had finally made up my mind to go straight in at first light and clear health, customs and immigration in the normal way. Grand Harbour was no more than forty miles away, five hours' motoring at an economical eight knots, which meant three-hour watches for each of us, starting with Luis at 21.00.

It seemed an awful long time that I lay awake thinking

about Malta. So much history, and the pale, honey-coloured limestone seeming to sprout churches, barracks, ramparts and fortresses everywhere, with hotels and every other type and period of building in such profusion that it hardly seemed possible there were farms scattered all over the island, secreted behind the endless stone walls. I had spent just over a year there, first training, then training others. Later I had gone back to stay with a Maltese family, one of those that are descended from the Knights, proud people whose forebears fought the Turks in the Great Siege of 1565. That was when I met Soo.

Now, with all the vast stone familiarity of the place a short night's sleep away, my mind kept going over and over the future and its problems, recollections merging with thoughts of Gareth Lloyd Jones, wondering whether his ship would be there, how much the island would have changed, what the attitude of Soo's relatives would be. Her mother's father was still alive I knew, and the younger brother, who had gone into the Church, was vicar of the big church in Birzebbuga when last heard from – the elder brother had emigrated to Australia and was running a cattle station up north in Queensland. Soo herself had a cousin, Victoria, who was married to a lawyer and living in Sliema; the male cousins had both got themselves jobs in the States. I had met the lawyer once, a man of about my own age, very conservative in outlook, but a good underwater swimmer and he liked sailing.

I heard the watch change and the muffled beat of the engines starting up, felt the change of movement. We were under way again and after that I slept until Carp gave me a shake just after 03.00. 'Gozo just coming abeam,' he reported, 'and I can now see the light on the St Elmo breakwater.'

It was a bright, starlit morning, the dark sprawl of Gozo clearly visible under the swinging beam of the lighthouse high up in the centre of the island. I was alone at the wheel then, virtually no wind and the engines purring us along at eight knots, dawn gradually filling in the details of the landscape on our starb'd hand. I could make out the hotel I had once stayed in at St Paul's Bay, which is the spot where the disciple is supposed to have been shipwrecked. So many places I remember, and when the sun came up in a ball of fire the honey-coloured buildings of Sliema and Valetta took on a rosy glow, the whole urban complex that surrounds the great harbour inlets of Marsamxett and Grand Harbour looking fresh as the phoenix still engulfed in flames.

I steered close under the old fortress of St Elmo, heading for Gallows Point, and when I turned into Grand Harbour itself, I called Luis and Carp to come up and see it, neither of them having been to Malta before. To come in like this, from the sea, is to see it as the Turks saw it in May 1565, as all one hundred and ninety of their ships passed slowly across the entrance to bring the greatest fighting force then in existence to attack the Knights of St John in the stronghold they had retired to after being driven out of Rhodes.

We hoisted the yellow Q flag, and heading up the harbour, there on the port hand was Kalkara Creek and the massive ramparts of St Angelo and Senglea either side of Dockyard Creek. And right in front of us, bang in the middle of Grand Harbour and looking as though it owned the place, was the solid grey armour of a cruiser flying a red ensign with hammer and sickle on it. How many British admirals, I wondered, had turned in their graves at the thought of all the other nations that now used *their* harbour? There was a Libyan freighter at the quay further in, a small Cuban warship moored off, and a gaggle of coastal patrol vessels among the ferryboats in the creek. And then I caught sight of a pale grey shape, awkwardly placed right behind the Libyan freighter and tucked in against the dockyard quay right under one of the cranes. It looked like a Royal Navy ship. A gaily pinted *dghajsa* was being rowed across our bows, the man at the oars calling to ask us if we wished to be taken ashore. But by then one of the harbour launches was coming out to meet us.

CHAPTER TWO

Things had been difficult enough during the Mintoff era, which is why we had only been back twice since our marriage, but now the bureaucracy, as represented by the puffed-up little immigration officer who came out to us, seemed to have become even more rigid and unco-operative. No doubt he had his orders, for as soon as I said my name he demanded to see my passport, and when I told him I had lost it overboard, he nodded, smiling, as though that was what he had expected.

I had been hoping, of course, that by now Martin Lopez would have had time to straighten things out, but when he ordered us to move nearer the dockyard area, presumably so that they could keep a closer watch on us, and said that nobody was to land, it was obvious the Menorcan authorities had been in touch with them. I pointed out to him that we had been at sea for almost four days and must send somebody ashore for fresh food, but the brown eyes in the smooth dark face stared at me uncomprehendingly. In the end he told us to arrange with one of the *dghajsas* to supply our needs. 'If you go ashore before you have clearance,' he said, 'you will be arrested.'

I was too tired to argue with him and shortly after he had left a Harbour Police launch appeared and under their direction we shifted to the industrial part of the harbour, anchoring just north of the largest of the dry docks, which was occupied by a Panamanian-registered cruise ship. Our new anchorage was noisy and smelt strongly of oil and sewage, the water thick and dark, the viscidity of its surface gleaming with a bluebottle iridescence in the bright sunlight.

The RN ship was a frigate; we could see her quite clearly now, but not her name, only the number on her side prefixed F. She was berthed alongside a quay on the Senglea shore of French Creek at about the spot where the Turks had tried so desperately to tear down the improvised palisade the Knights had erected to protect their southern flank. Maltese swimmers, armed with knives and short swords, had driven them off, and then on July 15, in the full heat of summer, Mustapha Pasha had launched what was intended as a final crushing blow against the Knights of St John. I remember the date because it was the day Soo and I had been married. The Janissaries, the Spahis, the Iayalars, the Levies were all thrown in, the galleys as well that had been dragged overland from Marsamxett. Three thousand fanatical Muslims died that day.

How much had changed! Yet over the long gap of four centuries, the forts, ramparts and ravelins of the Knights still stood massive in the sunshine – Senglea and St Michael, Birgu and St Angelo, and Fort St Elmo away to my left on the Valetta side of Grand Harbour. I had been reading up on the Great Siege when I first met Soo and it was she who had taken me to all sorts of places I would otherwise have missed. It was, in fact, the Great Siege that had brought us together, the beginning of our love, and seeing it again all bright on that cloudless morning brought a lump to my throat.

A sudden flurry of activity on the deck of the frigate brought my mind back from the past. The gangway staff had been alerted by the approach of a launch speeding across from Valetta. I watched as it came alongside the accommodation ladder, sailors with boathooks fore and aft and a naval officer stepping out and climbing quickly to the deck above. There was a twitter of bo's'n's pipes and I wondered if it was the Captain returning from a courtesy visit. Was it Lloyd Jones? Would he know about the Great Siege? Would that spark I had seen explode between them compensate for all the things Soo and I had shared? And then, more practically, I was looking at the frigate's super-structure, the tangle of radio and radar equipment. There, if the worst came to the worst, was the means of communicating with the outside world, if he would play.

That thought stayed in my mind all day. I needed to know what was happening back in Mahon, what my position was. I had been so convinced I would be in the clear by the time we reached Malta, and Evans? . . . surely they would have searched the villa by now? Lying in the broad double bunk in the port hull my mind went over and over the stupidity of it all. To fall into such a heavily baited trap – me, with all the experience I had of sailing close to the wind – Christ! It was unbelievable.

And then, when I finally got off to sleep, there was the jar of a launch alongside, Maltese voices and the thump of feet on deck. It was the customs back again, this time with orders to search the boat, which they did from end to end, peering into all the bilges, prodding cushions and bedding and searching every locker, the engine compartments, too. Periodically I asked them what they were looking for, but each time the senior officer replied, 'A routine search. Nothing more. Just routine.'

They were on board the better part of two hours. When they left I was advised once again not to go ashore. 'And don't send any bags, laundry, anything like that ashore. You wait here until you are cleared, okay?'

Nothing is more demoralising than being confined on board a sailing boat in port and at anchor, nothing to do but wait, and so many things I could have been doing ashore. Carp retired philosophically to his bunk, but though I followed his example, I couldn't sleep. After lunch I got the inflatable into the water and the outboard fixed to its bracket in readiness. If I had been on my own I think I would have risked it, but I had Carp to consider and so I sat there in the helmsman's chair watching the world go by, the sun hot on my bare shoulders, a drink in my hand and the sounds of Malta at work all about me.

Nobody else came out to us and time passed slowly. The flamboyantly painted *dghajsas* and ferries full of tourists scurried to and fro across the water between Valetta and Kalkara or Vittoriosa, and there were launches and service craft constantly moving among the vessels at anchor. Just before five the launch lying alongside the frigate's gangway was manned again and an officer appeared on the deck above. I got the glasses, but I couldn't be sure it was Lloyd Jones, the peak of his cap casting a shadow across his face. He was taken across the harbour to land by the Customs House where a car was waiting for him. Inside of an hour he was back on board. By then the sun was sinking over the Marsa township and the honey-coloured limestone of the older buildings ashore began to glow with a warmth that turned rapidly from gold to a fiery red.

By then the shipyard noises had been briefly swamped by the engines and horns of the rush-hour traffic. Lights appeared in the streets and on the wharfs, the windows of buildings blazed like a myriad fireflies, and suddenly the frigate was lit from end to end, a circlet of electric light bulbs. I think it was this that finally made up my mind for me. I went below, changed into a decent pair of trousers, put on a shirt and tie, then asked Carp to run me over to the frigate.

He looked at me hard for a moment, then he nodded. 'Okay, if that's what you want. You can always say it doesn't count – as going ashore, I mean.'

It took us less than five minutes to cross the flat calm strip of water that separated us from the frigate. The launch had been hoisted into its davits so that, once I had checked that Lloyd Jones was the frigate's captain and the Quartermaster had satisfied himself I really did know him, we were able to go straight alongside the accommodation ladder. 'Want me to wait for you?' Carp asked as I seized one of the stanchions and swung myself up on to the grating.

'No.' I didn't want it made that easy for them to get rid

of me. 'Either they'll bring me back or I'll have them flash you up on their signal lamp.'

By the time I reached the frigate's deck Carp was already on his way back to the boat and a very young-looking officer was waiting for me. He confirmed that Lloyd Jones was the Captain and when I told him I was a friend, he asked me to wait while he phoned. He came back almost immediately with Gareth Lloyd Jones. He looked very smart in an open-necked shirt, immaculately white, black trousers and cummerbund, and the gold of his new rank bright on his shoulder boards, a smile on that pleasant open face of his. 'Mike. It's good to see you.' He held out his hand, seeming genuinely pleased. 'John, take Mr Steele up to my cabin,' he told the young officer, 'and have Petty Officer Jarvis get him a drink.' Then to me he said, 'You'll excuse me for a moment. There's a party going ashore for supper at the invitation of a Maltese wine company and I want to have a word with them before they leave.'

He left me then, climbing the ladder to the helicopter flight deck ahead of me and disappearing round the hangar on the port side. John Kent, a dark-haired, dark-browed young man, who proved to be one of the seamen officers, led the way for me, up to the flight deck, for'ard past the illuminated funnel and in through a watertight door to a passageway that led across to the curtained entrance to the Commanding Officer's day cabin. 'Make yourself at home, sir, while I find the Captain's steward.'

The cabin was a roomy one with a desk, two armchairs and a couch with a coffee table in front of it, and there was a small dining table by one of the two portholes with utilitarian upright chairs. The portholes, which had grips for steel shuttering, gave me a view of the concrete wall at the back of the quay and the lit buildings behind it rising to the back of the Senglea peninsula. There was nobody on the wharf or at the end of the shore-side gangway, which I could just see a short distance aft of where I was standing. The only sounds that penetrated the cabin were shipboard sounds of whirring machinery and air-conditioning.

On the wall by the desk there was a telephone communications system, also a microphone and loudspeaker, and on the desk itself there was a naval manual of some sort, a Folio Society edition of Fitzroy's *Voyage of HMS Beagle*, a paperback copy of one of Patrick O'Brian's sea stories, also a framed photograph of Soo sunbathing on a rock. It looked like a picture I had taken myself, at Cala d'Alcaufar when we had first come to Menorca. It was a shock to have this visual evidence of how much my wife now meant to this man living a monastic existence on one of Her Majesty's ships.

'What would you care to drink, sir?'

I turned with a start to find a round-faced young man in dark blue, almost black, Navy trousers, and white shirt gazing at me curiously from the doorway. I ordered a gin and tonic and moved back to the porthole. There was movement now, a steady stream of sailors, all in civvies, looking clean and smart with their hair well brushed, moving down the gangway on to the wharf. I counted twenty-seven of them as they walked briskly across the wharf, separating into little groups as they disappeared from view round the corner of a storage shed. A moment later Gareth Lloyd Jones came in. 'Nobody offered you a drink?'

'Yes, it's coming,' I said.

Now that I had a chance to examine him more closely I thought he looked tired and edgy, as though his new command was getting him down.

The steward came in with two large gins on ice and a bottle of tonic. 'Fifty-fifty, plenty of tonic?' Gareth gave me a quick grin, poured the tonic, then took a long pull at his own drink before subsiding on to the couch. 'Well, what brings you here? That's your catamaran over by the dry dock, is it?' He must have caught sight of Soo's photograph then, for he suddenly bounced up, went over to the desk, and under the pretext of looking at some papers, turned the picture face down.

Briefly I explained what had happened, finally asking him whether there was any way he could find out what the attitude of the authorities in Menorca was to me now. 'Have you anyone there you can contact by radio?'

He hesitated. 'Yes, but . . .' He got to his feet and went back to the desk, lifted the mike off its rest and press-buttoned a number. 'Captain. Is the Yeoman of Signals there? Ask him to have a word with me.' He put the mike back on its rest. 'Funny ship, this,' he said. 'It's an antique really, but after being mothballed for several years and threatened with the knacker's yard twice, their lordships suddenly hauled it back into service, gave it a quick face-lift, and then fitted it out with the latest in communi-cations systems so that to that extent we must be the envy of the Fleet. We also have sonar equipment that's on its last legs and an Ops Room that belongs to the Ark and is on the blink . . .' There was a tap at the door and he said, 'Come in, Yeo.' He turned to his desk, reached for a message pad and began to write as a thin man with a dark pointed beard pushed aside the curtain. When he had finished, he said, 'Have that sent and make it immediate. And they're to stand by for a reply. This is Mr Steele, incidentally. Petty Officer Gordon, my Yeoman of Signals.'

The beard and I smiled at each other, and as he left Gareth said, 'It may be a little time before we get a reply to that. Meanwhile, perhaps you'd join me for my evening meal.' And when I demurred, he said, 'No, of course not – no trouble at all. I'll be glad of your company anyway. Occasionally I mess in the wardroom, and I have messed with the Senior Rates once, but mostly I feed alone. It's the custom, you know. So as I say, I'll be glad of your company.' He called to the steward to bring us another drink. 'I never drink at sea, of course –' He spoke as though he had been in command for years – 'but now that we're tied up alongside . . .' He gave a little shrug, as though the fact of being tied up to a quay absolved him of some of the responsibility of command.

But as time passed I began to realise that his position weighed heavily on him, more heavily than it should, even for a man newly appointed to the command of a ship. It was as though he had something on his mind, and the only clue he gave as to what it might be was when he suddenly said, apropos of nothing, 'You know, it's a strange thing, here I am flying the White Ensign, but tucked away against this filthy little quay, as though the Maltese didn't want to recognise the flag that's flown here for so many years. I'm out on a limb. Nobody wants to know us. Officially, that is. We're sort of pariahs. I've been here four days and not a day has passed but the authorities have dropped hints it's time we left. We have in fact flashed up the boilers so that we are ready to sail at short notice if we have to.'

He paused then, but two gins had loosened his tongue and he went on, talking fast: 'They don't want to make a thing of it, tell us outright to go, but they've made it very clear they don't want us here. You see, wherever we are, in this ship – any RN ship – we're a bit of the UK. That's what the Union flag is telling them, and they don't like it – not now, not any more. Politically, here in Grand Harbour, we stick out like a sore thumb.' And he added with a wry smile, 'Our visit isn't a bit like it was for the last frigate that showed the flag here.'

'That was the first courtesy visit in seven years if I remember rightly,' I said.

'Well, not quite. The Brazen was the first ship to visit Malta after the British Forces finally left the island in 1979. She had the C-in-C Fleet embarked. Prince Charles came later with ninety thousand Maltese cheering and waving flags.' He made a face, shrugging his shoulders. 'That's what the papers said anyway. And look at us, tucked away in a corner where nobody can see us, and that bloody great Russian cruiser lording it in the centre of the harbour. That's why I had the lights rigged.'

'I don't think La Valette would have approved of their presence here,' I said.

He smiled, 'Ah, so you know what happened. More than four centuries ago and we still talk of St Elmo's fire.' He had read Ernle Bradford's book, knew the whole incredible story, the astonishing bravery of the Maltese when led by men like the Knights and motivated by religious faith and the fear of being captured and sent to the Turkish galleys. 'And now they are under the hand of another Muslim ruler.'

There was a knock at the door and a thickset, bull-headed Lieutenant Commander with greying hair entered, cap under his left arm, some papers gripped in his hand. He was a good deal older than his newly-appointed captain. His name was Robin Makewate. 'MEO,' Gareth said, explaining that it meant Marine Engineer Officer. It was a state-of-the-engines routine visit, and when he had gone, Gareth said, 'He's forty-three, started as a stoker at the age of nineteen after studying engineering at night school. Volunteered for the job here, even though he knew he'd be serving under a much younger man.' He finished his drink, saying as he did so that it was odd being in command of a ship that was filled partly by volunteers, partly by throw-outs from the rest of the Fleet.

That wry smile again, his eyes not looking at me, not seeing anything but what was in his mind as he went on, speaking so quietly I could hardly hear him: 'I've a total complement of well over two hundred, and of those, fifty-seven are volunteers. Why? I don't know, and I'm the Captain. They don't know, and they're the ones who volunteered. Something dangerous, that's all some of them have been told. There's one or two I picked myself. The Appointers were generous in that respect – my Navigating Officer, Peter Craig. Also the SCO – that's my Communications Officer, Lieutenant Woburn – and Tony Draycott, my Weapons Engineer Officer. I've also got a CPO who was at *Ganges* when I was there. Most of the key people, they're volunteers, but there's others, fifty or sixty at least, who've been quietly wished on me by other ships' captains as though word had been put around that *Medusa* was a sort of personnel dustbin and I was a sucker on whom they could foist all the yobbos and troublemakers they wanted to be rid of. Oh, well . . .' Again the wry smile, the slight shrug. 'Let's have some food. I'm hungry. You must be, too, listening to me.'

He called for the steward, and over the avocado and shrimp cocktail we talked of Libya and the PLO, Beirut and the effect of the Gulf War. A daily signal from Fleet Headquarters at Northwood near London plus the World News of the BBC kept him very well informed. He needed to be, I thought, tied up here like a sitting duck in a little independent country that was set in the very centre of the Mediterranean like a stepping stone to the most volatile and unreliable country in Africa. And even as I was thinking about that, full of curiosity and wondering whether I could ask him about his plans, what orders he had received, and if he was headed for Menorca next, he was called on the intercom loudspeaker. It was the Officer of the Day reporting a little crowd beginning to gather on the quay.

I got to my feet then and looked out of the nearest porthole. It was almost dark on the concrete apron, only one small light still showing at the corner of the storage shed opposite. A dozen or so figures stood silent against the corrugated metal sheeting of the shed. It was like a stage set with others drifting in from the wings in ones and twos.

'Have you informed the First Lieutenant? They could be dockers waiting to unload. Is there a ship coming in?'

'Not that I can see, sir, and the First Lieutenant's trying to contact the port authorities to see if they can tell him what it's all about.'

'All right, tell him to report anything he finds out. And keep an eye on them. Let me know if their numbers noticeably increase.' He switched off, had a quick look through the other porthole, then returned to the table, muttering to himself, 'I don't like it.'

He didn't talk much after that. The main course was roast lamb and he ate it quickly, jumping up every few minutes to glance out of the porthole. Coffee came and we both stood at the window to drink it. The numbers had grown. It looked as though there were at least forty or fifty men down there lounging in the shadows. 'What the hell are they waiting for?' He turned at a knock on the entrance bulkhead. 'Well, what's the form?'

His First Lieutenant was a thin gangling man with what I suspected was a permanently worried expression. He had to duck his sharp-nosed halberd of a head to enter. He looked forty-fiveish, but perhaps he was less. His name was Randolph Mault, and his rank was the same as Gareth's. 'I don't know,' he said slowly. 'Looks like they're waiting for something to happen.'

'Trouble?'

'Could be a demonstration.'

'Against us?'

The executive officer hesitated. 'We know there's an anti-British — anti-West at any rate — element in Malta. We've been briefed on that. And it's supposed to be quite deliberately fostered and well organised.'

Gareth Lloyd Jones turned back to the porthole. 'Yes,' he said. 'That's probably why our people advised us to anchor out in the middle of the harbour. I thought at first it was because we'd be more conspicuous there, something to counteract the presence of that Russian cruiser, but it did cross my mind, when the Maltese authorities insisted on our lying alongside in this God-forsaken spot, that besides making us as inconspicuous as possible, it also made us more vulnerable to some shore-based whipped-up anti-Western feeling. Pity we didn't rig the lights right round the ship.' He stood for a moment, gazing out at the darkened quay and the figures grouped in the shadows.

The First Lieutenant had moved nearer so that he could

also see down on to the quay. 'What time is the shore party due back, do you know?' he asked.

Gareth shook his head. 'No time was specified on the invite.' He glanced at his watch. 'Soon, I would think. And I told them to be sure they remained sober. Do you think they'll be sober when they return?'

'It's not just a wine company, you know. It's also a distillery. They produce a local brandy, also a sort of gin. I found one of their brochures in the wardroom bar. Apparently we've shipped some cases of their wine, or maybe it was a present – I'm not sure.'

Gareth turned abruptly from the window. 'Very well.' His voice was suddenly different, sharp and incisive. 'Have young Kent go over to the company's office – my apologies to the Director, but something has cropped up and the shore party is to return to the ship immediately.' He produced a key from his pocket and passed it across. 'Tell him to take the car we hired yesterday. It's parked behind the shed there. And he'd better take somebody with him.' He glanced out of the window. 'And tell him to get a hustle on. I have a feeling all they're waiting for now is someone to give them a lead.'

'Aye, aye, sir.' The First Lieutenant turned and ducked quickly out.

'I'd better leave,' I said, but Gareth didn't seem to hear me, standing very still at the porthole, watching. 'If you'd be good enough to have one of your people signal to *Thunderflash* . . .'

He turned then. 'No, no. You wait here till we get an answer from Menorca. Shouldn't be long now.' And he added, 'I'm going up to the bridge – care to join me?'

We went up a flight of steps just outside his cabin. The bridge was dark and empty, only the glow of various instruments and a solitary figure, a senior petty officer, who came in from the head of the ladder leading down to the sidedeck. 'Lieutenant Kent's just leaving now, sir.'

'Who's he taking with him?'

''Fraid I don't know, sir.'

'Hastings.' It was the First Lieutenant. He had just come on to the bridge. I recognised the rather high voice.

'Good choice.' Gareth Lloyd Jones nodded and turned to me with a quick smile. 'He's our PT instructor. Keeps us on our toes and the flab under control. That's the theory of it, anyway.'

He went out through the bridge wing door on the port side and I followed him. From the head of the ladder we watched as the officer who had met me on arrival went quickly down the gangway, followed by a broad-shouldered, powerful-looking seaman. As they reached the quay there was movement among the shadows, voices sounding in the night, Maltese voices plainly audible above the continuous thrum of the ship. Suddenly a solitary voice was raised above the rest and the movement became purposeful, the shadowy figures coalescing into two groups and moving to block the way round the end of the storage shed.

'Have the ten-inch signal lamp manned and put out a call for the photographer.'

'Aye, aye, sir.' But before the petty officer could move Mault had reached for the bridge phone. He had been followed now by several other officers. 'I've closed the duty watch up, sir,' one of them reported.

'Good.' The acknowledgement was barely audible and Gareth didn't turn his head, his hands gripped on the rail, his body leaning intently forward as he watched the two figures advancing in step and without hesitation towards the group that now stood in a huddle blocking the exit at the eastern end of the shed. For a moment everything seemed to go quiet, the Maltese all standing very still, so that the only movement was the two uniformed figures advancing across the quay. I thought I could hear the sound of their marching feet, and then they had reached the group blocking the exit and were forced to stop. The young lieutenant might have made it. He was standing there, talking to them quietly, but whatever it was he was saying could not be heard by the group at the other end of the shed. They were starting to move, a little uncertainly, but their intention was clear. They were headed for the foot of the gangway to cut the two Navy men off.

'Shall I recall them?' It was the First Lieutenant and he had a microphone for the upper-deck broadcast system ready in his hand.

Lloyd Jones's hesitation was only fractional, but then one of the Maltese shouted something and in the instant the whole quay was in an uproar, the figures moving like a shadowy tide to engulf the dark blue uniforms. 'Lieutenant Kent to report back to the ship.' Mault's metallic, magnified voice seemed to fill the night. 'Both of you at the double.'

Lloyd Jones suddenly came to life, seizing the microphone from the First Lieutenant's hand, his voice booming out of it as he countermanded the order for the men to double and called for the signal lamp to be switched on to the quay. Instantly the whole concrete apron was flooded in a harsh light, the figures no longer shadowy, but leaping into focus, a sea of faces. They checked, and while they were held there, like a crowd scene under the glare of a film-set spotlight, Kent and the burly PO marched smartly back to the gangway. 'Where's the photographer?' Lloyd Jones's voice was crisp.

'Here, sir.' A man in a crumpled sweater with his equipment slung round his neck stepped out on to the wing of the bridge.

'I want pictures. Clear enough to identify individuals.' He raised the mike to his lips again. 'This is the Captain speaking. I don't know why you have gathered on the quay in front of my ship, but I would ask you all to disperse now and allow my officer to proceed. I should add that my photographer is now taking pictures so that if he is impeded going about his duty each of you will be identifiable

179

when I raise the matter personally with the authorities here in Malta.'

I think he would have succeeded in getting them to disperse, for some of them, particularly those nearest the ship, had turned away their heads as soon as the signal lamp had been switched on and quite a number of them began to drift away at the threat of being photographed. But then a motor bike appeared round the corner of the shed and a man in black leather, like a Hell's Angel, thrust it on to its stand and began haranguing them in a voice that was almost as powerful as Gareth's had been with the use of the loudhailer.

It checked the backward flow, but by then Kent had reached the bottom of the gangway and was standing there staring up at us, white-faced in the hard light, waiting for orders. 'What do you think, Number One – can he make it?' Lloyd Jones was still leaning on the rail, still looking down on the scene, the bullroarer gripped tight in his right hand. 'Take a party to the foot of the gangway,' he ordered. 'See what a show of strength does.' He leaned over the rail, his voice quite calm as he ordered Kent to proceed. 'But you'll have to move fast when you get to the roadway, before that man whips them up into a mood of violence.'

Kent and the Leading Hand moved smartly back across the quay, the Maltese watching them and the motor cyclist shouting at the top of his voice. They reached the corner of the shed, and then, as they disappeared from view, the crowd began to move, Gareth yelling at them through the megaphone to hold fast while men from the ship tumbled down the gangway to form up at the foot of it. The mob took no notice, all of them streaming out towards the roadway, to come to a sudden halt as the lights of a car went blazing past, the engine revving in low gear.

Standing as I was, right next to Gareth, I heard his breath come out in a sigh, saw him relax momentarily. But then he braced himself, turning slowly as he gave orders for the men on the searchlight to be ready. The quay was almost empty.

'You think they'll be back, sir?'

''Fraid so. This has been planned. It was planned before ever they allocated us a berth alongside this bloody quay.' He spoke quietly, more to himself than to his First Lieutenant. 'And have a full Damage Control Party closed up, fire hoses ready to be run out and full pressure on the pumps when we need it.'

'Internal Security platoon, sir?'

Gareth hesitated.

'A show of strength, as you said,' Mault added. 'It might do the trick.'

Gareth didn't answer, staring down at the quay. Already the crowd was drifting back, a group of them gathering round the motor cyclist. He was a barrel-chested, tough-looking man, his face almost square with a thick nose, and he had black curly hair that covered his head like a helmet. 'All right, have the arms issued. Say twenty men under the command of that Marine sergeant.'

'Simmonds?'

'Yes. Perhaps it's for this sort of thing he was posted to the ship.' Gareth's face creased in a grin. 'I did wonder.' And he added, 'But keep them out of sight. A parade of arms is the last thing we want.' And then, half to himself, he said, 'About time I sent a signal to CINCFLEET telling them what's going on.' He went back into the bridge to telephone, and after that it was a long wait. Finally we returned to his day cabin. 'No good my hanging around the bridge, looking anxious. They'd begin to get the jitters.'

'What about you?' I asked.

He laughed. 'Oh, I've got the jitters, of course I have.' His steward appeared and he ordered some more coffee. 'Care for a brandy with it? Or would you prefer Armagnac? The wardroom shipped some Armagnac at Gib, really first-rate stuff.' But he wasn't drinking now so I thanked him and said I was all right. We drank our coffee in silence, listening to the reports that began to come in over the loudspeakers: damage control first, then MEO confirming there would be full pressure on the hydrants, WEO to say the searchlight was manned. Finally the First Lieutenant's voice announcing that the IS platoon was at readiness and fully armed. 'God! I hope we don't have to resort to that.'

'You think it might come to that?' I asked him.

He shrugged and went to the window, standing there, looking out, his coffee gripped in his hand. 'That bunch isn't gathered out there for nothing.' There was a knock on the bulkhead by the curtained doorway and the Yeoman of Signals poked his bearded face in. 'Signal from CINCFLEET passing a telex from Menorca, sir.'

Gareth took it, read it through, then handed it on to me. 'Sorry about that. It looks as though you're still suspect.'

The telex was short and to the point: *Ref your query Michael Steele, his sudden departure confirmed authorities in their suspicions. Legal proceedings now being initiated for extradition Malta. For your information weapon used by Barriago still not found.* There was no signature, and when I asked him who had sent it, he shook his head. 'Everything on this ship that's connected with Communications is classified. But as far as I know the source is absolutely reliable.' He held out his hand for the signal. 'Too bad. I wish I could have provided you with better news.'

I thanked him and got to my feet. 'I'd best be going,' I said.

He shook his head. 'Not now.' He glanced at the clock on the bulkhead above the desk. 'Five minutes to get them off the company's premises, ten more for them to reach the quay here.' He finished his coffee and reached for his cap. 'Time to go up to the bridge. Coming?'

I followed him into the passage and up the ladder to the bridge. The scene had changed very little, except that the crowd seemed to have grown larger. We went out on to the wing. A big searchlight was mounted now and manned, and the damage control people were lowering hoses on to the quay. No sign of the boarding party, but a Marine sergeant was standing by the davits on the deck below. Gareth called him up to the bridge wing. 'I'll give you the order, Sergeant, when I want your men paraded on the quay. Once there you'll have to act as the situation demands. Your job is to see that all the ship's personnel get back on board unhurt. But just remember this, any action you take will have political repercussions and will ultimately be exposed to the full glare of publicity.'

The sergeant stared at him impassively. 'Aye, aye, sir.'

Silence then, just the thrumming of the ship's machinery, a slight trembling of the deck plates underfoot, and men everywhere around the deck waiting and watching, while down on the quay the excited, nervous babble of Maltese voices came up to us as an audible complement to the constantly shifting pattern of the waiting crowd. I could see the motor cyclist in his black leather talking and gesticulating to the little group gathered round him, and there were others, shadowy figures, among the various groups.

The Marine sergeant was back with his men on the deck below and Gareth was glancing at his watch for the third or fourth time. The brass nozzle of a fire hose hit the ship's side with a clang, then a sudden shout and a flurry of movement on the quay, the crowd pouring through the gap between the east wall of the shed and the neighbouring building. A horn blared, shouts and yells, and a small red car appeared in the gap, almost totally submerged in a flood of people. The noise increased, the sound of fists pounding on roof and bonnet, the horn now blaring continuously.

Gareth raised the megaphone. 'Searchlight.' The white glare of it was so brilliant and so sudden that all movement ceased abruptly. For an instant there was silence. Then the car's engine revved, nosing into the crowd, spearheading a path for the men following in its wake.

There was a shout, one word, not a Maltese word, but French – *Attaquez*, and on the instant the scene changed, a rush of movement, the car was picked up bodily from one side, the engine screaming as it was pitched on to its side and the wheels came free of the ground. Screams and shouts, and the two fire hoses, run out now across half the width of the quay, bulged, their nozzles hissing like snakes, water bursting out in a broad arc. But the car and the crowd were too far away. The jets of water barely reached them. I heard Mault's voice, but before he had even given the order, the Marine sergeant and his men, all in uniform and with bayonets fixed to their self-loading rifles, came thundering down the gangway.

If they had moved in before the shore party had reached the quay, if they had broken up the crowd, grabbed the ringleaders and the other agitators . . . But that would have meant taking the initiative with the Navy blamed for everything that followed. As it was, the men forming up in a compact body at the foot of the gangway and then advancing might still have been sufficient intimidation to get the sailors back on board. Instead, the sergeant ordered them to charge, and that was just the catalyst needed to turn an ugly little incident into a political bombshell.

The crowd round the car were already opening out. In a moment they would have run. But then it happened, a spurt of flame, the sound of a shot, and Lieutenant Kent, climbing out of the car, all of his torso reared up in the open window on the driver's side, threw up his hands and began to scream. And as he lost consciousness, his body sagging to lie crumpled across the side of the vehicle, I saw the man who had fired the shot drop his pistol, turn and slide away to the rear of the crowd.

I saw him, but I don't think the others did, for their attention had switched to the armed party. They had suddenly stopped, the sergeant's voice ringing out as he gave the order to fire over the heads of the crowd. The volley was ragged, but the noise of it and the sight of those men in blue with their rifles raised and the bayonets glinting in the glare of the searchlight was enough. The crowd broke and ran, melting away so quickly that for an instant the only figure left on the scene was the motor cyclist trying to kick-start his bike into life. Finally he threw it down and ran.

I think the enormity of what had happened was immediately apparent to Gareth, for he stood there on the bridge wing, his face white with shock, too stunned, it seemed, to take command. It was Mault who ordered the armed party back on board, sent for the medical orderly and a stretcher party to get the young lieutenant to the sick bay, and had the shore party drawn up at the foot of the gangway and checked against a list of names to make certain nobody was missing. They were coming back on board and the damage control men were rolling up their hoses before Gareth finally came out of his state of shock. 'Lieutenant Commander Mault.'

Mault turned, an interrogatory lift of his straight, very black eyebrows.

'Time we got out of here. Come to immediate notice for sea and go to harbour stations as soon as you're ready. We'll move out into the open harbour and anchor seaward of that Russian cruiser. After that we'll see.' He turned abruptly, going back into the bridge housing. 'Find Chief Petty Officer Gordon and tell him to have a word with me,' he said to one of the seamen. 'I'll be in my cabin.' And he disappeared hurriedly through the door at the back.

I realised then that he had understood more than any of the officers around him, including his First Lieutenant, the full implications of what had happened – an armed party had landed from a Royal Navy ship and had opened fire on a crowd of Maltese. Never mind that they had fired in the air, that their action had been provoked and an officer had been shot, it had been done on Maltese soil. An invasive and hostile act, that's how it would be presented, to the Maltese and throughout the Third World and the non-aligned states. He had forgotten all about my presence on the ship, and I couldn't blame him.

The main broadcast suddenly blared out, Mault's voice ordering the crew to harbour stations. I waited until he had finished his announcement, then suggested he signal *Thunderflash* to come and collect me, but he shook his head. 'Sorry. You'll have to wait until we're anchored.' He had hung up the mike and now had glasses trained on the main dock area where a crowd had gathered at the slip by Somerset Wharf. 'The whole place will soon be in an uproar.' He turned to the chart table, shaking his head. 'Bad business.'

He shouldn't have said that, not in front of me, and certainly not with the Navigating Officer standing beside him. And the way he said it, as though it were nothing to do with him – I knew then that he was trying to distance himself from his captain. At the time, of course, I put it down to the fact that he was older, a resentment at being passed over. Later I was to discover his grandfather had been an admiral in the First World War, his father killed at sea in the Second, and he himself had come up through the traditional officer education of the Navy, Pangbourne, Dartmouth, then service at sea. What had damaged his career was volunteering for submarines and then, when he was posted to HMS *Dolphin* for a submariners' course, finding he was subject to claustrophobia and unable to concentrate when submerged.

In the circumstances it was a bit hard to find himself serving under a man who had joined the Navy as a boy seaman at *Ganges* and been commissioned out of the lower deck, was several years his junior and newly promoted to Lieutenant Commander, a rank he had held more years than he cared to remember. Added to which, he had never had command of a ship in his life, and now this raw young

186

Welshman was plunging him straight into a first-class Mediterranean balls-up. That was his choice of words, and he went on: 'There's Chinese in the dockyard here, one of the latest Russian cruisers anchored in Grand Harbour, and the Libyans barely two hundred miles away. We should never have come to the wharf here. We should never have agreed to tie up alongside.' He turned away, muttering something that sounded like, 'He should have had more sense.' Then he was giving orders for singling up and sailors were letting go all but the head and stern ropes and the springs.

The bridge had now filled up with the special sea duty men, the Navigator standing in the middle by the pelorus. Mault, watching from the bridge wing, finally told him to inform the Captain the ship was singled up and ready to proceed.

I was watching the quay, so I didn't see Mault's face as the Pilot put the phone down and told him the Captain was in the main communications office and he was to take the ship out to the new anchorage himself, but I did notice the sharpness in his tone as he gave the order to let go aft and, picking up the mike to the wheelhouse below, said, 'Port thirty, slow ahead port, slow astern starb'd.'

I could feel the beat of the engines under my feet, saw the stern swing clear of the quay, then we were backing out past the rust-patched freighter moored at the Parlatorio Wharf. 'Harbour launch, sir, coming away from Gun Wharf, heading towards us.'

Mault nodded his acknowledgement of the lookout's report, the ship still going astern and turning. As soon as we were clear of the freighter and had sea room to complete the 180° turn, he went ahead, the long arm of the harbour opening up in front of us as we turned the end of Senglea Point with the massive fortress of St Angelo showing beyond it. The harbour was a broad lane of flat water ablaze with lights on either side and at the end of it the swinging beam of the St Elmo light flashing three every fifteen seconds, with the small light on the end of the breakwater winking steadily.

Mault moved to the chart table, calling to the Pilot to join him. 'Plan to anchor about there,' he said, pointing his finger to a position roughly south-west of what used to be Gallows Point but was now shown on the chart in Maltese as Il-Ponta Ta'Ricasoli.

'Right in the fairway?'

'Well no, a little in towards Bighi Bay.'

The Navigating Officer nodded. 'Nine Fathoms Bank. You'll have eighteen to nineteen metres. That do you?' He had the plot going and there was a PO on the radar. Through the sloping windows I could see the Russian cruiser looming large and brilliantly lit. 'Harbour launch on the port quarter, sir. About one hundred metres off. He's signalling us to stop.'

'Thank you, Stevens.'

There was a little group closed up around the capstan on the fo'c's'le and I could see men on the deck of the cruiser. She looked enormous as we ran close down her starb'd side and it crossed my mind that if the Russians became involved in any way it really would be an international incident. And then I saw a man with a rag in his hand waving from the open door of the helicopter hangar aft and the thought was suddenly absurd.

'Matey, isn't he?' The Pilot smiled at me. 'The way they behave sometimes you'd think they were our comrades-in-arms. And that's one of their *Kresta* class – very lethal!' He was a short man with a round face, a puggy blob of a nose and a twinkle in his eyes. 'My name's Craig, by the way. Peter Craig. I'm supposed to see my lords and masters here don't scrape their bottom along the seabed or hit a headland.' He waved at the chart. 'That's where we'll be anchoring.' He indicated a little cross he had pencilled in. 'Then we'll start explaining ourselves to the harbour master.' He glanced at his watch. 'Twenty-two minutes to go till the next news. Think they'll have it on the World Service?'

A sub-lieutenant, standing beside the chart table with his back to the bulkhead, said quietly, 'If the BBC includes it in the news, then the PM will be tearing the guts out of the C-in-C and we'll be in the shit good and deep. Thank your lucky stars, Pilot, you're just a common navigator. I wouldn't be in Taffy's shoes right now . . .' He stopped then, glancing at me apologetically. 'Sorry, sir, no disrespect, but all Welshmen are Taffy to the boys, just as anybody called Brown is Buster and anybody with a name like Randolph, our Chief, becomes Randy. No disrespect, you see.' Like the Pilot, he was a Scot, a Glaswegian by the sound of his voice. His name was Robinson and he was a seaman officer-under-training, one step up from midshipman. I thought he was probably not more than nineteen or twenty years old.

The Pilot was concentrating now on the approach to the anchorage and it was an older officer standing by the radar who answered him. 'You shoot your mouth off like that and it's you who'll be in the shit.' And he added, 'Right now nobody wants to be reminded what could happen following that little incident, so forget your old man's on the ITN news desk and keep your trap shut. Okay?'

There was a juddering under my feet and I turned to see the ship was slowing: 'Harbour launch close abeam, still signalling Stop.' Mault ignored the report. He came back to the chart table, took a quick glance at the position the Navigating Officer had pencilled in, then asked him to report how far before letting go the anchor as he moved to the port bridge wing and took up one of the microphones. Everyone was silent now, waiting, the ship slowing, small alterations of helm, the shore lights barely changing position. 'Let go!' I felt, rather than heard, the rumble of the chain, then the voice of the officer on the fo'c's'le was reporting how many shackles of cable had gone out.

'Well, that's that.' Craig checked the time, entered it on

the chart against the fix he had taken as the anchor was let go. Behind him, the bridge began to empty. 'Care to join me for a drink in the wardroom, sir?'

I hesitated, then nodded. Lloyd Jones would be as anxious to get rid of me as I was to go, so no point in making a nuisance of myself. Besides, I was interested to know what his officers thought of it all.

The wardroom was two decks down on the starb'd side. Half a dozen officers were already there and all of them silent, listening for Big Ben on the loudspeaker set high in the corner. It came just as Peter Craig handed me the horse's neck I had asked for, the solemn tones of the hour striking, then the announcer's voice giving the headlines. It was the third item and followed bomb blasts in Belfast and Lyons – 'A frigate of the Royal Navy on a courtesy visit to Malta was involved this evening in an incident in which a shore party had to be given protection. Shots were fired and one officer was injured.' That was all.

'Playing it down,' Craig said, sucking eagerly at his drink and turning to look around him. 'Where's young Robbie? Hey, Robinson – tell yer dad he'll have to do better than that. The people at home should know what really happened.' His words about summed up the view of the others. A put-up job, that was their verdict, and then Mault came in. 'Mr Steele. The Captain would like a word with you. He's in his cabin.'

I nodded, finishing my drink, but waiting for the news broadcaster to come to the end of the Lyons outrage and move on to the Malta incident. It was padded out, of course, nothing new, and nothing to upset the Maltese, no indication that it was they who had fired the first shot, or that the ship had been deliberately moored alongside Hamilton Wharf so that an anti-British mob could move in from the nearby Malta Dry Docks and threaten the lives of British sailors returning from a wine party that had almost certainly been organised solely for the purpose of luring them ashore.

I thanked Craig for the drink, excused myself and went up to the Captain's cabin. It was empty, a cup of black coffee untouched on the desk. I went to one of the portholes. We had swung to our anchor and were now bows-on to the harbour entrance so that I was looking straight across to the cathedral and the domes of Valetta with the signal flagstaff towering above them. The harbour launch had been joined by two police launches, all three of them keeping station opposite to the bridge on the port side. An officer on the leading police launch had a loudhailer to his mouth, the words coming muffled as they reached me through the shatter-proof glass: 'You will plees to lower your gangway. I wish to come on to your ship and spik with the Captain.' And the reply, from somewhere above me – 'When you bring the British High Commissioner out we can discuss things. Okay?'

The steward put his head round the pantry door. 'Captain's apologies, sir, but he's been called to the MCO. Can I get you a drink?'

I shook my head. 'Another cup of coffee would be nice though.'

He nodded, retrieved the untouched cup from the desk and, as he was taking it back into the pantry, he hesitated. 'Excuse me asking, sir, but do you know the Captain well? I mean, you're a friend of his, aren't you?'

I didn't know how to answer that, so I just gave a bit of a nod and waited.

The steward stood there with the cup in his hand as though trying to make up his mind. Finally he said, 'I can't tell him, sir, but perhaps you can. There's a lot of rumours going round the ship. In the seamen's messes, I mean. They say the Captain's –' again the hesitation – 'well, bad luck, if you get me. A sort of Jonah. And it's not just the Captain. It's the ship.'

'Any particular reason?' I asked.

He stood there awkwardly, feeling no doubt he had said too much already. 'There's quite a few – misfits on board, sir.'

'Troublemakers, do you mean?' I asked.

He gave a little shrug, shaking his head. 'Hard to say, sir. Toughies certainly. Real toughies. Some of the lads feel they've been landed with a load of shit – if you'll excuse me – men that other ships wanted to be rid of.' And he added, 'These are the comments of lads that volunteered, you understand, specialists most of them, real good lads who thought *Medusa* was intended for some sort of special service. That's why they volunteered.'

I took him up then on the use of that word 'specialists' and he said they had been on courses, some of them, that weren't the usual run of courses sailors got sent on – demolition, assault, urban guerrilla warfare. 'There's even men on board here who've been trained by the SAS.' And he added, 'They volunteered for something out of the ordinary. At least, that's what they thought, something that sounded to them like it was as near to active service as you could get in peacetime. Instead, they find themselves on a ship that's got a hardcore of throw-outs in the crew. Tell him, will you, sir? Privately. He should know the feeling.' He said that quickly, almost in a whisper, and as he turned to go into the pantry, the entrance curtain was swept aside and Gareth entered, his face white, his lips a hard, tight line, and he was scowling. 'Get me some coffee, Jarvis.' He had a sheet of paper in his hand and he went straight to his desk and sat there, staring at it. He seemed completely oblivious of my presence. The main broadcast began to sound through the ship, Mault's voice ordering special sea duty men and the cable party to close up. 'All action stations to be manned and gun crews closed up.'

I couldn't believe it. I stared at Lloyd Jones. He'd heard it, but he made no move to counteract the order. 'Can you drop me off now?' I asked him. 'The harbour launch . . .'

He was staring at me, his eyes wide, that shocked look on his face as though suddenly aware that he had a civilian witness to what was happening on board. He shook his head. 'Sorry.' He held up the sheet of paper. 'Orders. No contact with the shore and put to sea immediately. Resist any attempt to prevent departure. Ministry of Defence. Whitehall's orders.' He put his hand to his head, leaning forward. 'Downing Street by the sound of it. Christ!' And then he suddenly seemed to get a grip of himself. He smiled. 'Glad to have you aboard. My God I am!' The steward brought him his coffee and he gulped it down, then reached for his cap and jumped to his feet. 'Make yourself at home. I'm afraid you'll have to put up with us for some time now.' He stopped in the doorway, his face grim as he said very quietly, so that only I could hear him, '*Medusa* is to leave now – immediately.' He hesitated, then added, 'It's Menorca. Port Mahon. I'm sorry, but those are my orders.' He turned then, putting his hat on and dropping the curtain behind him. There were feet pounding the deck, the throb of engines again and a clanking for'ard, the chain coming in.

I went up to the bridge. Everyone was back at their stations and the officer on the fo'c's'le reporting the anchor up and down, the shorelights beginning to move as the ship got under way. The harbour and police launches were maintaining station on the port side and one of their officers shouting through a loudhailer, his amplified voice clearly audible and nobody paying attention, the beat of the engines increasing, the ship gathering speed. Port Mahon! Why Mahon? Why was *Medusa* ordered to Menorca immediately? Regardless of the Maltese.

'Vessel putting out from Kalkara, sir. Looks like a patrol boat.'

It was Mault who acknowledged the lookout's report, the Captain merely raising his glasses to look at it.

'They're signalling, sir. An order to stop.'

Gareth nodded. 'Maximum revs as soon as you're clear of that ferry.'

I had tucked myself as inconspicuously as possible

against the rear bulkhead, between the chart table and the echo-sounder, which was clicking away over my left shoulder. I saw the ferry emerge virtually from under our bows as we sliced into its wake, the rising hum of the engines almost swamped by the surge of the bow wave as Gareth pulled open the port-side door to look back at the launches.

'That's not a patrol boat.' Mault's voice sounded high and a little tense. 'It's that big customs launch.' He strode across the bridge to Gareth. 'What happens if they open fire?'

'They won't.' Gareth's voice was firm and absolutely calm.

'You mean they won't dare. Then what about that cruiser?'

Gareth spun round. 'Our orders are specific. Leave Malta immediately. Are you seriously suggesting the Russians would risk an international incident of such magnitude? To open fire on a British warship in a friendly harbour would amount to something very close to a declaration of war – against us, against Nato.' He had spoken with sudden heat, an outburst almost. It indicated the pressure he was now under, the nervous strain. I also realised that his words were spoken for the benefit of everybody on the bridge, and thus for the ship as a whole.

He turned to the open doorway again, his back and the raising of his glasses indicating that the subject was closed. Nobody spoke after that, except for essential orders and reports, the hum of machinery, the sound of water, the shuddering and clattering of loose items, everything building to a crescendo as the two double reduction geared turbines piled on full power and the ship's twin props reached maximum revs. We were out past Gallows Point, the end of the breakwater approaching fast and the light at the end of it swinging across us so that every five seconds we were caught in its beam. Nobody fired at us, nobody followed as we pounded past it and out to sea, where we turned to port and set course to clear Gozo and leave the volcanic island of Pantelleria to port.

Craig pulled out Chart 165, and looking over his shoulder as he pencilled in our final course past the southern tip of Sardinia, I saw on the extreme left of it the eastern half of Menorca. Six hundred miles, say thirty to thirty-four hours at full speed. Why the hurry? And what would my position be when we got there? Customs, health and immigration would come on board in the usual way when we arrived and it was very unlikely Gareth would attempt to conceal my presence.

'If you care to come with me, sir, I'll show you to your cabin.' It was Petty Officer Jarvis and he had a bag in his hand. 'I've looked out some clothes of the Captain's – shirt, sweater, pyjamas, socks, that sort of thing. He thought they'd fit all right, you being about his size.'

The cabin was two decks down, just aft of the room housing the gyro compass machinery. It had two berths, both unoccupied, and when I finally turned in, lying there, conscious of the movement of the ship and unable to sleep, I couldn't help thinking how odd it was to be wearing the pyjamas of a man who would probably cuckold me within the week, may indeed have already done so. But that hardly seemed so important now as I stared into the darkness, my mind going over and over the events of the day. I thought of Wade, that telephone conversation, the trouble he had taken to trace my background, that bastard Evans trying to implicate me, and now this ship, sent to Malta, then, just after a nasty little shooting incident, sent off on a wild dash to Mahon. Why? And we had actually left Grand Harbour at action stations with gun crews closed up. Turning it over in my mind it seemed so incredible that at length I couldn't think of anything else.

III

MERCENARY MAN

CHAPTER ONE

I must have slept, for the next thing I knew was the shrill note of the bo's'n's pipe echoing over the main broadcast followed by a metallic voice declaring the start of another day: 'Call the hands, call the hands, call the hands.' It was 06.30 and since the movement had become a jerky roll and an occasional shivering crash for'ard, I guessed we had now cleared the western tip of Sicily with the full fetch of the Tyrrhenian Sea on our starb'd beam. The cabin door lurched back and Petty Officer Jarvis entered balancing a cup with a saucer on top of it. 'Captain's compliments, sir, and would you join him for breakfast as soon as you're ready.'

The tea was dark, strong and very sweet. I drank it quickly, then staggered along the passageway to the heads. It took me some time to shave and dress because of the unpredictability of the ship's movement, so that by the time I reached the Captain's day cabin he had finished his meal and was seated at the desk reading through a clip-board of signals with the Yeoman standing by. 'Sleep well?' It was a perfunctory query, his mind concentrated on the sheets in his hand, his face drawn and tense, dark shadows under his eyes. After a while he said, 'Very good, Yeo. Better send it now. They'll need to have all the details.' And then he turned to me. 'The BBC had it on the six o'clock news and it was also referred to in the round-up of the day's papers. *The Times* called it The Malta Incident and one of the tabloids had the headline: NAVY SCUTTLES OUT OF GRAND HARBOUR.' He smiled, but without humour, and he didn't refer to it again, the routine of a ship taking over as the Marine Engineer Officer came in to report engine and fuel states, followed by other officers with reports and queries.

I had finished breakfast and was having a final cup of coffee when he suddenly stood up and reached for his cap. 'Care to come round the ship with me?'

I followed him out into the passageway and down the ladder. For that moment we were alone, the first opportunity I had to ask him if he knew why he'd been despatched to Mahon in such haste.

He looked at me, tight-lipped. 'I seem to remember I told you, last night. I shouldn't have done, but I did.' And he added, 'I wasn't quite myself, a bit tensed-up.'

'You told me you'd had orders to leave, and you mentioned 10 Downing Street. But nothing else.'

'That's it – orders.'

'But why?'

He stopped then. 'This is the Navy, Mike. Politicians make the decisions, we carry out the orders.'

'But you must have some idea of the reasons for those orders.'

'Some idea, yes.' He said it slowly, hesitantly. 'The rest I'm having to guess at.' He started down the next ladder to the deck below. It was then that I passed on to him what Jarvis had said about the mood on the mess decks. He turned on me. 'I know about that. It can't be helped.' And when I persisted, suggesting that some hint of the reason for the orders he had received would make his men, and myself, a good deal happier, he gripped hold of my arm and said angrily, 'Leave it at that, will you. I'm pleased to have you on board, but don't ask questions.'

He went on ahead then, down a long passageway to the sick bay, where we found Kent pale but cheerful, sitting up bare-chested and heavily bandaged. 'Pity we've no helicopter,' Gareth told him. 'But another twenty-four hours and we'll either have a Spanish surgeon here on board to get that bullet out or we'll fly you home.'

'I'd rather have it out on board, sir.' But as we left him

there were beads of perspiration forming on his forehead, his skin very white. Gareth said to me quietly, 'Good man, that. He'll leave a gap I'll have great difficulty in filling.' And he added, 'If we'd had a helicopter, we could have flown him ashore from here.'

The tour of inspection took in three decks and lasted just over half an hour, and all the time Gareth was making an effort to imprint his personality on the officers and men he talked to and play down what had happened at the wharf in Malta. Finally we reached the flight deck, going through the hangar to look down on to the quarterdeck below where the white of our seething wake and the roar of water boiling up from the twin screws made it almost impossible to talk. 'What's wrong with the helicopter – out of service?' I shouted to him.

He shook his head. 'I haven't been allocated one.'

'So what do you keep in the hangar?' I was curious because the shut steel doors had seals on the locks.

He didn't answer that, looking at me sharply, then turning away. Later, talking to the Pilot on the bridge, I learned that those seals were inspected by the Captain or WEO personally mornings and evenings, that they each held a key to the doors and it required both of them present in person to unlock them.

But by then I was less interested in the sealed hangar than in the political repercussions of the Malta affair. It was, in fact, the main topic of conversation, not just on the bridge or among the officers, but throughout the ship. At first it was no more than a small item at the end of the early morning news. By 09.00 the BBC had slotted it in as a major news item immediately following the latest exchange of notes between the Kremlin and the White House, and it was clear from the way in which the incident was being presented that it was being blown up into a major political row. Later the World Service of the BBC announced that the British High Commissioner had been summoned to the office of the Maltese premier where he had been handed a note of protest to the British Government for the 'high-handed, irresponsible and internationally outrageous behaviour of one of HM ships in opening fire on innocent people when on a courtesy visit'. Almost simultaneously the Maltese High Commissioner in London had been called to the Foreign Office. The Opposition spokesman on foreign affairs had put down a question for the Prime Minister to answer at Question Time in the House that afternoon and there was even some talk of an emergency cabinet meeting later in the day.

The repercussions of all this bore heavily on Gareth, who spent most of the day at his desk replying to the stream of signals that came in, one of them from 10 Downing Street itself demanding an immediate personal report of the affair direct to the Prime Minister's Office.

And on top of this, in the late afternoon, there was a sudden flurry on the bridge, messages flying around the ship and the Captain himself finally being called. We were then approaching Cape Spartivento at the southern end of Sardinia with the wind increasing from the north-east, the surface of the sea flecked with whitecaps and the sky so overcast it looked as though night was about to fall.

It was the Communications Officer who first alerted the officer of the watch. He was a flamboyant, cocky lieutenant with a round, smiling face. His name was Woburn, so everybody referred to him as The Smiler. But he wasn't smiling when he appeared on the bridge in the late afternoon, his face set as he and the Pilot searched the murk through the bridge glasses. We were on collision course apparently with a section of the Sixth Fleet, which had left the Bay of Naples the previous day and was now spread out over quite a large area of sea.

Night had fallen before we sighted the aircraft carrier. It came up over the horizon like the gas flare of an oil rig, so bright and red was the masthead light, and then, as we closed it, two American destroyers powered towards us at full speed, swirling round and stationing themselves between us and the carrier like protecting sheepdogs. When we passed it we were so close that the side of it was like the blurred outline of a harbour wall, and always the destroyers tracking alongside us, close enough at one point for Gareth to slide open the starb'd bridge door and exchange greetings with one of their captains over loudhailers. Then they peeled away and for the next half-hour we were threading through a litter of radar blips that only occasionally resolved themselves into fleeting glimpses of actual ships.

As a result our evening meal was later than usual. It was also a rather hurried one with Gareth hardly saying a word, his mind concentrated on the problems facing him. One of those problems was, of course, my presence on the ship. Due to the decrease in speed while crossing the track of the US ships, and the fact that we had to alter course to starb'd, our ETA at Mahon the next day had been delayed by about two hours to 08.45. It was hardly likely he would risk putting me ashore in daylight, and once we were tied up at the Naval Base . . .' 'What are you going to do about me?' I asked him.

He looked at me vaguely. Then his eyes focused as though suddenly recalling my presence in the cabin. 'I haven't decided yet.' He got suddenly to his feet, hesitated, then crossed to his desk. 'This came in just after we cleared that carrier.'

Time of receipt of the message he passed to me was 21.13. It read: *Weapon that killed Jorge Martinez found in home of Michael Steele. Police statement just issued indicates Steele arrived Malta on twin-hulled yacht Thunderflash then disappeared. Recent owner of yacht name of Evans also wanted for questioning; thought to be on fishing expedition. Political situation here still tense. In view of what happened Malta suggest you anchor off Villa Carlos well clear of Mahon port area.*

I was still in a state of shock, reading again the first lines of that message, when he said, 'You understand, I hope – the sooner you're off my ship the better.' I began to protest that I had had nothing to do with the Martinez killing, but he stopped me. 'Whether you were involved or not is immaterial. The gun was apparently found in your house and I've got troubles enough –'

'It wasn't in my house. It was in the port engine compartment –'

'I don't care where it was,' he cut in. 'I want you off the ship and the sooner–'

'For God's sake, listen will you . . .'

'No, you listen.' His hand was up, an abrupt, imperative gesture. 'I'm sorry, but you must understand. You're dynamite in my present circumstances.' He took the paper from me, staring down at it and muttering something about 'he was bound to be mixed up in it somewhere', then folding it and slipping it into his pocket with a bitter little laugh as he told me I was probably the least of his worries, everybody blaming him for the Malta Incident. 'And the PM insisting I act with more circumspection in Menorca. Circumspection! That'll be the Foreign Office putting their oar in.' The boyish smile flashed out, but it was only a glimmer, then he banged his cap on his head and was gone, hurrying down the ladder to the Communications Office.

I finished my coffee, my mind in turmoil. Finally I went back up to the bridge, preferring contact with the outside world to the confines of the cabin, where I had nothing to do but think about Soo and what the hell had been going on for that gun to have been found in the house.

The watch was just changing, and shortly afterwards young Davison, a fresh-faced, tow-headed officer-under-training appeared at my elbow to say the Captain had phoned to enquire if I would join him for a drink.

I found him sitting hunched over his desk, the reading light pulled down to spotlight the pad on which he had been making notes, hs face, his whole body set rigid, and a cigarette smouldering in a scallop-shell ashtray. He looked up, his eyes blank.

'What is it?' I asked. And when he didn't reply, I said, 'You asked me down for a drink.'

'Oh yes.' His eyes blinked quickly and he seemed to pull himself together, jumping to his feet and waving me to a seat at the low table. He picked up the bottle standing there. 'Real cognac, or would you prefer brandy and ginger ale?' I opted for the cognac, and as he poured it the neck of the bottle rattled against the rim of the glass. That, and the awkward silence as he helped himself to a Coke and sat down opposite me, was an indication of how tensed-up he was.

'You're thinking about tomorrow,' I said.

He nodded, stubbing out the remains of his cigarette, lighting another, then leaning back, drawing the smoke into his lungs as though he were at high altitude sucking in oxygen. In the silence that followed I was conscious of the engines, the far-off sound of the bow wave surging along the frigate's side, the rattle of crockery in the steward's pantry.

'I was wondering . . .' But it's not easy to ask a favour of a man who's in love with your wife. 'Why don't you drop me off on one of the islands as you go into Mahon?' I asked him finally, very conscious of the hesitancy in my voice. He was the Captain of a Royal Navy ship on an official visit and my suggestion was tantamount to smuggling a wanted man back into Spain. And when he didn't say anything, I made the point that I hadn't asked to stay on his ship. 'You virtually kidnapped me.' And I added, 'Drop me off. Forget I was ever on board.'

'Yes, I've thought of that.' He nodded. 'But there's over two hundred men on this ship and most of them know you're here.' He got up, pacing back and forth behind me so nervously that I began to think it must be a more personal matter he wanted to discuss. He and Soo had probably been corresponding while he was in Malta, or before he had left Gibraltar. They might even have made up their minds already. But then he said, 'How well do you know Pat?'

'Evans?' I swung round in my chair.

'Yes.' He had stopped pacing. 'What do you know about him?'

'Not very much.' I paused. 'No more really than Carp has told me.'

He leaned down, staring at me. 'Tell me something.' His dark eyes fixed themselves on my face. 'The murder weapon – a rifle was it?'

'An AK-47,' I told him. 'The sniper version with folding butt.'

'So you've seen it?'

I didn't say anything. It had been such an easy trap and I had fallen for it.

'Where did you see it? Did that man Barriago give it to you?' He didn't wait for an answer. 'Was Pat involved?'

'Yes,' I said. 'I'm pretty certain he was and I was trying to tell you when you shut me up. I don't know whether he acquired the weapon for Barriago, but he certainly disposed of it.' He listened to me then as I told him what had happened, how I'd found the gun tucked away at the stern end of the starb'd engine compartment under the prop shaft, how I'd taken it up to the villa and concealed it under the floorboards in the kitchen.

'And now they've found it.'

'Apparently.'

Silence then and the sound of a door slamming, both of us thinking about that message from Menorca. Suddenly he laughed. 'So you paid him back in his own coin, and now he's fixed you again.' His laughter was without mirth. 'Par for the course,' he muttered. 'And now?' He stared at me as though expecting an answer, then shrugged and sat down opposite me. 'I gather that fellow Carpenter has told you about my being sent to live with Moira Evans at

Felixstowe Ferry, and then Pat arriving?' He nodded. 'He would know, of course – all the gossip, all the things they said. Felixstowe Ferry! My God!' He was smiling and shaking his head. 'Lost my innocence there, found a no-good bastard of a half-brother – then, years later . . . But you know about that.'

'The Haven buoy?'

He nodded. 'That Haven buoy episode hangs round my neck like a millstone. It's the cause . . .' He put his head in his hands, rubbing the palms of them over his eyes. 'He crucified me. He didn't know it at the time. He thought he was saving my life, but he crucified me – and now the agony begins.'

'What agony?' I asked. His face had gone very pale, his eyes half-closed. 'You all right?' He looked as though he might pass out. His eyes flicked open then, his mind on something else. I asked him about his use of the word bastard. 'Did you mean that literally? Is Evans your father's illegitimate son?'

He didn't answer for a moment, then suddenly he burst out laughing. 'Is that what Carpenter told you, man? If so, he's got it the wrong way round. Whatever else Pat is, he's legitimate.' And then, his mood changing again, he put his elbows on the table, his head thrust forward. 'Look now, I'm going to tell you something I haven't told anyone else. In confidence, mind you. You'll see why. You've heard part of it, so you may as well know it all. Especially as it's my belief you've now got the boat they brought the stuff ashore in.' He nodded towards the bottle. 'Help yourself. This may take a little time.' He leaned back, drawing on his cigarette. 'The King's Fleet mean anything to you?'

'By the entrance to the Deben River, isn't it?'

He nodded. 'I heard you visited Woodbridge and Felix-stowe Ferry a while back when you were searching for a boat. The Fleet was used by the Vikings, and the Romans before them. Now it's cut off from the river by a high flood bank. But there's still a few stretches of water left. When I was about fourteen and living for a time at the Ferry, Pat and I used to bird-watch there. It was a great place for nesting swans, some of the rarer water birds, too.' And he added, 'It was only later I discovered Pat's real interest — he liked to smash the eggs with steel balls fired from a catapult, or try and put out a swan's eye with it.'

'Charming!' I murmured, but he picked me up on that. 'It wasn't viciousness, you understand. It was a question of marksmanship. Later he acquired an airgun. It was the challenge, you understand. He didn't think about the cruelty of it. He hasn't that sort of imagination.' He shook his head, staring vacantly at his empty glass, his mind back in the past. 'Perhaps he doesn't have any imagination at all. I'm not sure.'

'What happened?' I asked. 'You were going to tell me what happened there.'

'Oh yes.' He nodded. 'Over four years ago now. I was on leave, the first since my wife and I split up. I thought it would be fun to go back to Suffolk, stay at the Ferry, particularly as it was November, a good time for bird-watching.' He leaned back, his eyes half-closed again. 'The second night I was there, after the evening meal, I took some chocolate biscuits and a Thermos of coffee and rum and walked along the Deben bank to the King's Fleet. Half a mile or so in from the river there's a series of little Broads-type lakes. The farmer had parked a trailer there part-loaded with bags of fertiliser. It made an ideal hide and I hadn't been propped up there, my back against the bags, more than half an hour before I heard the beat of wings. They passed almost directly over my head, five dark shapes against the Milky Way, the beat fading, then strengthening again as the birds circled. Suddenly I had them in the glasses, coming in low, the wet glimmer of the Fleet shattered, a flurry of water as they breasted it, then only ripples and the five shapes gliding ghostly white. Five Brent, and if nothing else happened that night it would have been worth it just to see the way they touched down. It was magic.'

Recalling the pleasure of that night was, I think, a sort of displacement activity for him. It helped to relieve some of the tension, his eyes half-closed, his mind totally concentrated and the Welsh lilt in his voice suddenly quite pronounced, the words with a poetic touch: '. . . a slow, heavy beat, a single bird this time and quite invisible until the splash of its touchdown showed white on the black pewter surface of the Fleet. It was a swan, but it carried its neck stiff like a column, with none of the graceful curve of the ubiquitous mute. It looked like a Bewick, a juvenile, the feathers drab instead of white. And then I thought it might possibly be a whooper. It would be unusual, but by then it was past midnight and I felt anything could happen, having already had a very good night with the sighting of a goosander as well as three grebes among the coots.'

He was smiling to himself, reliving a night that was indelibly etched on his mind. 'I drank the last of my coffee and rum with the buildings of Felixstowe Ferry sharp-etched against the light of the rising moon, the dark line of the sea's horizon just visible. When the moon finally rose above the sea the patches of water close by me were full of shadow shapes, coots bobbing their white-blazed heads, mallard and pochards motionless, the swans gliding slowly; no zephyr of a breeze, everything frozen still, a light winking far away in the approaches to Harwich. I remember I started thinking about another night, when I had come out to the Fleet with Pat and his father; then suddenly my thoughts were interrupted by the sound of an engine.'

His eyes flicked open, dark pupils with the glazed look of jet. 'It came from beyond the hill where an old farmhouse stood among some trees, a low hill that marked the limit of what had once been the great marsh that was part of the vanished port of Goseford. I waited for the sound of it to fade away towards Kirton village and the main Felixstowe–Ipswich road, but instead it gradually increased, no lights and a shadow moving on the road down from the farm.'

Through his glasses he had seen it was a van, the engine quieter as it coasted without lights down the slope to the Fleet. Duck shooters was his first thought – poachers. There were two of them in the van and they had driven straight on, finally parking against the high grass bank that shut the Fleet off from its entrance into the Deben. 'I didn't worry about them after that, presuming they were fishermen. Now that the moon was clear of cloud I could see that what I had thought was a goosander, the pinkish breast showing pale and the down-turned bill just visible, was in fact a red-breasted merganser, a much more likely bird to see close by an East Coast estuary. I watched for another half-hour, and then a breeze sprang up, blowing in little gusts off the North Sea and bitterly cold. There was a dampness in the air, too, so that a rime of frost formed on my anorak. My fingers were numb by then and I got to my feet, climbing down off the trailer, and after picking up my knapsack with the Thermos flask in it, I headed down the track towards the Deben. Several times I stopped to watch the Fleet, my breath smoking and the birds mostly hidden now among the reeds, or still shadows fast asleep. It was just after one when I reached the grass-grown bank of the river.' He paused. 'That was when I heard the sound of voices and the clink of metal on metal, the clatter of a halyard frapping.'

He was staring straight at me, his eyes blacker than ever in the glare of the wall light. 'It was a little unnerving really. I was alone, you see, and yet I couldn't help it. I had to know what it was all about. So I clambered up the bank, and as soon as my head cleared the top of it, I stopped.' He paused again, and it was almost as though he did it for effect. Then he went on, his voice very quiet: 'Tide was at the full, and it was a spring tide, the river and the inlet of the King's Fleet almost brimming over with water, otherwise they would never have got it in there. I just stood there, gaping at the thing, it was such an incredible sight – a large catamaran, black-hulled, its single aluminium mast gleaming like silver in the moonlight. It was moored stern-on to the bank with an anchor out in the middle of the Fleet, and there were men passing cases up through a hatch in the starb'd hull to others on the bank.'

His hand was gripped on the edge of the table, the stub of his cigarette burning unheeded in the ashtray. 'The quick furtiveness of their movements, their faces covered by stocking masks, gave a weirdness to the scene, the moon bright now and everything very clear and sharp in the frost. I snuggled down in the whitened grasses. Smugglers! I wasn't sure, but clearly something was being run ashore at dead of night, and that meant contraband of some sort.' His eyes flicked up at me. 'What the hell do you do in a situation like that?' And he went on, softly as though talking to himself. 'I was alone, you see. I trained my glasses on them. There were three on deck, two ashore, and another passing the cases up. Six altogether, and one of them standing with his hand on his hip . . . I focused the glasses on the case being passed up over the stern, searched the growing pile on the bank. That's when I began to be really scared.'

He was silent for a moment, staring into space. 'It wasn't drink, you see, nor drugs. It was arms! I wasn't in any doubt. There were long cases that could only contain hand-held rocket-launchers, others that looked more like rifles, but it was the ammunition boxes – I'd seen too many of those not to recognise them instantly.'

He stopped then, stubbing out his cigarette, and in the silence I was conscious again of the ship's sounds, and of the movement, too. 'Maybe he caught the glint of my binocular lenses in the moonlight,' he went on slowly. 'Whatever it was, he was suddenly looking straight at me.

Then he said something to the others and they froze, their stockinged faces all turned towards me.' He shook his head. 'It was unbelievable. The coincidence of it. The two of us . . .' His voice faded into silence.

'You mean it was Evans?'

'Yes. Pat.' He nodded. 'And now — again. Out here. It's as though some devilish fate . . .' He left the sentence unfinished, and when I asked him what had happened, he shrugged. 'What you'd expect, considering the cargo they were running. They had a man in the outfield, hidden in the tall grasses by the sluice. I ran straight into him. Big fellow. Rose up right in front of me and knocked me out, cold. Next thing I knew I was lying on the wooden grating of the catamaran's steering platform with Pat bending over me.' And after a moment he said, 'Lucky for me. They'd have killed me if he hadn't been there.' He lit another cigarette, his eyes closed, his mind far away so that I had to get the rest of it out of him by question and answer.

When he had come round the catamaran was already under way. He could hear the winches clicking as the sails were hoisted and hardened in. Then the engines were cut and Evans whispered urgently to him to lie still. 'I could hear voices on the deck for'ard, Irish voices, and Pat with his mouth right against my ear telling me he'd slip me into the water as close to Woodbridge Haven buoy as possible. He told me they'd tied up to it on the way in, waiting for the tide to make over the bar. The warp hadn't been double-ended, so instead of slipping it, they had cut it.'

He stopped there, apparently lost in the memory of that night and what had happened after they'd crossed the bar.

'And that was the rope you used to lash yourself to the buoy,' I prompted.

He nodded slowly. 'He had me flung overboard up-tide of the buoy so that I pretty well drifted down on to it. They were Irish on board, not East Coasters, and they didn't understand. They wanted me dead, but not with a bullet in my guts. Found drowned –' He smiled wryly. 'Nobody can ever be accused of murder if you're picked up out of the sea with your lungs full of water.'

'But why did he do it?' I asked. The blood relationship was all very well, but the man was running arms to the IRA in England . . .

'There was a condition, of course.' I hardly heard the words, they were spoken so softly.

'But you couldn't possibly keep quiet about it,' I said. Anyway, he hadn't attempted to conceal the fact that he had seen them landing arms at the King's Fleet. 'Or was it just his identity you promised not to reveal?'

He nodded. 'I swore I'd never tell anyone I'd recognised him. I wouldn't have done, anyway,' he murmured. 'He knew that. But he made me swear it all the same.'

'Then why have you told me?' I asked him.

He got up suddenly and began pacing back and forth again, his shoulders hunched, the new cigarette burning unheeded in his hand. When I repeated the question, he said, 'I'm not sure really.' He stopped just behind my chair. 'To show you the sort of man Pat is. That's one reason. A warning. And at the same time . . .' He went over to his desk and sat down, pulling the message slip out of his pocket and going through it again. 'God in heaven!' he murmured. 'Why doesn't he get the hell out? Now, while nobody knows he's involved.'

And then he turned to me. 'He's not all bad, you see. And to end up in prison. A life sentence. He's not the sort of man who could bear imprisonment. Freedom is everything to him. That's why he deserted from the Navy, why he couldn't stand any ordinary sort of job. It's against his nature, you understand.' He was pleading with me, trying to persuade me to keep quiet about where I had found that Russian gun. I remembered Soo's words then, wondering what exactly the relationship had been between this man, who was now the Captain of a Royal Navy frigate, and his half-brother, who was a gun-runner, what they had felt for each other when they were both young-sters at *Ganges* and Pat Evans had got him down from the top of that mast.

He looked up at me suddenly. 'How old's that catamaran you sailed to Malta?'

'It was built six years ago,' I said.

He nodded perfunctorily as though it was what he had expected. 'The hulls are painted white now, but under-neath – any sign of black paint?'

'You'd have to ask Carp,' I told him. But neither of us were in any doubt it was the same boat.

He didn't say anything after that, sitting hunched at the desk the way he had been when I had come down from the bridge to have a drink with him, his mind closed to everything else but the signals lying there under his hands.

The loudspeaker burst into life, a muffled announce-ment about the deadline for posting letters home. He listened to it briefly, then returned to the papers.

'About tomorrow?' I reminded him.

He looked up, frowning. 'I'll think about it. Meanwhile, if you've finished your drink . . .' He returned to the papers, his withdrawn manner making it clear the period of intimacy was over. 'See you in the morning.' But then, as I was going out, he stopped me. 'Ever done any board-sailing?' And when I told him I had run sailboard courses when I first came to Menorca, he nodded. 'That might help.' And he added, 'I'll think about it. Let you know in the morning.'

I went up to the bridge then, standing inconspicuously by the radar, watching the knife-like bows rise and fall beyond the twin barrels of the 4.5-inch guns, the white glimmer of the bow wave either side, my body adapting to the pitch and roll as we drove north-westwards through breaking seas. The wind had backed into the north and was blowing about force five. Standing in the dark like that, conscious of the engines vibrating under my feet, the sound of them overlaid by the noise of the sea, and the watch on duty still like shadows all about me, there was an extraordinary sense of isolation, of time standing still. I was thinking of *Thunderflash* and the voyage to Malta, all the other occasions when I had been alone at the helm, just the sea and my thoughts for company. But now it was different. Now I had the feeling I had reached some sort of watershed.

Tomorrow! And my life slipping through my mind. Nothing achieved, never anything solid, all I had built in Menorca breaking in my hands, Soo, the business, everything, and now that bloody catamaran . . . 'Care for some coffee, sir? Or there's kai if you prefer it.' One of the leading seamen was standing at my elbow with a tin tray full of mugs. I chose the chocolate and took it over to the chart table, where the Navigating Officer was now checking our position against the plot. 'Do you know where we'll be anchoring?' I asked him as he completed the log entry.

For answer he pulled open the topmost drawer and extracted the chart that gave plans of Mahon and Fornells harbours, as well as two in Ibiza. 'About there, we reckon.' He indicated the Mahon plan, where he had pencilled a cross just south of Cala Llonga right opposite Villa Carlos. 'ETA is now 09.30 approx.' He looked at me curiously. 'You staying on board or is the Captain arranging to put you ashore?'

'I'm not certain,' I said.

He nodded, smiling at me. He understood the problem. 'It might interest you to know he's just rung me to say he wants one sailboard with wet suit and goggles ready on the flight deck by 09.00. I'm in charge of sailing, you see.' And he added, 'Sorry about the board, but it's the best we can do. No dinghies, I'm afraid.'

It was probably nervous exhaustion that finally got me off to sleep that night for I was dead to the world when Petty Officer Jarvis shook me into consciousness. He was earlier than usual. 'Lieutenant Craig would like you to select whichever one fits best.' He dumped three wet suits on the foot of the bunk. 'They're the only sizes we have on board.' And as he went out, he asked me to leave the two I didn't want and any borrowed clothing on the rack above my bunk.

By then the bo's'n's mate was rousing the ship, and shortly afterwards Gareth's voice announced: '*This is the Captain. Just to bring you up to date. We are now approaching Port Mahon, the main harbour and capital of Menorca, one of the Spanish Balearic islands. For obvious reasons we shall not be tying up alongside. Instead, I propose to anchor well clear of the town in the approaches opposite Villa Carlos. In the circumstances, I do not see any possibility of shore leave. I will let you know how long this courtesy visit is to last as soon as I can. That is all.*'

His cabin was empty by the time I arrived for breakfast. 'Captain's on the bridge,' Petty Officer Jarvis told me. 'And there's no choice this morning.' He placed a heaped plateful of bacon, sausages, eggs and fried bread in front of me. 'He thought you might appreciate it. Later in the day, that is.'

I was still working through it when Gareth appeared. 'We shall be abreast of St Carlos Point and La Mola in approximately fifteen minutes. Things will begin to hot up then. As soon as you've finished, I'd be glad if you'd return to your cabin and wait there until Petty Officer Jarvis comes to take you down to the quarterdeck. Chief Petty Officer Clark will meet you there. He will have . . .' The Sinbad loudspeaker interrupted him, a voice from the bridge reporting that revs were now being reduced. 'Also, there's a small vessel lying off Lazareto. Spanish Navy by the look of her, sir. Could be coastal patrol, or one of those small minesweepers, can't tell yet.'

Gareth reached for the mike. 'Very good, Simon. I'll be up.' He turned to me again. 'That could complicate matters. I didn't expect an escort.'

'You've decided have you – to get me off the ship by sailboard?'

'Yes, didn't Peter Craig warn you last night?'

'All he told me was that you'd ordered him to have a board ready on the flight deck by 09.00. I didn't know you'd made up your mind till your steward brought me a choice of wet suits with my tea this morning.' I hesitated, but this looked like my last chance to question him. 'Has Wade been in touch with you?' I asked him.

'Commander Wade?'

I nodded, watching him closely as he said he couldn't discuss official contacts with me.

'Particularly Wade I suppose?'

He didn't answer. I think he had intended having a cup of coffee with me, but now he put his hat back on his head. 'I'll try and arrange it so that *Medusa* is between you and the escort when we drop you off. The engines will be stopped for that moment and I'll get as much of the way off the ship as I can. You've got a good breeze, so with luck you'll be on the board and sailing fast enough to remain hidden from the escort vessel as we gather way again. Okay?' He smiled then and held out his hand. 'Good luck, Mike!' And as we shook hands he had the gall to add, 'If you make it to Bloody Island you'll be able to hide up with that archaeological Amazon of yours.'

There is something about a Navy ship that instils a sense of something akin to discipline even in a civilian visitor like myself. I could have turned left, gone up to the bridge and watched our approach to Mahon. Nobody would have stopped me. I could have got my things, found my way aft down to the flight deck and waited there. Instead, I did what Gareth had told me and went straight to my cabin. I wished I hadn't. Sitting on the bunk, staring at nothing except the opposite berth and the cabin fittings, time passed slowly. There was no porthole and even if I had had something to read, the ceiling light was too dim, so that I would have had to stretch out on the bunk with the little bulkhead light on.

Shortly after 08.40 I felt the engines slow, then Mault's voice called for the watch on deck to muster and put fenders out on the starb'd side. Somebody was coming aboard, presumably from the patrol boat. The engines stopped, feet pounding on the deck and orders shouted, then a slight bump as the other vessel came alongside. This was the moment they should have dropped me over the side, but nobody came and the beat of the engines started up again.

It was 08.55 when Petty Officer Jarvis knocked at the cabin door. 'Everything's ready, sir, if you'll bring the wet suit with you. And the Captain asked me to give you this.'

'What is it?' I asked as he handed me a nasty-looking bit of black fur in a plastic bag.

'A beard, sir. Compliments of our entertainments officer. The Captain thought it might help if somebody had their glasses on you.'

There was a CPO waiting for us on the flight deck. The sailboard was propped against the hangar doors, mast and sail rigged, and a thin line attached to the bows was coiled ready. To starb'd the cliffs of La Mola and the brown of the military casements came into view. 'We'll be approaching the narrows at the southern end of Lazareto Island in a few minutes,' the CPO said. 'Lieutenant Craig estimates the distance from the buoys marking the narrows to the spot where we'll be anchoring as roughly nine cables. He'll stop engines when we come abreast of the little island immediately beyond Lazareto. That will be the signal for you to go.'

I stripped off my clothes and he helped me into the wet suit, zipping me up and slipping a bum-bolster round my buttocks. ''Fraid the harness isn't exactly a speed seat. You'll have to adjust it as you go. And the board's just an ordinary production job for funboard sailing, so if you want air, you won't find it.' Looking at it, I could see it was no jump board, more a beginner's board, which suited me in the circumstances. 'Got any goggles?' I asked.

He reached into his pocket and produced a narrow, almost slit-eyed pair with black surround. I put them on and adjusted them to fit my head. 'Don't forget the beard, sir.' He was grinning. 'You look like you could play Mephistopheles in that. Nobody could possibly recognise you.'

By then the conical buoy with its flashing light marking the channel on the starb'd side was already bobbing in our wash, the sharp southern point of Lazareto, Punta de San Felipet, appearing at the same instant. The engines were slowing now, the speed dropping off. 'How long do you reckon?' I asked the CPO.

'Seven, eight minutes.'

The beard was close-fitting and warm, the sea goggles on the tight side. They wrapped up my clothes and taped them into a plastic bag, which they tied firmly to the base of the sailboard's mast in such a way that it did not restrict its pintle fitting. Petty Officer Jarvis excused himself. He had to attend to the needs of the Captain and his visitor, who was the Spanish Navy's *Jefe*, Capitán Perez. The long brown line of Lazareto went slowly by. Peering out to port, I could see the buildings of Villa Carlos coming closer. Soon now, and I was wondering whether Petra would be back from burying her father, whether she would be on the island, and how the hell I was going to live with the police watching for me and no money. All I had in the pocket of my trousers, now screwed up in a plastic ball, was £235 in traveller's cheques which I couldn't cash because it meant going to a bank or a hotel.

Cala Pedrera. Punta de Medio. I could see Punta de Cala Fonts coming up, and beyond the point, the Villa Carlos promenade with its hotels and restaurants and the Cafayas light. 'Stand by, sir.' The engines were slowing, the sound of water slipping past the plates dying away. I caught a glimpse to starb'd of the Plana de Mahon light. 'Ready?' The CPO took one end of the sailboard, I took the other.

A few steps, a heave, and it was overboard, the slim board surfing alongside as he held it by the line. 'Away you go, sir, and whatever you do, hang on to the beard. Entertainments want it back.' He was grinning as he clapped me on the shoulder. Not quite a shove, but it reminded me of the one occasion I had parachuted under instruction. I jumped, my head in my arms, my knees up in a foetal position. Wham! I hit the water, the ship still moving, its displacement dragging me under. And then I was up, the grey stern moving past, the board within yards, anchored by the sail which was lying flat on the surface.

It was over two years since I had been on a sailboard. The technique doesn't leave one, but, like skiing, the muscles lose their sharpness. I flipped on to it all right, but instead of getting myself and the sail up in virtually the same movement, it was all a bit of a scramble. The wind was funnelling down the harbour, a good breeze that had me away on the starb'd tack and going fast before I was visible to the escort vessel, which was on the far side of *Medusa* and lying a little ahead of her, one of the old minesweepers by the look of it.

There was a moment, of course, when I felt naked and unsure of myself, but as my arms and knees began to respond to the drive of the sail, confidence returned, and after I had snapped the harness on I began to enjoy myself, steering close to the wind, my weight a little further aft and the speed increasing, my exhilaration, too. I found I went better if I railed it down to leeward. Gradually, as I became more relaxed and let the harness take some of the strain off my arms, I was able to glance over my shoulder at the pale grey shape of the frigate with its bristling antennae. I was paralleling her course and going faster, so that I was soon abreast of her for'ard guns. There was a little group of men gathered on the fo'c's'le ready for anchoring and the four international code flags flying from the yardarm. Ahead of me, and beyond Villa Carlos, I could now see Bloody Island, with the old hospital buildings looking even more like a stranded steamer.

I swung round, passing the sail across as I went through the wind on to the other tack. I was heading directly towards the patrol boat now and there were other boats about – a launch, two motor cruisers and a sailing yacht, several rowing boats and a tug moving across to Cala Figuera to perform its regular job of taking the small supply tanker in tow. Without thinking I put my hand to my chin. I knew the beard was still there. I could feel it. But I still had to touch it, to be sure nobody could recognise me. By then I had worked the board up to about twelve knots and it was really skimming across the flat surface of the water. The tug hooted, and as though that were a signal, *Medusa*'s anchor splashed down, the clatter of the chain running out echoing back from the rocky shore, a cloud of seabirds rising from the small boat gut in the middle of Villa Carlos.

I turned again, driving the board hard on the wind through the gap between Bloody Island and the shore, heading straight for the north side of Cala Figuera until I could see the quay I'd built and the chandlery and my home tucked tight in against the cliffs. There were two boats moored stern-to by the quay, figures moving about their decks and the chandlery door wide open. So the business was still operating. I passed within two hundred metres of it. No sign of Soo, but the office balcony window was open. I was then heading straight for the Club Maritimo, and seeing a big inflatable coming out from the huddle of yachts moored at the pontoon, I swung away towards the other shore.

If I hadn't been distracted by a small freighter coming out of Mahon itself, I would have recognised that inflatable sooner. Or would I? The fact was that I was thoroughly enjoying myself now, the water and the sailboard having temporarily divorced me from reality, so that perhaps I had no desire to recognise it, subconsciously aware that reality and all the problems of the future were at the helm. I ploughed my way into the freighter's wake, swinging down-wind and surfing in the turbulence. And then, when I was almost back at Bloody Island and could see the inflatable heading straight for it, I knew, and in the instant I couldn't resist the joke of heading straight for it, just to see what she'd do, a bearded stranger sailboarding along-side.

It was Petra all right. She smiled and waved, her features half-hidden by that ridiculous sombrero she sometimes wore. She held up the tail end of a rope, offering me a tow, and I felt a pang of jealousy, seeing her suddenly as a girl on her own making overtures to an unattached male. Or did she guess who it was? I swept round and chased her all the way to Bloody Island, running the sailboard in right behind her and flopping into the water alongside the inflatable. 'I thought we might have dinner together,' I suggested.

She was out on the rock that did service as a quay, leaning down, her shirt gaping. Her eyes lit up. 'Where?' She was smiling that big-mouthed smile of hers, the lips open so that her strong features looked all teeth.

'Here,' I said. 'On the island. I'm told you have a tent . . .'

'That beard of yours.' She was squatting down on her hunkers, her eyes very wide and bright in her tanned face. 'It's crooked.' She began to giggle uncontrollably.

Reality closed in on me before I had even hauled the sailboard out of the water, words pouring out of her, a rush of information as she moored the inflatable and began unloading her stores. There had been several quite large political demonstrations ahead of next week's election and during the night a bomb had gone off in the little square in the centre of Villa Carlos. Two soldiers on sentry duty outside the military HQ and one of the *Guardia* had been injured, and it had affected the telephone exchange, all lines between Villa Carlos and St Félip being cut. 'Two-thirty in the morning. It woke me up. I thought one of the big guns on La Mola had gone off. And now I've just heard there was another bomb went off in that big new hotel at Santa Galdana and fires started at several of the most congested *urbanizaciós* – St Tomas in particular and St Jaimé. None of your properties are involved. At least, Lennie doesn't think so.' She asked me what I had been up to. 'You've been in Malta, I gather. Were you mixed up in that disturbance? I was picking up newsflashes about it as I waited at Gatwick for my plane.'

I told her a bit of what had happened as I helped her hump her shopping up to the camp, which was in the lee of one of the hospital's standing walls, close by the old burial ground and the dig. There was just the one big tent. Now that the hypostile was fully excavated she was using that as an office-cum-storeroom, the big stone roofing slabs covered with vegetation providing protection from sun as well as wind and rain.

Her father was dead and she had only been back a few days, having stayed on after the funeral to help her mother move up to her sister's in Nottingham. 'I've traded in my car, by the way. The little CV2 had just about had it and that old rogue Flórez offered me a Beetle – very cheap!' I asked her if she had had time to see Soo since she had arrived back in Mahon and she said she had been talking to her only a few hours before.

'How is she?' I asked.

'Oh, she's fine, and very full of what her Lieutenant Commander has been up to, and now that he's right here . . .' She was grinning at me and I told her not to be bitchy, but she only laughed. 'You can't blame her when every time she looks out of the window now she can see his ship anchored there.' And then she switched to her work. 'You remember the drawing on the cave roof I took you to see?'

'The night of the Red Cross barbecue?' I stared at her angrily. 'I'm hardly likely to forget it.'

She ignored that, telling me how she had checked on it

while she was in England. 'They don't think it can be anything important, probably done with a burnt stick in roughly the same period as the megalithic remains. Certainly no older, which is a pity because Lennie knows of some more drawings – drawings that are fully exposed, human figures as well as animals – in a passageway leading back into the headland above that big underwater cave Bill Tanner told me about at Arenal d'en Castell.'

By then she had disposed of the stores she had brought out and, still talking, she began to help me off with my wet suit. I asked her for more details about the night's bombings, whether she had picked up any gossip about the reaction of the authorities, but she had no official information, only what she had heard from Lennie when she had met him coming out of the chandlery. 'He said it's been panic stations since the early hours with the *policia* and the *Guardia* rushing around all the major foreign developments.' The violence had been directed exclusively against foreign-owned property. 'Except for the Villa Carlos bomb. It was in a parked car and they think it may have gone off by accident. There's talk, too, of disturbances in Alayór and Ciudadela, but nothing serious – just demonstrations, no bombs.'

'Well, that's something,' I murmured and asked her for the loan of a towel as she pulled the wet suit clear of my feet. But instead of handing it to me she insisted on towelling me down with the inevitable result that we finished up in each other's arms arguing hilariously as to how we should proceed, her camp bed being designed strictly for one person and the floor being bare earth and rock. We had just settled for a sleeping bag opened out and spread on the floor when we were interrupted by the sound of an outboard coming steadily nearer. 'Oh hell! I forgot.' Petra pulled herself away from me and glanced at her watch, which by then was the only thing she had on. 'Lennie! I told him to be here by ten.'

'Why?' I was annoyed and frustrated, suddenly suspicious. 'Lennie should be painting a villa over by Cala en Porter.'

'Well, he's not painting it today,' she said, struggling into her trousers. 'Or any other day.' God! She was a big, powerful girl. I watched her button up her shirt, no bra and her breasts big and round as melons, and suddenly a picture flashed into my mind of her wrestling with Lennie on that narrow bed of hers, the morning sun heating the canvas of the tent above them. And then she said, 'Lennie's old-fashioned, you know. Shot his mouth off to Soo about her playing around with a Navy officer when her husband was in trouble. Said it wasn't fair on you and she shouldn't have had Gareth up to the house when you were busy with that catamaran and under suspicion of being implicated in a political murder. Tore her off quite a strip. She didn't like it, so she fired him.' The engine note died. 'I told him he could come and work for me. This whole complex is opening out. Just before Daddy had that crash I found what I thought was the base of a fallen taula.'

She slipped her big feet into a pair of flip-flops, tied her scarf round her neck, and standing there, looking down at me, she said with that endearing giggle of hers, 'It's a foine upstanding figure of a man you are, Mike, lying there on the floor of my tent without a stitch on. But I think you'd better get dressed.' And then she was gone, and as I reached for my bundle of clothes, I heard her calling a welcome to Lennie, her voice powerful as a bullroarer.

Lennie was one of those men who seem to wear the same clothes year in, year out, who will doss down anywhere and have no interest in the ownership of anything. He had no car, not even a motor bike, and would go to endless pains to cadge a lift or avoid paying for a drink. He was one of the meanest men I had ever met, except where scuba diving was concerned. For that he treated himself to the very latest equipment, his diving boat a replica of one of those big inshore lifeboats that have an alloy hull with inflatable surround, the power of the outboard such that the sound of it was unmistakable and the boat packed with all the latest gadgets for locating objects on the seabed.

While he was fussing over the mooring of it, the battered remains of an Aussie-type hat jammed on his head and the tails of his khaki shirt flapping in the breeze, I walked over to the dig, which was on the north side of the island about fifty metres from the flashing beacon and facing across the narrows to the shore just west of Cala Llonga. The exposure of a flat stone surface about eight feet long was the only change since I had last seen the site over six weeks ago, except that it was now a riot of wild flowers, even the rock steps leading down into the hypostile half-hidden by a tangle of some blue rock creeper. The hypostile itself was an extraordinary place, a large chamber with walls of up-ended stone slabs and a stone slab roof supported by stone columns. There were rock couches, or perhaps sacrificial altars, around the walls, and the human bones that showed here and there between the roofing slabs were a grisly reminder of the wars that had filled the island's hospital. It was the result of reading a letter from a soldier to his girlfriend in England after he had had his arm amputated at the hospital that had started Petra digging on the burial site, and looking down into the stone chamber she had uncovered in the shadow of the hospital ruins, it was difficult to disassociate the two and see it as a megalithic religious complex.

I remember that moment very well, the hospital ruins dark against the sun, the entrance to the hypostile yawning open at my feet like some ancient burial vault, and my mind on what Petra had told me. The political implications of what had happened in the night were disturbing enough, particularly if the army were unable to stop a recurrence of the violence, but I was thinking of the haste with which we had left Malta. Remembering Gareth's tenseness, I wondered what information he had received that had despatched him so abruptly to Mahon. And now, in the sunlit morning, everything appeared so deceptively peaceful, the town white above the waterfront, the surface of the great harbour inlet barely ruffled by the breeze and the only sound the murmur of traffic moving between Villa Carlos and Mahon.

The rattle of tools made me turn. It was Lennie wheeling a barrow with an assortment of picks, spades and shovels. 'Looks like the prospect of two of us on the island with nothing better to do has gone to the lady's head.' He parked the barrow and shook my hand. 'Glad to see the Navy delivered you safe and sound. And the beard kinda suits you.' He looked me over, a gap-toothed grin lighting his craggy features. 'Stable door's wide open, mate. Better zip up before I jump to any conclusions.' He took a pick from the barrow and approached the exposed slab of pale stone, standing there waiting for me to fix my trousers. 'Petra says to work round it with care, like it was a piece of Ming porcelain. She's making some coffee for us.' He hesitated, looking across to where *Medusa*'s superstructure showed above the back of the island. 'Chris'sakes, that's an old frigate. I was in the Navy once, so whether they're Aussie or Pom, I don't much go for Navy ships, but by God I'm glad to see that one here. You heard what went on last night?'

I nodded. 'Petra told me.'

'Okay. Well, while we're trying to clear a little more of the rubble round this stone she thinks is a taula, I'll tell you what happened to me last night. It concerns you in a way since it was your boat until a few weeks back.' He cocked his head at me sideways. 'I haven't told her this, so keep it to yourself. She thinks we're going to have a look at rock drawings.' He began picking gently away at the weed growth along one side of the exposed stone as he told me how Miguel had taken him over to Arenal d'en Castell one evening to show him some plastering work he wanted done in one of the hotels. They had then driven back by way of the villa he had been building on Punta

Codolar. 'Up there, you know, you look across to that cave and the villa above it where I did a bit of work on the side.'

He grinned at me, leaning on his pick, waiting I think for me to complain that he had been working for two people at the same time. 'It was a funny sort of night, no wind and black as hell with the clouds hanging right on top of us. I wouldn't have seen it except that Miguel had to turn the car and on the slope there the beam of the headlights swept across it. Your boat.' He nodded. 'The old *Santa Maria*. No doubt about it. I had Miguel turn back and hold the headlights right on her for a moment.'

Apparently she had been lying close in, right opposite the mouth of the cave. He couldn't see whether she was anchored or not. What he did see was that there were men on deck lowering a case into the water. He paused there and I asked him what he thought they were up to. 'Well, I tell you this, mate, they weren't fishing.'

'So what did you do?'

'Had Miguel turn the car and drive off, double quick. You see something like that, you don't hang around.'

'No.' I was thinking of Gareth Lloyd Jones and the King's Fleet. 'So what are you planning to do tonight?'

'Go and look at rock drawings.' He gave that funny grin of his and turned back to picking at the weed growth round the stone slab. 'You want to come?' And he added, 'But don't let on to Petra what I've told you. She'd be thinking of what happened that night at Cales Coves.'

The paths leading one deeper and deeper into trouble can be very tenuous. If Lennie hadn't shot his mouth off to Soo on my behalf, if Petra hadn't heard he was out of a job and asked him to help out on Bloody Island, if his arrival there hadn't coincided . . . But there are so many ifs in life, and the threads that weave the pattern of our existence seem so haphazard that we are inclined to attribute to accident what older races of men put down to fate. At that moment, on Bloody Island, I thought I couldn't be more deeply involved than I was. And yet, standing there in the sunshine, with all of Mahon and Villa Carlos spread out before me, the Golden Farm of Nelson fame red-roofed across the water on the long peninsula that ran out to the military casements and the big gun positions of La Mola, and the stone of the hospital ruins dark in shadow, I was on the threshold of something that would make my present circumstances seem totally irrelevant.

But I wasn't thinking about that. I was watching the Spanish patrol boat steaming back to the naval quay and passing through the narrows so close I could have thrown a stone on to its deck if I'd been standing by the beacon. And there was movement on *Medusa* now, a launch manned by bluejackets coming out from under her stern and pointing its bows to pass the other side of Bloody Island. There was an officer standing in the stern and somehow I knew it was Gareth, knew where he was going. I climbed to a vantage point at the south end of the hospital ruins and watched as the launch powered past me, cutting an arrowhead wake that pointed straight at Cala Figuera. A few minutes and it was alongside the quay we had built, Gareth clambering out and going straight across the road and in through the open door of the chandlery.

He was only there a short time. No reason for me to feel hurt, but I did, and when I returned to the dig, neither Lennie nor Petra made any reference to my absence. They were drinking coffee, and when we had finished, the three of us got to work.

All through the day we were hard at it, picking and shovelling with care and carting the rubble away. At one point we were involved in the awkward removal of a complete skeleton, and then, after only a short break for lunch, we hit what I thought at first was the island's bedrock. Petra was back by then, and as we uncovered more of it, she became very excited, her conviction growing that what she was unearthing really was a fallen taula. She had reason to be excited, for if it was a taula it would confirm the site as a megalithic religious complex. The centrepiece of such sites was always a huge stone monument of two rectangular slabs, one slotted into the top of the other in the form of a T, the upper slab like a lofty table raised sometimes as much as twelve to fourteen feet above the ground. Occasionally two slabs supported the top.

Petra's excitement was infectious and my mind gradually became concentrated on the dig. Before her father's death she had been working largely on her own. Now in one day the three of us had exposed all one side of a fallen upright, also part of the jointing of the capping slab, which unfortunately was broken into three pieces. I knew of at least eight taulas in Menorca, some of them either raised up or still standing, but this was the first I had ever seen on one of the subsidiary islands.

We went on until just after sunset, when we went back to the tent, lit the pressure lamp and had a celebratory drink. There was no doubt then about what it was we had uncovered. 'A taula here on Bloody Island –' Her eyes were bright in the sizzling light. 'If only the professor I saw at the V and A about that cave drawing had been a little more enthusiastic, then with what I have discovered here I could have developed my theory on the growth of the Mediterranean culture to the point where I could have written a paper on it.'

CHAPTER TWO

We had a quick meal and left shortly after dark. Petra wasn't all that keen. I think she had accepted that any cave drawing she discovered on Menorca would be what she would call recent. It was Lennie who insisted on our taking a look at the water-worn passageway he had discovered by accident below the villa where he had been moonlighting. He was very determined I should see it. It was all open country, he said, and even if we were stopped the chances of my being recognised were slight. Anyway, I wanted to know what Evans had been doing with the *Santa Maria* moored above that cave entrance.

Petra had a bag full of archaeological papers to justify her journey in the unlikely event that we ran into a roadblock, also she had fastened the beard more securely to my chin with some adhesive tape. Having forced myself to wear it all day, I had become quite used to it and she assured me it was a great improvement in my appearance. 'Very macho,' she whispered to me with a grin as she finally stuck it in place.

It was a clear night, no wind, and the stars very bright. We only passed two cars between the turn-off to the little fishing port of Es Grau and the crossroads where we turned right for Macaret and Punta Codolar. The warm air coming in through Petra's open window was full of the resin scent of pines and the more pungent smell of the maquis growth that blanketed much of the gravel country we were passing through.

The villa to which Lennie directed her was only a short distance from the half-completed one I had traded for *Thunderflash*, and as we swung down the western slope of the headland, I caught a glimpse of it, still with the scaffold up and what looked like a big removal van parked outside it, the box-like shape momentarily in silhouette against a naked light bulb shining from one of the downstair windows. I wondered if it was Evans and how he would react if Petra dropped me off there and I walked in on him. But then we were on the eastern arm of Arenal d'en Castell's little horseshoe cove and Lennie was telling her to drive on past what he called the cave villa. 'We'll park down by one of the hotels.'

The villa was in darkness, one of those architect-designed summer homes built into the rocky slope on several layers, its garden stepped in terraces. The owner was apparently a German bank executive, and Miguel, who looked after it for him, had told Lennie he was not expected until the middle of June. We left the car at the first hotel, parked among a covey of hired Fiats, and climbed back up the hill, Petra with her bag of archaeological stuff slung over her shoulder, Lennie and I with the torches, pressure lamp, a bottle of wine and a coil of rope taken from his boat. The driveway swung off direct to the garage, which was built into the hillside at the bottom of the garden. 'We had to blast that out of solid rock.' Lennie had done the blasting. 'That was what he wanted me for.' He had worked at one time in one of the Kalgoorlie mines. He had been a prospector, too. 'It's limestone here, nice easy stuff. That's why there's caves and blowholes.' We climbed up the terraces and let ourselves in through the garden door, the house very dark inside and smelling faintly of paint and sea damp. 'Better not show a light.' Lennie closed the door and pocketed the key. 'Had it copied,' he said with a wink. 'You never know.' And he added, 'You two wait here while I locate the cellar door.'

The cellar itself was reached by a curving flight of half a dozen concrete steps. It had been blasted out of the solid rock, an area of about thirty square metres lined with wine racks. He swung his torch over the array of bottles that hid the naked rock of the walls. 'Got some good stuff here, certainly has. Haven't been in the cellar since he got it fully stocked.' He went over to the far corner where there was an olive-wood table and two seats made out of oak-staved barrels standing on a sheet of corrugated iron. When we had shifted the furniture and pulled the tin sheet aside, there was a jagged-edged hole dropping away into what looked like nothingness with the slop and gurgle of water faintly audible.

'Well, there it is,' he said to Petra. 'Down you go. Turn right at the bottom and you'll find the drawings on the roof about twenty yards away. If you get to the rock fall where I blasted out the blowhole to make the garage you've gone past it, okay?' He was fastening one end of the rope to the base of one of the bottle racks, then he put a couple of foot loops into it before passing the end of it down the hole. ''Bout ten feet, that's all, then you're into the blowhole.' He passed Petra one of the torches and held her while she got her foot into the first loop. She looked very strange, her body disappearing into the floor, shadows flickering on the walls and the bottles watching with a dusty glint.

We lit the pressure lamp and passed it down to her. Then we lowered ourselves into the cave-like passageway beside her. It was wider than I had expected, the walls very irregular, and quite different to the cellar, for the rock here had not been blasted, but was carved out by centuries of pressurised sea water as the waves of the tramontana crashed against the coast.

'We'll leave you for a moment,' Lennie told her.

'Why? Where are you going?'

Lennie nodded in the opposite direction. 'We'll head down the slope. I want Mike to see how the blowhole drops into the cave. Won't be long.' We left her then, moving quickly down the irregular passageway. At times we were almost crawling, then suddenly the passage would open out into an expansion chamber so that we could walk virtually upright. Here and there Lennie paused, the beam of his torch directed at the scuffed dust of the floor, and all the time the sound of the sea increasing as it slopped and gurgled in the cavern ahead. Round the first bend he paused. 'I wasn't telling Petra this. She's hooked on cave drawings and such. But this is what I came to check on.' His hand was on my arm, a tight grip as he pulled me down to take a closer look at the floor. 'A lot of stuff has been dragged along here. Heavy stuff in cases, I'd say. And here and there the imprint of a shoe. Look!' And he let go my arm, tracing a blurred imprint in the dust.

'Smuggling?' I was thinking of Gareth, all the questions he had asked over that lunch at Fornells – and that story of his about Evans in the King's Fleet. 'You say you saw the *Santa Maria* lying off here?'

'Sure did.' Lennie straightened up. 'Come on. And be careful now. It gets steeper. Then I'll show you how it's done.'

We continued on, another expansion chamber opening up, the sound of the sea suddenly very loud. At the far end the blowhole tunnel fell right away, an almost vertical drop, the nearside of which had been heavily scored as though by a large shovel or scraper. Rigged across the hole was a lattice of small scaffolding poles bolted together to hold a heavy metal pulley. We slithered down till we could clutch the scaffolding, then, leaning out over the abyss and probing downwards with our torches, we could see the surge of the waves in the cave mouth, the water in the cavern itself rising and falling against a steep little beach of dark sand and round, water-rolled stones that gleamed wetly.

There was also something else, a heavy old anchor, brown with rust and half-buried in the beach. A heavy-duty purchase of the type used in large yachts before the switch to winches was shackled to the eye of the stock, and nylon sheets or warps ran through the pulleys and out into the sea. 'That's what I came here for.' Lennie's voice was a whisper as though at any moment he expected one of the smugglers to rise like a genie out of the blowhole. 'To see how they did it.'

'So what do you think they were bringing ashore?' I asked him.

'Dunno, mate. I thought it would be just ordinary household things, TV sets, electric cookers, glassware, jewellery, anything that was taxable. But after last night . . .'

'What are you suggesting – arms?'

'Well, it certainly ain't drugs. The Menorquins haven't gone for that so far and the villa people . . .' He stopped abruptly as Petra slithered down to join us, the pressure lamp casting her shadow behind her, lighting up the latticework of steel tubing on which we leaned.

She was panting, her eyes wide and a little wild. 'Some silly bugger's been playing around with candles. They're not cave drawings at all.' She gulped for air. 'But it's not that. I thought I heard voices, the sound of an engine.'

'Where?' Lennie asked.

'Beyond the garage.' She took a deep breath, pulling herself together. 'There's no cave-in there, no rock fall. It's all been cleared away.'

'You mean you went inside the garage?'

'No.' She shook her head, the dust stirring in her shoulder-length hair. 'No, it was boarded up. A jagged hole stopped up with what looked like fresh matchboarding.'

Lennie didn't wait to hear any more. He pushed past her and started back up the slope, clawing his way up on all fours. I followed, dragging Petra after me. We were all together in a bunch as we ducked past the rope we had rigged from the cellar and came to the boarded-up hole into the garage. 'Look at it!' Petra held the pressure lamp up and her voice was an angry whisper as she rubbed at the blurred black outline of some four-legged animals on the roof. 'Candle-black.' She showed me the palm of her hand. It looked as though she had been handling a badly

235

printed newspaper, and the head of the beast was smudged. 'The sort of thing a schoolboy would do, and I was fool enough to hope . . .'

Lennie's hand clamped suddenly over her mouth. 'Listen!' He opened the valve of the pressure lamp, his torch switched off, the hiss of the gas mantle dying away and in the darkness the scrape of a door sounding muffled and a voice, very faint from beyond the boarding, instructing somebody to back right up to the door. An engine revved, more directions, then a babble of whispering voices barely audible as the engine noise died away and was suddenly cut. A tailboard slammed and somebody said, 'Quiet! Keep everything quiet.' There was no more talking after that, only the sound of heavy boxes or crates being loaded.

'The cellar,' Lennie breathed. 'Follow me and keep hold.'

We felt our way back down the blowhole till we came to the rope again. Lennie went first, then Petra. My foot was in the first loop, ready to follow her, when the crash of breaking wood sounded hollow along the passageway. I froze, thinking for a moment they had heard us and were breaking through from the garage. Somebody swore, a muffled voice – 'That was my fucking foot, you bastard.' An answering voice, then the two of them arguing until somebody shouted at them to cool it. By then I was on to the second loop and reaching up to clutch hold of Lennie's hand. As soon as I was out of the hole he unhitched the end of the rope, coiling it and slinging it over his shoulder, then he swung the torch to show us the steps leading up to the cellar door. 'Just follow me.' Black darkness as he switched off the torch again and we felt our way up to the room above.

Back at the garden door we waited, listening. No sound now, only the door squeaking as he pulled it gently open. The garden was in three terraces, dropping away steeply to the garage driveway. Two cars were parked there, and where the garage itself disappeared into the hillside, the protruding section was merged with the body of a truck that looked like the one we had seen parked outside the Punta Codolar villa. A figure appeared out of the garage, heading for the nearest car, then turning towards us and slowing. Finally, beside the thin pencil point of a cypress, he stood quite still, feet apart, head thrown back, staring straight at us.

Could he see us in the starlight? Could he see that the door we were peering out of was half-open? We stood there, the three of us, absolutely still, waiting. The man bent his head, both hands to his front, as though holding a weapon. Then he turned and went back to the garage. 'Pissing.' Lennie breathed a sigh of relief, and Petra giggled under her breath as he added, 'It was his cock, not a gun. He was just relieving himself.' He closed the door and led us up through the villa's three levels, up into a large room that faced both ways.

From a circular porthole window we looked out on to the hilltop where barely twenty metres of shrubland separated us from the road. Here a low stone wall marked the limit of the property and a brick arch framed an elaborate wrought-iron gate. A gravel path flanked by stone urns planted with cacti led to the heavy cedarwood door beside us. Lennie eased the catch and pushed it gently open, leaning his head out through the gap. The stars were very bright. 'Looks clear enough.' His scrawny neck, the lined, leathery features, the way he cocked his eyes over the landscape – I had the sudden impression of a turkey checking that nobody was going to grab him for their Christmas dinner. My mind also registered a picture of Gareth being grabbed as he ran from the King's Fleet towards Felixstowe Ferry.

'Shut the door,' I hissed.

He turned, eyeing me curiously. 'Wot's up? Nobody there.'

'If it's Evans loading that truck, he'll have somebody hidden up this side of the villa, just in case.'

'Okay. So we wait.'

He was just shutting the window when we saw lights approaching, and heard the sound of an engine. It was a car, moving fast, and as it passed the villa's gate Lennie sucked in his breath. 'Jesus Christ!' he muttered and half leant out of the window as though to call to the driver. 'Why the hell does he come out here now?'

'Who?' I had only caught a glimpse of the car, a battered estate. I hadn't seen who was driving it.

'Miguel,' he said, still peering out of the window as the car slowed on the dip and turned into the villa's driveway. 'The poor stupid bloody bastard – to come here now, just when they're loading up.' The car's lights flickered through the shrubbery, then they were gone, snuffed out by the corner of the building. The engine note died abruptly.

We listened, but there was no sound – no shouts, no outcry or altercation. Just nothing.

We felt our way across to the other side of the room, standing at the window there, looking down across the flat-topped roofs of the villa's lower levels to the truck, the whole shadowy shape of it now visible as a sort of elongated extension of the garage. And beyond it, on the sweep of the drive, as well as the two cars they had come in, there was the estate car standing black and seemingly empty.

A hand gripped mine, Petra's voice in my ear whispering, 'What is it?' Her fingers tightened convulsively, but it wasn't fear. It was excitement. Her breath was warm on my cheek, her hair touched my ear. 'Is it to do with what happened last night?'

I couldn't answer that. I didn't know. In any case, I was wondering about Miguel. Was he one of them? Was that why he was here? Or had he walked right into it, unarmed and unprepared?

'It's arms, isn't it? It's an arms cache.' And when I still didn't say anything, she whispered urgently, 'If it's arms, then we have to notify somebody, warn the authorities.'

'Not yet – when they've gone . . .' And I added, 'Maybe we can follow them.'

She had moved her head slightly so that it was outlined against the window. I saw the shape of it nod against the stars, her hand still in mine, still the grip of excitement, so that I was reminded that between school and college she had done a VSO stint in the Andes, trekking alone on the borders of Chile, Peru and Bolivia looking for old Inca remains. I don't think she knew what fear was, otherwise she would never have been able to go it alone at such high altitude with only the Quechua Indians for company. 'What's the time?'

Lennie glanced at the luminous dial of his diving watch. 'Twenty after midnight.'

'Do you think it's arms?' she asked him.

'Yes, I do.'

'Then if they're going to use them tonight they'll have to get a move on.'

At that moment, as though the hoarse whisper of her voice had carried to the garage below, the dark shadow of a man came hurrying up through the garden, leaping the steps between the terraces and angling away to the right. Abreast of the upper part of the villa he put his hand to his mouth and gave a piercing whistle on two notes like the call of a bird. A figure rose out of a dark mass of shrubbery beside the road some two hundred yards away, glanced quickly round, then hurried to join the man below. The two of them went back down the terraces to the garage where half a dozen men were now heading for the parked cars. The slam of a door came to us faintly, then the truck's engine started up. The men got into the cars, all three of them, including Miguel's estate, and the little convoy moved off, slowly and without lights, then swung left at the driveway end and from the front of the villa we watched them pass along the road, dark shapes in silhouette against the stars heading for Punta Codolar.

'What do we do now – get the car and follow them?'

'Depends how good you are at driving without lights,' I told her.

She laughed. 'Won't be the first time.'

Lennie had the door open and we were out into the night, slamming it behind us and running to the road. It was all downhill to where Petra had parked the Beetle and took us barely two minutes. 'Where now?' she asked breathlessly as she started the engine. I hesitated. There was only one road out until the crossroads junction with the main Mahon–Fornells road, unless they were heading for the ports of either Macaret or Addaia. 'Back up the hill,' I said. 'It's just possible they'll stop at the Punta Codolar villa.' If Evans was involved and they were operating to an exact timetable, then I thought they might be using it as a rendezvous.

She drove fast, a lot faster than I would have cared to drive in that dim light, up past the villa where they had been loading the truck, over the shoulder of the cove's sheltering arm and out on to the bleak empty heathland beyond. There was more light here, cliffs all round us dropping to the sea which reflected the starlight, and against that milky glimmer the Punta Codolar villa stood out solitary and square like a concrete pillbox, and beside it, also outlined against the stars, was the black rectangular shape of the truck.

Petra slammed on the brakes and we rolled to a stop. 'Where now?'

We had just passed a service road under construction and some two hundred yards away to the right there was a road roller hull-down in the heathland. I told her to back up and park beside it. Close against the road roller, our front wheels hard into the rubble of an open trench where an electricity cable was being laid, the Beetle was almost indistinguishable from the heavy mass of the roller's iron.

For almost the first time since I'd known her Petra's obsession with the island's megalithic past was overlaid by more immediate concerns as we speculated about what they planned to do and when, the villa hull-down and indistinct on the heathland's horizon. I asked her whether she had any glasses in the car. She reached over to the back seat, grabbed the bag that contained her archaeological gear, and after rummaging around in it, produced a pair of those very small, high-magnification binoculars. I rolled the window down and with some difficulty managed to focus them on the villa. The field of vision was very small. 'I was only once involved in a political upheaval.' Petra's voice was low and intense as though she were afraid of being overheard. 'I was in the Cordillera Real just north of La Paz and a ragged bunch of them passed through my camp. Defeated revolutionaries are very unpredictable. South American revolutionaries, anyway, and I had found an Inca tamba that nobody had discovered before. All very exciting, worked stone blocks jigsawed together so that they wouldn't be toppled by earthquakes, and these exhausted men in fear of their lives flopping down in the undergrowth I'd cleared. There was a thick cloud mist, everything very damp and cold. They lit a fire, huddling round it.'

It was strange to be watching the villa through glasses. Last time I had seen it I had been breaking in by the garage window and there had been nobody there. Now it was just as dark, but the cars and the truck were clear proof that there were men inside it. They must be sitting there, waiting.

'What is it? Can you see something?'

I shook my head. All the glasses showed me was the Moorish front with its arched colonnade, the low wall that separated it from the road and the blockhouse shape of it against the night sky with the cars tucked in against the garage and the truck left out in the road.

'Go on, Petra.' Lennie leaned forward, his head between us. 'What happened? Did they mess you about?'

'If you mean what I think you mean, the answer is no,

they were too bloody tired. But they did something worse. They ate up everything I had, all my stores, then went off with my tent, even my sleeping bag. I think they'd have had the clothes off my back if I'd been a man, they were that ragged and desperate. Only their guns looked in good condition.'

I thought I saw the glow of a cigarette. It was there for a second, then Lennie knocked against me and I lost it. It had come from the last arch of the villa's colonnaded front, and focusing on it, I thought I could just make out the darker outline of a figure standing there. I heard Petra say something about trekking more than twenty miles through snow and ice and a blazing midday sun before she managed to hitch a ride with some geologists into La Paz.

'And what happened to the men who pillaged your camp?' Lennie asked.

'Oh, the Army caught up with them in the end. About a dozen of them were gunned down from a helicopter, the rest were tracked down, tortured and hanged. The usual thing. There's no mercy in the Andes.'

'I never experienced anything like that,' Lennie said quietly. 'And I've been around. But nothing like that.' And he added, leaning his head further forward between us, 'You think there's going to be a revolution here?'

She didn't tell him not to be ridiculous. She didn't comment. She just sat there, not saying a word, and at that moment a bright star shot up from the sea to our right, blazing a vertical trail that burst into a blob of white so bright that even at that distance it lit up our faces. 'Bloody hell!' Lennie pushed his nose almost against the windscreen. 'What is it?'

'Pyrotechnic.' The pop of its burst came to us faintly as I jumped out of the car, steadying my elbow on the top of it and searching with the glasses for the ship that had fired it. A second stream of sparks flew up, a second burst, but this time green. I still couldn't pick out the shape of the vessel, so it was presumably close in below the line of the cliffs.

'That a distress signal?' Petra asked, but I think she knew it wasn't, because her head was turned towards the villa. Through the glasses I saw shadows moving, followed almost immediately by the sound of a car engine starting up. Doors slammed, the cars emerging on to the road. Then the truck's diesel roared into life and it began to move, one car in front, the other behind. The time was 01.32. Miguel's estate stayed parked against the wall.

'What now?' Petra had already started the engine.

'Go back,' I told her. 'Back down towards Arenal, then take the main development road and we'll wait for them just short of where it joins the Alayór highway.' Either they were meeting up with a ship at Macaret or else somewhere further up the long inlet that finished at the new quay just beyond Addaia.

'I don't get it, mate,' Lennie muttered in my ear as Petra felt her way along the dark strip of the road without lights. 'What do they want with a ship when their truck's already loaded? They can't be picking up more.' But I was thinking about Wade then, that first visit of Gareth's to Menorca, the questions he had asked me over that lunch. And on board *Medusa*, the suddenness with which we had left Malta, the way he had looked that evening when I went back down to his cabin from the bridge, his sudden decision to tell me about Evans.

We reached the crossroads and Petra pulled in to the verge. We sat there for perhaps five minutes, but there was no sound and nothing passed. I told her to drive straight across and head for the high point above the entrance to the Addaia inlet. From there we would have a clear view of Macaret itself and the seaward entrance to the harbour. We would also be able to look southwards down the length of the inlet to the two small islands that protected the final anchorage.

When we got there we were just in time to catch a

glimpse of a small vessel heading down the pale ribbon of the inlet. 'Fishing boat by the look of it,' Lennie muttered.

Out of the car again, I was able to fix the glasses on it. No doubt about it. The boat was the *Santa Maria*. I jumped back into the passenger seat and told Petra to turn the car, go back to the main road, then take the cut-off down the steep little hill to Port d'Addaia itself. 'But go carefully,' I warned her as she swung the Beetle round. 'They may have dropped somebody off to keep watch. And stop near the top so that we can check if they're there or not.'

When we reached Addaia she tucked herself into a little parking bay where we had a clear view of the quay across pantile roofs and the steep overgrown slope of the hillside, and it wasn't just the truck from Codolar that was waiting there. I counted no less than five trucks, all parked in line along the concrete edge of the quay and facing towards us. There were more than a dozen cars, too, and a lot of men, most of them gathered round the back of the last truck, where crates were being dumped on the quay, prised open and the weapons they contained handed out.

'Christ! See that, mate. They got rocket-launchers. The hand-held type. What do the bastards want with them?' Lennie had followed me out of the car and across the road. From there we had a clear view of the anchorage where I had joined Carp for the voyage to Malta. And there, as though I were seeing it all again, like on video but from a different angle, was the *Santa Maria* motoring in through the narrows that separated the humpbacked outline of the second island from the muddy foreshore and the huddle of fishermen's dwellings. The boat was headed straight for the quay, and as she slowed and swung her stern to lie alongside, I saw she had a stern light showing.

That was when we heard the rumble of engines coming from seaward, and a moment later we saw the dim shape of a flat box of a vessel. There were two of them, old LCTs dating from the days before they called them logistic landing craft. I recognised them immediately, one of them having dropped me off at Loch Boisdale on its way to St Kilda some years back. The *Santa Maria* had clearly been leading them in. Now she was alongside and a man had jumped ashore. I watched him through the glasses as the men on the quay gathered round him. Even in that dim light I was certain it was Evans. He was head and shoulders taller than most of them, standing there, hands on hips, issuing orders. He wore a kepi-like forage cap and camouflage jacket and trousers, and the way he stood, the arrogance and the air of command, I was suddenly reminded of early pictures of Castro.

A splash, and the first of the logistic vessels had dropped its stern anchor, the big drum winch on the afterdeck reeling out the hawser as the ship nosed into the quay. The bow doors opened, then with a clank and a crash, the ramp dropped on to the quay. By then the second vessel was coming in alongside it and a moment later the vehicles inside the two slab-sided hulls, their engines already running, began to trundle out. They were half-tracks, each of them mounting what looked like a heavy Bofors gun, and as they came off the ramps they were joined by small detachments of the men on shore.

Behind the half-tracks came men, dozens of them, dressed in some drab uniform and loaded down with equipment, each of them pausing for a moment as they stepped on to the terra firma of the quay's concrete edge. It was as though they needed to find their feet. Some, as they stood there, arched their backs and stretched. A babble of human voices reached up to us. It was the natural reaction of men who had been cooped up in a confined space for some considerable time and for a moment the scene below us was one of disorder, almost chaos. Then somebody shouted. I think it was Evans, and the men standing around the parked trucks began splitting up and moving to join the new arrivals, the mêlée gradually sorting itself out as they formed up into units and marched off to embark in the waiting trucks or climb on to the backs of the half-tracks.

It was less than ten minutes from the time the LCTs had put their ramps down to the moment when the local vehicles were all loaded and the whole convoy beginning to move off, and by then I was convinced that what we were witnessing was the start of an armed usurpation of the political power in the island. Who the men were that had landed from the two LCTs, where they had come from – that was of no importance for the moment. What was important was to alert somebody in Mahon to the danger. I saw it all in a mental flash, dissident elements, gathered from the various towns, meeting here to be given arms and then to be distributed amongst the newly arrived mercenaries, or whatever they were, to guide them to objectives that had already been decided on.

It seemed ridiculous on the face of it. There couldn't be more than a hundred and fifty to two hundred men down there on the quay and the military garrison of the island I knew to be somewhere around 15,000. But if what Petra had told me was correct, the effect of the previous night's violence had been a redeployment of the available forces, so that the towns, and particularly the *urbanizacións* inhabited by foreign visitors, were fully protected. As a result, the men below me had not only the advantage of surprise – essential in an operation of this sort – but also the certainty that the island's defences were thinly spread and the targets they would be aiming at that much more vulnerable. In such circumstances anything was possible.

All this passed through my mind in a flash as the vehicles moved out on to the steep road up from the port and Lennie and I flung ourselves back across the road and into the car. 'Mahon,' I told Petra. 'Lights on and drive like hell.'

She didn't hesitate. She had seen the ships, the mustering men. She swung out on to the Alayór road, her foot hard down and the elderly Beetle shaking and swaying at the rear. 'Who are they?' She was taking a bend fast, pines rushing at us. 'What are you going to do?' And when I said

I had to get to the frigate, she started to argue, asking why I didn't stop off somewhere and phone the nearest *Guardia Civil* post or Military Headquarters in Mahon.

'For God's sake! Who would believe me?' I started to remind her then that I was suspected of complicity in the Martinez murder. 'Anyway,' I added, 'they'll almost certainly have cut the telephone wires.'

'Alayór then. Alayór is nearer than Mahon.'

'No, Mahon,' I told her. It was Gareth I needed. He had all the means of communication there on board, the whole world at call. And then I was briefing her what to tell Soo after she had dropped us off at the Maritimo pontoon, who to telephone, very conscious that it would be the early hours of the morning, everybody asleep and in no mood to believe that danger was imminent.

'You'll have to come with me,' she argued. 'Even if I can get through to somebody in authority . . .'

'No,' I said. 'I've got to make contact with Gareth.'

But the frigate was something too remote for her to grasp, and anyway she did not want the responsibility of alerting people locally. 'You know what they are. They won't believe a woman. I'll never get it across to them.' And even when I told her she was one of the few people outside of government they would believe, that as an English archaeologist she had the standing of a scientist and therefore would be regarded as a reliable witness, she went on arguing until the crossroads came up in the headlights and I put my hand on her knee and told her to turn left for Mahon or I'd switch the engine off, drive the car myself and leave her at the side of the road.

An angry silence filled the car after she had made the turn, the road snaking through a forest of pine, with the scent of resin all-pervading, then straightening out with no sign of lights anywhere. Something flapped across the beam of our headlights, a kite probably. We reached the turn-off to Faváritx, and still nothing on the road. In fact, we did not see another vehicle until we were running into the outskirts of Mahon. Where the road curved down the hill from the main Ciudadela highway we had to wait for a small convoy of three army trucks which swung into the road in front of us, then turned off to the left, almost certainly bound for the Zona Militar barracks out on La Mola.

'Why not try the Naval Base?' Petra said. 'Fernando likes you. He would believe what you told him.'

I had already thought of that. It was very tempting, the Naval Base so close we were almost at the entrance to it. But how long would it take me to get through to Perez? 'No,' I said. 'Gareth is a safer bet.' I was watching the tail-lights of the convoy climbing up the hill beside the Base, the white beam of their heads shining on the heath-land scrub with its pillboxes and old stone fortifications built to stand against Napoleon. Another ten minutes, maybe quarter of an hour, and other vehicles would be rolling up that road on to the long peninsula that formed the northern arm of the finest deep-water natural port in the Western Mediterranean, and at the end of that peninsula was La Mola with its barracks and casements and those huge guns. I had absolutely no doubt that this would be one of the main objectives, La Mola being little more than an island, the neck joining it to the main arm of the land so narrow it could readily be sealed with mines, the whole garrison then cut off. 'Keep going,' I told her. 'I haven't time to argue with the Navy guard at the entrance. And Perez might be in Ciudadela, anywhere.'

We passed the turning to the Base and over my left shoulder there were lights on a freighter lying alongside the new quay, and beyond it, lights flashing green on the naval jetty. Then we were under the mass of Mahon itself, hammering along the waterfront past the commercial quay. There was a ferry lying there and out beyond Bloody Island I could see the dim shape of *Medusa* lying broadside to the town. A minute later we had rounded Punta Maritimo and Petra was bringing the car to a halt at the pontoon. I remember telling her to say something nice to Soo for me as I flung open the door and leapt out, the black, limpid water of the harbour washing lazily at the concrete of the roadway, the wooden boards of the pontoon moving under my feet. 'You reck'n they'll go for La Mola?' Lennie asked as he cord-whipped the outboard into life and we nosed out past the mooring lines of a big French sloop, the bows lifting as he increased the revs, heading to pass just north of Bloody Island where the frigate's bows were pointing towards Nelson's Golden Farm.

I nodded, the noise too great for conversation.

'They could just concentrate on the town, you know,' he yelled in my ear. 'Seize the town hall, take a crack at Military HQ and occupy the radio station. Wouldn't that be enough?'

I shrugged, unable to answer him, thinking ahead to my meeting with Gareth. I could imagine him asking me just those questions and what the hell would I say? We passed the quick-flashing red beacon close to the dig, Lennie cutting it so fine I could see the wheelbarrows still full of the rubble we had been shifting, and then the businesslike outline of *Medusa* was looming nearer. 'Which side?' he shouted in my ear.

'Starb'd,' I said, and he swung in a tight arc, passing so close under the bows I thought he would smash into the anchor cable. The engine slowed, then died with a cough as he brought the inflatable alongside where the accommodation ladder had been lifted clear of the water. By then I had Petra's big torch beamed on the bridge, flicking the switch on and off – three dots, three dashes, three dots – hoping that whoever was on watch would realise the SOS was to signify urgency, not just some drunk from the shore playing silly buggers. I could hear the hum of the ship's machinery now, sense the power of the organisation that was in her. 'Ahoy there, *Medusa!*' I was shouting for the Officer of the Day, the Captain, anyone, my voice raised high, desperate with the need to be got on board quickly.

A face under a sailor's hat leaned out above me. 'Wot you want?'

'The Captain,' I shouted up to him. 'Tell the Captain it's Mike Steele and it's urgent. Every minute counts.' A door slammed and a beam of light was directed straight at me, my eyes blinded, and a voice said, 'Good evening, sir. You come to return that beard we lent you?' It was young Davison, the officer-under-training, and he was grinning. 'The Captain!' I yelled at him again.

'The Captain's asleep, sir.'

'Well, wake him up. And get me on board. I have information for him that must be transmitted to London immediately.'

He stood there for a moment, mouth agape, gazing down at me. I could see his brain working, trying to decide whether this was a joke or something deadly serious. Fortunately the beard was in my pocket, where it had been for some time now, otherwise he might have thought I was fooling. 'Hurry, man! For God's sake hurry!'

He nodded, suddenly seeming to pull himself together as he ordered a sailor to lower the ladder, then turned and ran to the bridge. He was back by the time I had scrambled up to the deck. 'This way, sir. Captain says to take you to his cabin.'

Gareth was in his dressing gown as I was shown in, his face pale, his hair tousled. 'Thank you, Davison. That'll do.' He turned to me. 'Now, what's this all about?'

I made it as short as possible, but before I had finished he had reached for the phone, flicking a switch. 'Captain. Call all hands. Lieutenant Commander Mault to my cabin immediately.' He had pulled out a notebook and was flicking through the pages. 'Anchored out here we're not on a land line, so we have to slot in to the telephone system through ship-to-shore. However, I can contact the Naval Base on UHF.' He was reaching for the phone again when Davison's voice broke in on the loudspeaker – 'Captain, sir. This is the bridge.' He sounded a bit nervous, very excited. 'There's what sounds like shots coming from the direction of La Mola – and, sir, we're just picking up bursts of machine-gun fire from the town now.'

'Very good, I'll be up.' Gareth turned to glance at the wall clock, picking up a comb and smoothing his hair. The second hand flicked to the vertical. It was exactly 03.31. 'From what you've told me, looks like the time of attack on all objectives was zero-three-thirty.' And he added, 'I've been expecting something like this.' He slipped out of his dressing gown and began pulling on trousers and white polo-necked sweater over his pyjamas. 'But not those logistic craft.' He had me describe in detail the scene on the quay at Addaia. 'You're certain it was Pat? He was on that fishing boat of yours and led them in?'

'Yes,' I said. 'And he was organising them ashore.'

'The whole thing – I mean, the men who came ashore from those LCTs as well as the locals? You're sure?'

'I think so.' It was obvious he didn't want to believe that the man was totally involved, but when I told him it was bright starlight and I had ten-magnification glasses on him, he sighed and said, 'I suppose I should have expected that.' He was buttoning up his jacket. 'Well, no good trying to alert Capitán Perez now. His boys can hear the shooting just as well as we can here. Let's go up to the bridge.'

Outside the cabin all was bustle as the ship came to readiness, men in various stages of dress hurrying to their posts, the bridge itself beginning to fill up. As soon as we reached it, we could hear the firing out on La Mola, for they had both wing doors open. We went out on to the starb'd wing and stood there looking at the black outline of the peninsula sprawled against the stars. 'When do you reckon first light, Pilot?'

'With the sky as clear as this, sir, there should be a glimmer in the east within the hour.'

'An hour's darkness.' Gareth nodded, then turned to me. 'Nice timing, the whole thing highly organised.' And he added, 'That will be Pat. He's had a lot of experience –

Angola chiefly, Mozambique, with the Polisario, and Wade says they thought he had done a spell with the Contras, so he's had the benefit of American as well as South African training.'

Mault appeared at his elbow. 'I was ordered to report to your cabin, but you weren't there.'

'No, I'm here.' Gareth's voice was sharp. 'Have the launch brought alongside and go across to the Base. Try and see Capitán Perez personally. Offer him any assistance he needs. Oh, and tell him the entire force at the disposal of the insurgents at this moment in time is not more than two hundred. They are supported by professional troops landed from two small logistics craft at Addaia. I have an eye-witness of the landing here on board *Medusa*.'

Mault hesitated, glancing at me. 'Wouldn't it be better if I took Mr Steele with me?'

'No.' Gareth's voice was even sharper. 'Tell the *Jefe* he can interview him here on board if he wants to.' And he added, 'Now hurry, man. Things are happening, and happening fast. Perez needs to know that the whole thing can be controlled and suppressed if he acts quickly enough.' He turned to Davison. 'Is somebody looking after that inflatable and the man who was with Mr Steele?'

'Yes, sir. He's been taken to the petty officers' mess for some coffee.'

'Good.' He turned back into the body of the bridge as the Yeoman of Signals appeared at his side with a piece of paper in his hand. 'A sit-rep, sir. The Communications Office were alerting the radar unit on top of the Toro rock when the radio contact suddenly went dead, there's a small foreign outfit in Alayór, nobody knows yet what nationality but Arab by the look of them, and there's a ham of sorts broadcasting Independence Day messages from Ciudadela.'

Gareth glanced through the paper, nodded, dealt with the little queue of officers waiting to be briefed, then went over to the nearest mike, his voice stilling all conversation as it blared out over the ship's main broadcast: '*This is the Captain speaking. We have a situation ashore that was not wholly unexpected and is to some extent our reason for being here in Port Mahon . . .*' And then he was outlining briefly what the firing was all about. He also indicated that there had been outside intervention . . . '*Whether by political sympathisers, mercenaries or some foreign power is not yet clear. I will keep you informed.*' Just as he said that there was a flash, followed immediately by the rumble of a heavy explosion, the rumbling muffled as though it were underground, and suddenly the highest point of La Mola was lit by a pyrotechnic display that was so colourful and went on for so long it was more like fireworks than the destruction of a military target. 'Looks like they've got the garrison's ammunition dump.' Gareth had a pair of the bridge binoculars fixed on La Mola. Davison said something to him and he lowered the glasses, frowning. 'Funny! I should have thought he would have been glad of a coffee, even a drink . . .' He turned to me. 'That Australian of yours. Seems he was worried about something, so he's pushed off. Said he'd be at the dig when you wanted him. Yes, Yeo?'

The Yeoman of Signals was at his elbow again. 'Looks as though they've taken the radio station, sir. They're playing local music interspersed with announcements of this sort.' He handed Gareth a slip of paper.

'Ismail Fuxá –' Gareth was reading it aloud – 'I imagine you pronounce it Fusha, the X is sh, isn't it? He's described here as leader of the Independent Movement and it says he'll be broadcasting an Independence Day message to the Menorquin people at 06.00. Apparently the speech will be repeated every hour on the hour throughout the rest of the day. What do you think?' He glanced up at me. 'The speech taped in advance?' And he added, 'Must have been. Which suggests a degree of organisation . . .'

The Navigating Officer interrupted him. 'Message from the Naval Base, sir. No answer from the garrison command post on La Mola. And the *Jefe* would like a word with you on UHF.'

The ultra high frequency set used by Nato service units was on the far side of the bridge. He picked up the headset with its boom-mike and though I couldn't hear what was said I saw the lines of strain on his face ease. He was talking for barely a minute and then he said, 'Well, thank God for that. They haven't got the Naval Base.' He said it loud enough for all on the bridge to hear, knowing I suppose that it would spread from there right through the ship.

'Launch coming back now, sir.'

He nodded, watching it come out from behind Bloody Island, making an arrowed arc as it swung to pass under the bows and come alongside the ladder. To seaward the first glimmer of the dawn was etching black the outline of Lazareto Island with the bulk of La Mola reared up behind it.

Mault, when he reached the bridge, reported that he had been received very formally. He had the impression that his visit was not welcomed and that the Spanish Navy *Jefe* was wanting to distance himself from the British naval presence in the harbour.

'You saw Perez himself, did you?' Gareth asked him.

'In the end, yes.'

'Would you say his coolness was dictated by higher authority?'

'Yes. He asked me to thank you for your offer of assistance, but to tell you it would not be necessary.'

'He's in touch with Madrid then?'

Mault nodded. 'I think so. But locally I had the feeling he was cut off. I was with him when the explosion occurred on La Mola. That was when he told me his Communications people could no longer talk to the garrison there. He seemed very dejected. In the circumstances the sensible thing would seem to be for us to withdraw to Gibraltar.'

Gareth looked at him, gave a short bark of a laugh and said, 'The sensible thing!' His voice was full of irony. 'Oh yes, Lieutenant Commander – that would undoubtedly be the sensible thing. Unfortunately, our orders are quite the opposite. We stay here.' And he turned on his heel, striding quickly up and down the bridge several times, his face tight-drawn, an expression almost of anguish on his face. He seemed to be struggling to make up his mind about something. Finally, he turned to me. 'Wait for me in my cabin.' He was moving towards the door and when I started to say something about it being time I was off his ship he turned on me angrily. 'Just do as I tell you. Wait in my cabin. I may need you if I manage to contact any of Soo's friends.'

He went below then and shortly afterwards the Navigator advised me to do as he said. His hand was on my arm, steering me to the door. On the stairs outside he suddenly stopped. 'He needs you, sir. You know the island and the people here, and you're not a part of the ship. That's important.' And he added, speaking quite urgently now, 'There's one or two of the officers here trying to dismiss him as a jumped-up little Welshman from the lower deck promoted too quickly and not big enough for the job. They don't know what the job is, of course, and nor do I, but I can tell you this – he's carrying a burden hardly anybody on board yet realises, a burden I can only guess at from hints dropped by Phil Woburn, our Communications Officer. I admire him.' He gave a quick embarrassed grin. 'So do as he says, will you? He needs you.'

It was on the tip of my tongue to tell him to keep the man away from my wife. But instead I nodded and went down to his cabin, wondering again why he had been given this particular command and what the hell the ship was supposed to do here.

I was there on my own for a good half-hour and for most of that time I was standing by the porthole which looked out past Bloody Island to the port and the Naval Base. Once one of the naval patrol boats put out heading for

Cala Figuera, but a few minutes after disappearing behind Bloody Island it emerged again and returned to base. Otherwise, there was virtually nothing moving in that section of the harbour and the waterfront was too far away for me to identify the few vehicles that were on the road.

To pass the time I had a look at the books on the shelf above the desk. They were most of them reference books, including the Admiralty Pilot for the Mediterranean Volumes I and II, also, surprisingly, Kemp's encyclopaedic work, *Ships and the Sea*, and beside that was Conrad's *The Secret Agent* and a rather battered copy of a collection of Kipling's verse. Opening it at a marker, I found he had underlined a passage from 'How Fear Came' – '*When ye fight with a Wolf of the Pack, ye must fight him alone and afar, Lest others take part in the quarrel, and the Pack be diminished by war.*' And earlier there was a ticket to the Shakespeare Theatre, Stratford-upon-Avon, marking 'The English Flag'. '*And what should they know of England who only England know.*' I felt the wrench of that second line, thinking of spring and blossom, chestnuts bursting. Then Petty Officer Jarvis came in to say he would be serving breakfast as soon as the Captain arrived, meanwhile could he offer me a cup of coffee? By then it was 06.09 and I wondered what Ismail Fuxá had said in his Independence Day message.

Gareth had listened to it on the radio, of course. But when he came in some ten minutes later he couldn't tell me what the man had said, apart from the fact that it was a declaration of the island's independence, but he seemed to have got a very vivid impression of Fuxá himself. 'A little like listening to a re-run of the German Führer speaking at one of the big Nazi rallies in the thirties – very emotional, the voice rising in pitch to the point of screaming, then suddenly falling away so that it seemed to be whispering in one's ear.' He slumped down on the settle, passing a hand over his eyes as though to rub out the weariness that showed there. 'Quite an exercise. Very compelling, almost hypnotic. I think we're in trouble.' He said it so softly I could hardly catch the words. 'They seem to have taken all the key points except the Naval Base, which suggests there were sympathisers among some of the military.'

He had contacted several of our English-speaking friends, but none of them, not even the Renatos, were willing to talk about what was happening ashore. 'In the absence of any effective opposition they're not prepared to stick their necks out.' Jarvis had brought him a tray of coffee and he sat drinking it and staring vacantly at the clock on the wall. 'It's up to the politicians now. Everybody's been informed – Madrid, London, Washington, and Moscow, of course. They'll have a finger in it somewhere, I suppose. That cruiser we saw in Grand Harbour sailed yesterday evening and a flotilla of Soviet ships has just passed through the Straits of Bonifacio. Elements of the Sixth Fleet, the ships we passed through yesterday evening, have put about and are headed back into the Western Mediterranean at full speed.' He poured himself some more coffee, drank it quickly and went out. 'Won't be long, then we'll have breakfast.'

This time he was gone the better part of an hour, and when he came back his face looked grim. 'The BBC News led off with it at seven o'clock. There was a short statement from Madrid to the effect that the Spanish Government was greatly concerned and would be watching events closely.' He was standing at the window looking out towards the town, the white of the buildings touched with gold as the sun rose above the northern arm of the harbour. It was one of those still mornings, the water glassy calm, a molten look that was a sure sign of heat to come. 'In other words, they're not sure of themselves and are waiting upon developments locally. No suggestion at the moment that they are prepared to take any positive and determined action.' He turned to me. 'How left is this man Fuxá, would you say?'

'We always thought of him as more of an anarchist than a communist,' I said.

'My information is that he has spent some time in the Soviet Union and is probably Russian trained.' He gave a little shrug, went over to his desk and sat down, staring vacantly at the litter of signals that covered it. 'Oh well, we'll know soon enough. If that's correct, then he'll almost certainly request recognition from Moscow, even perhaps some assistance if the going gets rough.'

He seemed to be using me as a sounding board, for he went on talking about how the situation might develop, the political repercussions outside of Menorca. At the back of his mind, of course, was the American bombing of Libya. 'Do you think they're involved?' He was staring at me, but I don't think he was seeing me at all, only what was in his mind, the question purely rhetorical. 'Russian warships, the American Sixth Fleet, and those big guns out on La Mola. If they know how to fire them, somebody's got to take them out before any naval ships hostile to this new regime can enter Port Mahon. There are Spanish Navy ships in Barcelona, but they haven't moved. Perhaps that's why.'

'Surely they could knock them out,' I suggested. 'An air strike . . .'

But he was shaking his head. 'The situation is too confused for them to do that. They don't know who they'd be attacking. Their own people perhaps.'

'What does Palma say?' I asked him.

'The Civil Governor has called for calm throughout the Province and appealed for the maintenance of democratic government. Usual sort of thing.'

'And the Military Governor?'

'Nothing so far from him. Not that we've been able to pick up, and nothing on the BBC News or even the World Service. Madrid seems to be keeping a low profile.' He banged his fist against the arm of his chair. 'Time is passing, and every minute counts. They don't seem to realise —'

'Nor do you,' I said.

He stared at me. 'How do you mean?'

'It's obvious, isn't it – they're afraid of aggravating the situation. If you'd lived in the islands you'd understand something of their history and how recent and how delicate is the matter of provincial autonomy.'

'I know that. But they're dithering and they haven't time for that.' His voice had risen almost to a note of shrillness. 'They haven't time,' he repeated more quietly, gazing into space. 'God almighty!' It was an invocation that seemed forced out of him by his lone position at the centre of events that were beyond his control. 'Better get some breakfast now.' He got up from the desk and led me over to the table under the portholes, calling for Petty Officer Jarvis.

'Your people knew something like this was going to happen,' I said as we sat down. 'That's why you were ordered out of Malta in such haste.' He didn't answer, his mind locked in on itself. 'Well, wasn't it? And wasn't that why you came to Menorca in the first place, before you took command of this ship?'

That got through to him, his eyes coming into focus and staring at me across the table. 'I suppose so.' Jarvis appeared with two plates loaded with bacon, sausage and fried egg.

'So what are you supposed to do? A British Navy ship, you can't take any part in a coup d'état like this.'

'No, of course not.'

'So, what's the point?'

'Toast?' He pushed the rack towards me, concentrating now on his food.

'You can't do any good here,' I told him.

He nodded, the broad forehead under the black curly hair creased in a frown. 'Jesus! Do you think I don't know that?'

'So why were you sent here?' I asked him.

'Why?' He looked surprised. 'For the same reason Nelson was here. And poor Byng – executed because he wouldn't face the French.' And he added, 'These people, they have this one priceless asset – the finest deep-water harbour in the Western Med. That's what it's all about. That's why I'm here.' He gave a hollow laugh. 'If there had been any opposition, if Madrid had reacted to the situation . . .' He stopped there, the loudspeaker breaking in on his thoughts: 'Bridge here, sir. There's a launch approaching. Harbour launch by the look of it.'

Gareth finished his breakfast quickly and a few minutes later the same voice announced that it was the harbour master himself wanting to speak to the Captain. Gareth asked for the man's name, then turned to me. 'Francisco Romacho. Is that right?'

'No,' I said. 'It should be Juan Terron.'

He nodded. 'They haven't wasted any time. A key appointment and he's in position already.' Then into the intercom: 'Does he speak English? No, well get hold of Sykes, then send the two of them up.' He suggested I conceal myself in the steward's pantry. 'See if you recognise him.'

The man who entered was short and very dark with an aquiline face. I had never seen him before. He was dressed in khaki trousers and camouflage tunic. He came straight to the point. 'Señor Fuxá – *el Presidente* – feels that, in the circumstances, he cannot accept the presence of a foreign warship in the port of Mahon.' Watching through a crack in the serving hatch, Victor Sykes came into my line of vision. He was another of the young officers-under-training, probably posted to the ship for his knowledge of Spanish. He looked a little scared, his voice low as he interpreted. The three of them were seated at the coffee table, Gareth pointing out that what went on ashore was not his concern, he was simply in Mahon on a courtesy visit and if there had been some change in the government of the island, he was sure the new regime would extend the same welcome to one of Her Majesty's ships as the old.

The interview went on like that for some time, Romacho insisting that *Medusa* leave Mahon, Gareth pointing out that his orders came from London and he had no authority to leave without new instructions. At one point he said, 'This is a matter for the Spanish and British governments.' And Romacho answered quickly, 'I don't think so. We are now an independent state.'

'Then I suggest your president takes the question up directly with the Foreign Office in London.'

'He cannot do that until we have recognition. In the meantime, he insists that you leave Mahon.'

'I have explained that my orders –'

'Your orders are to leave. Immediately.' Romacho had jumped to his feet. 'This is our water. Our port. You have no right to be here when we don't invite you. You will leave immediately please.'

Gareth had risen to his feet. 'Unfortunately we have a problem.' And he went on to explain that the high-pressure boilers delivering steam to the turbines had sprung some leaks and his Marine Engineer Officer had taken the opportunity to close the boilers down for maintenance work on the condenser pipes.

It was obvious that Romacho didn't believe him, but he couldn't very well demand to inspect the engine room. Instead, he said, 'In that case, we will have to arrange a tow for you. Fortunately the tanker that keeps the Cala Figuera depot supplied has just finished off-loading and we have our own harbour tug. I will arrange for the two of them to tow you to Palma in Mallorca.'

'That will not be necessary,' Gareth said.

'You will leave then under your own steam?'

'When I have orders to leave I will leave. Not before.'

'So! You are not going to leave?'

'No.'

'Very well, *Capitán*. I also have orders. *El Presidente* instructs me to say that you have until noon. If you are not away from Mahon by midday he will be forced to regard your continued presence here as a hostile act. You understand?' He gave a formal little bow, and without waiting for Gareth's reply, turned quickly and made for the door. His last words as he went out were, 'You have until midday.'

IV

BLOODY ISLAND

CHAPTER ONE

I remember standing by the taula on Bloody Island watching as the minute hand of my watch crept towards the vertical. Clouds were forming to the south over St Felip, the day already hot and airless, as I had known it would be, and the frigate lay to her reflection in the oily water, nothing moving on her deck, everything very still and silent. I was alone, and had been since *Medusa*'s launch returned me to the island shortly after eight that morning. Gareth had accompanied me to the head of the ship's ladder. 'You'll be going ashore, will you?' By that he had meant, of course, going across to Mahon. 'Give my love to Soo.' He smiled then, a funny, crooked little smile, and then he had said, 'Pray for me, both of you.' A perfunctory salute and he had turned on his heel and disappeared back up to the bridge.

It wasn't until after I had landed and the launch was on its way back to *Medusa* that the full import of what he had said began to sink in. By then I had discovered, not only that Petra's inflatable wasn't at the landing place, but there was also no sign of Lennie's semi-rigid diving boat. I was on my own and plenty of time to think about it. Also, I had no means of knowing what was going on ashore.

The odd thing was that everything seemed normal enough, the usual volume of traffic along the waterfront, so shops and businesses must be opening as usual. But on the water itself virtually nothing moved. As for the outside world, now that I was off the frigate all I had was Petra's little portable radio, and listening to the news bulletins I got the impression the media was deliberately playing down events in Mahon. The unilateral declaration of independence was referred to, but only briefly, and even the Overseas Service relegated it to a late spot in the World News. This could, of course, be the result of a local clampdown. It could equally be political pressure at home.

Sitting there in the sun, stripped to the waist as the day advanced, there was something quite uncanny about the brooding ruins of the hospital, the sense of isolation, and that lonely British warship riding there so peacefully to her reflection. She looked puny against the shimmering sprawl of La Mola and it was hard to realise that inside the battered plates of that grey hull the Communications Room must be humming with messages bounced off satellites as the well-known names of international politics, roused from their beds at an unaccustomed hour or called to their offices unexpectedly, endeavoured to grapple with the possible repercussions of Fuxá's seizure of power on a small island in the Western Mediterranean. Was Gareth right when he had said it was all because of this four and a half miles of deep, sheltered water that stretched away on either side of me?

Shortly after eleven a single mobile gun took up a position in the garden of a villa above Cala Llonga. Now, as I waited by the beacon beyond the dig, periodically checking my watch as the seconds ticked away to noon, I wondered whether it would actually open fire, whether there were other guns ranged on the frigate. La Mola had been very quiet since that early morning explosion.

Noon. And nothing happened. The sun blazed down, everything very still, the frigate's anchor chain hanging slack, the water flat like polished brass. Fearing the worst it was almost an anti-climax. Away to the south a plane rose from the airport. It looked like a military plane, but it flew west towards Ciudadela.

I stayed there, watching, and shortly after twelve-thirty a launch moved out from the commercial quay heading straight for Bloody Island. It was the same launch that had brought the new harbour master out to *Medusa*. I turned the glasses on to the naval quay. Still the same three ships there – a fast patrol boat, one of the big fishery protection launches and the old minesweeper that had escorted *Medusa* in. The launch came through the narrows, making for the frigate, and as it passed I could see a little group of three men in the stern of it. One was Romacho. He was now wearing an official cap and beside him was a man in uniform, an Army officer by the look of it. The third man was in civilian clothes and I wondered who it was. He had his back to me and it wasn't until he turned to speak to Romacho that I realised it was Fuxá himself.

So the RN presence was that important. The launch swung alongside the frigate's accommodation ladder where they were met by one of the officers, Mault I think, certainly not Gareth, and all three of them went on board.

I stayed there by the beacon, watching through the glasses, waiting to see what would happen now. They were on board exactly seventeen and a half minutes by my watch and it was Gareth himself who escorted Fuxá and his two companions to the head of the ladder, saluting perfunctorily, then turning away. The Army officer did not salute and there were no handshakes, the three of them hurrying down the ladder to the waiting launch without looking back.

I watched them all the time through the glasses, and all the way through the narrows they stood silent and grim-faced, none of them saying a word.

Nothing happened after the launch had returned to the inner harbour. Nobody else came out to the frigate, so I presumed the deadline had been extended. It was siesta time anyway. The day dragged on, no sign of Petra or Lennie, with the result that I was marooned in the midst of what now seemed something of a non-event, everything so quiet, so peaceful it was almost unbelievable, and only the absence of any movement in or out of the harbour to convince me of the reality of it.

I had time then to think about myself – my own life and

how sailing, and a fascination for the precision of target shooting, had given me the means to live by my wits in a world that seemed to be getting everlastingly richer as more and more successful businessmen decided to make the Mediterranean their playpen. It had seemed so easy. Exciting too. Then I had met Soo and the urge to build something solid, a business of my own, a family, had brought me here.

And now?

I went over it all in my mind, sitting in the blazing sun beside the half-cleared outline of that fallen taula – the night of that Red Cross barbecue in the Quarries, the cave and the loss of the child, the murder of Jorge Martinez, that big beautiful catamaran and the blind stupidity of my desire to own it.

And Soo. My mind kept coming back to Soo. The only sheet anchor I had ever had. And I had lost her. *Give my love to Soo*, he had said with that funny little smile. And he was there, on that frigate, and she could see the ship from her bedroom window. *Pray for me*, he had said.

Hell! It was I who needed praying for, sitting alone beside a religious monument fashioned by Bronze Age men some three thousand years ago, and wanted by the police.

Shortly after four, with Mahon active again after the three-hour break, a convoy of over half a dozen yachts left. There was activity in the port area now. But still no sign of either Petra or Lennie, and no means of crossing the water to Mahon. The narrows on the north side of Bloody Island are barely three hundred metres wide and I was greatly tempted to swim across, but it would undoubtedly be under observation, and apart from the Naval Base, I was certain the whole peninsula that formed the northern arm of the harbour was in the hands of the new regime. How much of Menorca they held, outside of the Mahon area, I had no means of knowing. Not all of it probably. Several times I thought I heard firing away to the south-west, in the direction of the airport. Then suddenly there was the sound of engines, a distant rumble from the far end of the port, by the new cargo quay.

It was the Libyan freighter getting under way, the harbour tug pulling her bows clear and swinging them round, so that they were pointed straight towards me. At the same time, the harbour master's launch left the Estación Maritima, accompanied by two other launches. I was standing by the red-flashing beacon again when they passed through the narrows, but I couldn't see who was on board the harbour launch. It was flanked by what looked like a harbour police launch and a customs launch. Only the harbour master's launch went alongside *Medusa*'s ladder, and though somebody attempted to go on board, his way was blocked by a burly petty officer standing immovably halfway up it.

The little tableau remained motionless for some time, the man on the grating gesticulating very energetically and an officer, Sykes probably, on the deck above. I watched them arguing through the glasses until my attention was distracted by the increasing rumble of ships' engines. The freighter, with the tug leading it, was approaching the narrows. It was low in the water, not yet unloaded, so it could hardly be intending to leave port. And behind me, just visible beyond the rocks above Petra's landing place, I could see the bows of the small oil tanker lying in Cala Figuera beginning to swing as she fetched her anchor.

The tug was through the narrows by then and headed direct for *Medusa*. The beat of the freighter's engines slowed as she passed so close to me I could see that the Arabic letters of her name had been painted over some earlier name, the outline of which suggested that she had originally been Greek, possibly Russian, for the faint lettering appeared to be Cyrillic. The rusty plates slid by, the bridge housing at the stern seeming to tower over me.

In the distance I could just hear the tug exchanging

words with the harbour launch over loudhailers, and at the same time Gareth appeared on the frigate's bridge wing. He had his hand to his mouth, holding a mike I think, because even at that distance I could hear his voice quite clearly, it was so powerfully amplified. He spoke in English, very simply: *'I have to warn you that any ship coming within two hundred metres of my anchorage will be regarded as having committed a hostile act.'*

He turned then and I think he must have given an order, for as Lieutenant Sykes hurried to his side and began repeating what he had said in Spanish, the turret of the two 4.5-inch guns slowly swivelled, the barrels no longer aimed at the heights above Cala Llonga, but being lowered, slowly and menacingly, to point directly at the freighter.

It flashed through my mind then what a chance he was taking – or was he bluffing? For a British warship to open fire on the ship of a country we were not at war with, however unfriendly that country might be, and to do it while anchored in the harbour of a Nato ally . . . It didn't bear thinking about and I almost held my breath as I waited to see what the freighter would do, wondering whether Gareth was acting on his own initiative or whether he was covered by explicit orders. I hoped, for his sake, that it was the latter.

Everything now was in slow motion. The launch had pulled away from *Medusa*'s side to join the others, the three of them in a close huddle as though the vessels themselves were discussing the situation. The frigate's guns stayed implacably levelled at the approaching super-structure of the freighter, which was now barely moving. A sudden swirl of water at her stern and she was stationary, everything held motionless as in a still picture.

The sun had begun to set, a lovely golden glow lighting up the grey slab-plated side of the frigate. Time passed, nothing happening, but the tension seeming steadily to increase as the sunset glow deepened to red so that the villas above Cala Llonga and Cala Lladró were all aflame, the bare scrubland above taking fire.

The police launch was the first to break away, ploughing back through the narrows at full speed. At the same time the harbour launch went alongside the tug. It was there for several minutes, then it made across to the freighter, going alongside on the port hand where I couldn't see it. Meanwhile, the customs launch had passed astern of *Medusa* and disappeared in the direction of Cala Llonga, or perhaps further along the peninsula, by Lazareto Island. I couldn't follow its movements because it was hidden from me by the frigate.

By now lights had begun to appear along the Mahon waterfront and in the town above. The clouds had thickened, darkness closing in early. I could still just see the harbour launch. It paused briefly to turn and run parallel with the tanker, which was already approaching the narrows. Then, when it had resumed course for the Estación Maritima, the tanker changed direction to pass out of my sight to the south of Bloody Island. At that moment *Medusa* leapt suddenly into fairy-like outline, her deck, upperworks and mast all picked out by strings of light bulbs – Gareth Lloyd Jones cocking a snook at the waiting ships and the shore. It was as if he was saying, 'Here I am, still anchored here and my guns ready. What are you going to do about it?'

After that I didn't stay much longer by the beacon. There was no point. It was already too dark to see what was going on ashore. The tug and the freighter had been joined by the tanker, all three of them anchored astern of the frigate and well beyond the two-hundred-metre protection zone Gareth had declared for himself. Stiff and tired, I went back to the camp, where I lit the pressure lamp, raided Petra's drink cupboard for a glass of brandy, and got the paraffin stove going to heat up one of her packets of instant food.

The sound of an engine sent me tumbling back to my

lookout point by the red-flashing beacon. It was the harbour launch, back again, and I watched as the dim shape of it passed through the narrows, making straight for *Medusa*. The frigate had swung with the slight movement of the tide, so that through the glasses I had an even clearer view of the launch as it went alongside the ladder. One man only got off and was escorted to the bridge. It wasn't Romacho, and it certainly wasn't Fuxá. This was a much taller man wearing a seaman's cap and dark jersey.

A stone clinked behind me and I swung round as a voice spoke out of the darkness – 'Your grub's boiling over, mate.'

It was Lennie. He had rowed across in a borrowed dinghy from the little gut in the cliffs below Villa Carlos known as Cala Corb. 'I turned the stove off. Better eat it now, then if you wanter go ashore I'll take yer.' He was staggering off towards the dark bulk of the hospital ruins. 'They've kicked most of the prisoners out of the jail and locked up half a dozen senior officers of the *Guardia* and the national police instead, including your friends Menendez and Molina. You'll be safe enough.' His voice was slurred and he moved with care for he had spent most of the day in the waterfront café-bars. No, he didn't know where Petra was, and he hadn't been near the chandlery nor seen anything of Soo. 'Wouldn't go near 'er, mate. I told yer. She fired me. Just like that. She can go to hell.' He was very drunk, holding himself stiff and erect.

His news, gathered at second hand in the waterfront café-bars, was that as yet the new regime controlled barely half the island. But they had the key points – La Mola and Punta de Santo Carlos to the south of the Mahon entrance, both airports, the radio and radar station on El Toro, also the town of Alayór. But in the country south and west of Alayór there were rumours of fighting between local factions. 'They say the Russians are coming.' But he admitted that was just bar talk. 'They're full of talk over in the port, wild talk.'

He waved away my suggestion that he joined me and get some food into himself. 'Don't wan' food – 'nuther drink.' He had found the cupboard with the Soberano in it. 'Their own bloody fault, yer know. Didn't think it through.'

'How do you mean?'

But his mind had switched to something else. 'Pinched my boat.' He slopped the brandy into the glass, the bottle clinking on the rim, then slumped into a chair. 'Left it at the Club pontoon, only gone an hour – well, mebbe two. Bloody bastards!' His eyes focused on me with difficulty. 'What was that you asked? Oh yes. Didn't cotton on, the fools – all that bombing. Two nights ago. An' next day, orders of the Military Governor over in Palma they say, all them raw young conscripts spread around the island to protect the *urbanizacións* and foreign property. Clever! Did the job, yer see. One night's bombing and it got them La Mola. Hardly any military left in the barracks there.' And he added after a moment's thought, 'But there's talk of some regulars over to Ciudadela that could act as a rally – a rallying point. Talk, talk, talk . . . In one bar – yer know, the one by the commercial quay – there was a trucker came in said he'd seen military vehicles moving towards Alayór, told us Fuxá wouldn't be able to hold the airport for long. Then some silly bastard starts talking about the Russians. Snow on their boots!' He snickered. 'That was a long time ago.' His voice trailed away, the hiss of the pressure lamp making him sleepy. 'Didn't think it through,' he said again. 'All part of the plan an' they fell for it. Clever!' His head was lolling. 'An' now that Navy ship, boxed in with a Libby bloody freighter sitting on 'er tail.'

He didn't seem to have anything more to tell me, so I asked him why he had slipped away from the petty officers' mess that morning. 'You left me stranded.'

He nodded, mumbling something about, 'It's all right for you'.

'You should have checked the chandlery, had a word with my wife and made certain Petra was all right.' His head was sinking into his arms. I reached out across the table and shook him. 'It wasn't the Australian Navy you deserted from, was it? It was the Royal Navy.'

'Wot if it was?'

'And that's why you got pissed.'

'Well, wouldn't you, mate?' There was a note of belligerence in his voice now. 'I do'n want ter think back to them days. And those petty officers – Chris'sakes! They could've picked me up jus' like that.'

I told him he was a bloody fool. All those years ago . . . But he was fast asleep, his head fallen sideways on to his arm. I finished my meal, then put what clothes I had on, turned the pressure lamp off and went down to the landing point. It was a plastic dinghy, and though he had been drunk, he had still hauled it out on to the rocks, stowed the oars neatly and made fast the painter.

The water looked inky black as I floated it off and stepped in, Mahon a blaze of light as though nothing had happened and it was just a normal evening. Fortunately there was no wind, for the boat was no better than a plastic skimming dish. Clear of Bloody Island the brightly lit shape of the frigate blazed like a jewel, the tug and the freighter in black silhouette, the tanker barely visible and no sign of the launches. I made straight for Cala Figuera and our own quay. My car was there, but nothing else, no sign of Petra's Beetle. No lights on in the windows of the house either and when I crossed the road I found the door to the chandlery standing half-open.

I think I knew by then there was nobody there. I called, but there was no answer, the only sound a sort of scratching as though a net curtain was flapping in the breeze from an open window. It came from above and as I climbed the stairs I had an unpleasant feeling there was something in the house, something alive.

I reached the landing and stopped. The scratching sound

came from the bedroom, and suddenly I knew. The dog! 'All right, Benjie.' The poor little beast couldn't bark and as I pushed open the door I could smell it, a mixture of urine and excreta. He flung himself at me, making that extraordinary singing noise in the head. I switched on the light. He was shivering uncontrollably. Apart from the messes and the smell, the bedroom looked much as usual. I got a bowl of water from the kitchen and he drank it straight off, lapping with desperate urgency. Clearly he had been shut in that room for some considerable time and Soo would never have done that. She doted on the animal.

I went through into the front room then, and as soon as I switched on the light my heart sank – a chair tipped over, Soo's typewriter on the floor, its cable ripped out as though somebody had tripped over it, a jug of flowers lying in a litter of papers, a damp patch on the Bokhara rug and an occasional table on its side with one leg smashed. There had been a struggle and I stood, staring helplessly at the evidence of it, asking myself why – why for God's sake should anybody want to attack Soo, and what had they done with her?

Anger, a feeling of desperation, of inadequacy almost, came over me, not knowing where she was or what to do. I got some food for the dog. He was hungry as well as thirsty. The fact that he hadn't been able to contain himself might be partly nerves, but clearly he'd been shut up for some time, so whatever had happened to Soo had happened quite a few hours back. I cleared up the mess in the bedroom, moving about in a daze, wondering all the time where she was, what had happened. I found myself back in the front room, in the office, staring out at the dark glimmer of the water. The dog was pawing at my trousers.

I took it down the stairs and out into the road, where it did what it had to while I stared across the water to the lit outline of the frigate. A bell sounded above the cliffs in

Villa Carlos. I glanced at my watch, scooped up the dog and ran back up the stairs. The news was already being read as I switched on the radio, the announcer in the middle of saying that the self-styled President of Menorca had called upon Moscow to recognise the new island republic and provide immediate assistance in dealing with dissident elements endeavouring to impose what was described as 'a reactionary fascist regime centred on the old capital, Ciudadela'.

I switched to the World Service where it was now the lead story, the announcer listing a whole series of countries who had been asked to recognise the island republic. So far only Libya and Albania had complied. Madrid had still not taken any positive action, but there was clearly intense activity on the political front. The Spanish ambassador had been to the Kremlin and it was reported that the Government had called upon all EEC countries to assist in maintaining Spanish sovereignty over the Balearic Islands. More practically, Spanish Navy ships in Barcelona had been put on alert and parachutists were standing by.

But, listening to that news, it was clear everybody was waiting upon Moscow, and Moscow was saying nothing, for the moment. Towards the end there was a reference to a British frigate being on a courtesy visit to the island, and the Foreign Secretary, in answer to a question in the House, had made a statement to the effect that if the ship was molested in any way the Captain would be fully entitled to take any action he felt appropriate. In other words, the responsibility for anything which might happen was Gareth's. No wonder the poor devil had asked us to pray for him!

Comments followed from BBC reporters in various capitals, but by then I was on the phone, enquiring about Soo. The Renatos first, but they were out and the others I contacted knew nothing. In desperation I tried the hospital, but the line was either engaged or out of order. I went down the stairs again. The store was locked and no sign of Ramón. But he had been there that morning for he had signed out paint, varnish and anti-fouling to Rodriguez who was the only one left working on the boats. Life went on, it seemed.

I returned to the office, put the typewriter back on the desk and sat there staring out of the window to the lit frigate, wondering what the hell had happened here, where they had taken her, and why – why, for God's sake? Until I knew that . . . A door slammed, feet on the stairs, and before she burst in I knew who it was. 'Thank God you're here,' she cried. 'I've been searching everywhere. Have you found her?'

'No. When did you discover she had gone?'

'This afternoon. Some time around four.' And she added, speaking breathlessly, 'Soo was all right this morning. We had breakfast together.' She had come straight here, she said, after leaving Lennie and myself at the pontoon and had phoned, first the Military HQ, then the Naval Base. 'I don't think it did any good. It took so long to get hold of anybody in authority.' She sank into the armchair by the window. 'God! I'm tired now. What do you think happened? The typewriter was on the floor, that chair broken, everything a mess. She'd put up a fight before they could drag her away. Who were they? Have you any idea?' Her eyes bulged as she stared at me. 'No, of course you haven't.'

'Did you go into the bedroom?' I asked.

'Yes, of course. I searched the whole house.'

'You didn't see the dog?'

'No.'

So the poor little beast had been so scared at what had happened it must have hidden itself under the bed. 'And there was no mess?' She shook her head. 'Then it looks as though they came for her late morning, around lunchtime.'

'Yes, but who?' She was slumped there, staring miserably at the water below, her big capable hands folded in her lap. One of the side zippers of her jeans had slipped to show a little bulge of brown flesh. She was as swarthy as an Indian. 'The police or these new people? Do they know you're back, here in Mahon? There must be a reason. There's always a reason.'

'We'll know in due course.' A note of resignation had crept into my voice.

'I'll make some tea.' She bounced to her feet, her face suddenly alive again, the relief of something positive revitalising her. 'Or would you prefer a drink?'

'No,' I said. 'Tea will do fine.' I didn't care what I had.

When she came back I was still sitting there. 'Noon,' I said.

'You think that's when it happened?' She poured a cup and passed it to me.

'No, he was given till noon.' I told her about the new harbour master, his visit to *Medusa* and how, after the deadline was up, Fuxá himself had gone out to see Gareth. 'But he hasn't moved. He's still there and lit up like a Christmas tree.'

'What are those ships doing there?' She had poured herself a cup and was sitting down again, lying half back in the chair.

'Waiting to tow him out,' I said.

'Well, why don't they?' She was staring out of the window towards the fairy outline of the frigate bright against the dark bulk of the peninsula behind. 'Oh, I see. They're anchored.' She turned and looked at me. 'Why?'

'Because he's threatened to blow them out of the water if they come any nearer.' And as I told her what I thought the purpose of his presence here in Mahon was I could see the same thought was in both our minds.

'What are you suggesting? That they've taken Soo because . . . Oh no, surely not. How would they know?' She was leaning forward now, staring at me, her eyes wide and appalled. We both knew what she meant.

'There was gossip,' I said. 'There must have been gossip.'

'Oh yes, there was plenty of that – after she lost the

baby. In a place like this, a tight little circle, tongues wag all the time. Gareth here, a British naval officer – they would have had their eyes on him anyway, but after what happened . . . And there was you and me. Our friends made a meal of it.' And she added, frowning, 'But are you really suggesting Soo could be used as a hostage in that way, to force Gareth to take his ship out of Mahon?'

'I don't know. They might think it a possibility.' I shook my head, the warmth of the tea comforting. 'Anyway, it's the only motive that occurs to me.'

'So who do we contact?'

There was only one person I could think of. 'Evans.' But how to reach him? 'Where's Fuxá established himself, do you know?'

'Esmerelda said he'd taken over the Military Government Headquarters block on Isabel II.'

'That makes sense. I'll phone there.' I drank the rest of my tea and was just getting to my feet when Petra leaned forward, peering intently through the window.

'Wait a minute. There's a boat coming in.'

As it came alongside our quay I saw it was *Medusa*'s launch. A young midshipman jumped ashore. It was a boy named Masterton. He glanced quickly left and right as though to make certain he wasn't going to be challenged, then scuttled quickly across the road. The bell sounded and I went down. 'Good evening, sir. Captain's compliments and would you be good enough to join him on board. He says it's important.' And he handed me a note.

It was very short and had clearly been dashed off in a hurry: *I am sending the launch for you. Something has occurred that you should know about. It concerns Soo. Hurry, it's urgent. Gareth.*

Petra was at my elbow and I passed it on to her. 'It's what we feared.' I grabbed my anorak. 'Look after the dog, will you? Take it round to the restaurant if you're not spending the night here. They look after it sometimes.' I found a key for her, checked that I had my own, and then I was across the road and into the launch. 'Is there somebody with the Captain?' I asked the youngster as we swung away from the quay and headed for the lit outline of the frigate.

'Not at the moment, sir. But I think he's expecting someone.'

'Who? Do you know?'

But he couldn't tell me that. 'There's been quite a bit of coming and going. First of all it was the President's personal aide in a speedboat out of Cala Llonga, then it was the President himself. That was just after midday.' There had apparently been other visitors, but they had come out from Cala Llonga, which was why I had not seen them. None of them, except Fuxá, had been allowed on board. 'The Captain says that's because we don't recognise the new government here.'

'What about the three launches that came out from Port Mahon just as it was getting dark?' I asked him. 'One man was allowed on board. Do you know who he was?'

'No, sir. A seaman of some sort.'

'Is he still there?'

'No. He went off towards Cala Llonga in the harbour launch. I heard him say he was going to fetch somebody. The other boats have gone, but we've still got three ships anchored near. They wanted to tow us out, but our Captain wasn't having that.' And he added, 'What's it like ashore, sir? It all looks very normal from where we're anchored, though we can hear firing sometimes away to the south, towards the airport.'

Excited to be caught up in an event that was world news, he chatted on like that all the way out to the green-flashing beacon on the south side of Bloody Island. It slid past us very close, the bulk of the hospital a solid backdrop, the tower outlined against the stars, and I was wondering what Gareth intended to do, how I could persuade him that Soo's life was more important than his career. I was leaning against the canopy, the beat of the engine pulsing through my body and the launch already swinging in a wide arc to come alongside, the lit outline of the frigate growing larger.

There was no other reason that I could see for what had happened. If somebody had told them the commander of the British frigate was in love with my wife ... But did they really believe the man would take his ship to sea without specific orders? Thinking it over, it seemed barely possible, but then men who live by violence often find it difficult to accept that others are governed by a code of social behaviour and operate within the framework of a disciplined order. I had seen something of that myself. The idea that every man has his price is mirrored in the belief that violence is totally effective in changing people's minds. Why else use torture?

It was that thought that was in my mind as we slid alongside the frigate's accommodation ladder and I stepped out on to the wooden grating. The sudden rush to leave Malta, the way Gareth had dropped his anchor in about the most conspicuous position in the whole long inlet, the blazing lights above my head – the ship was there for a purpose, and that purpose could only be to act as a block to any power thinking of supporting a rebel regime unopposed. If I was right, then Soo's life was of total unimportance as compared with the job Lieutenant Commander Lloyd Jones RN had been sent here to do. Her death, even her torture, could make no difference, and knowing that, I felt sick with fear as I climbed the gangway.

I was met at the top by one of the officers, I can't remember who. He took me to the Captain's day cabin where we had breakfasted – was it only that morning? I barely heard him tell me the Captain would be with me shortly as I tried to marshal my arguments, my mind perversely concentrated on all the forms of torture I had heard and read about, a picture there as vivid as the day I had seen it – on a beach in Mali, a palm-frond hut, and lying there in his own excreta with the flies crawling, the only man I have ever seen tortured to death. His face – I could see his face still, the lips chewed to ribbons, the teeth protruding white and the eyes starting from his head. And then I was thinking of Soo as I had last seen her, laughing as she had left me on the quay at Addaia.

I went over to the settee and sat down, suddenly tired, the two images merging, so that in my mind's eye I saw them as one, the Arab's tortured features superimposed on Soo's. I don't remember how long I sat there, numbed at the vision of what might happen to her if Gareth didn't take his ship out of Mahon. This wasn't just a matter of Ismail Fuxá and his personal ambitions. It was bigger than that, much bigger, Fuxá just a pawn in a game being played far away from Menorca behind closed doors. Political figures with hot lines and satellites at their disposal. A young woman, held as a hostage – that was nothing. A unit of flesh. Disposable. Just as this ship was disposable, the men I had lived with on the hurried run from Malta . . .

'Glad we were able to contact you.' His voice was flat. It seemed tired, and he didn't smile as he crossed the cabin, pulled up a chair and sat down facing me. 'I don't know how long we've got. Not long.' He sounded resigned, his face grey as though he hadn't slept for a long time. I thought he had aged since I had seen him that morning, the broad forehead puckered deeper, the lines at the corners of eyes and mouth more pronounced, and he just sat there staring at me dumbly.

'Where is she?' I asked.

He gave a little shrug. But he didn't say anything. It was as though he didn't know how to begin.

'They've contacted you, have they?'

He nodded.

'So where is she? Where is she being held?'

'Then you know.' He seemed relieved, the knowledge that he hadn't got to break the news to me releasing his tongue. 'I sent across to Bloody Island for you as soon as it was dark, but you weren't there. Then we saw lights in your place at Cala Figuera, so I took a chance and sent young Leslie Masterton in to see if you were there. I'm glad you were.' His eyes were fixed on me. 'What happened? Do you know?'

I told him briefly of the scene that had greeted me, and then, unable to restrain myself, I burst out, 'It wouldn't have happened if you hadn't pushed your way into our lives. It's your bloody fault. All your fault.' And seeing that image again in my mind's eye, I leaned forward and grabbed hold of him. 'Who was it came for her? Who were they that grabbed her so brutally. Benjie – that little dog of ours – was shit scared. He's always so clean, and a brave little beast normally. Those bastards must have been rough with her.'

'All right, all right.' He was holding up his hand, pleading with me. 'You've told me how they took her, and you're right, it's because of me. I'm sorry. It's my fault.' And then, his voice suddenly stronger, 'But it's happened. You have to accept that. We both do.' His tone took on a note of authority. 'The question now is how we handle the situation. They started piling on the pressure for me to take the ship out shortly after two o'clock local time, an emissary from some sort of military commander. He came out in a speedboat from Cala Llonga. I wouldn't allow him on board, of course, and I told him my position was unchanged – I could only put to sea when I had orders to do so. The same thing I had told that man Fuxá. Until then I would remain here. He came out once more, threatening to open fire on me, and I warned him that if he did so I had the authority of the British Government to take what action I considered necessary to defend my ship. In short, I asked him to tell his general not to be a bloody fool and push me that hard.'

'Soo,' I said. 'What about Soo?' My voice was too high and I tried to get a grip on myself. 'All you've talked about so far is your problem. I'm not interested. It's my wife I'm concerned about.'

'Do you think I'm not concerned? What the hell do you

take me for?' He straightened his shoulders, his hands clasped tightly. 'I'm sorry.' The anger was gone from his voice. 'My problems are my own. I agree. But they do concern you.'

'No, you,' I said. 'Not me. My concern –'

He suddenly banged the coffee table between us. 'Will you listen, for God's sake. I've told you. We haven't much time. And my position, as Captain of one of HM ships, is very relevant to what has happened to Soo. I have my orders, and the fact that she's a hostage –' He was interrupted by a knock and his eyes flicked to the doorway. 'Come in, Leading Seaman Stanway.' He was always very punctilious about rank and I had to sit silent while he went through a whole sheaf of messages.

'We may be an old ship,' he said, as he dismissed the young seaman, 'but they've fitted us out with a pretty sophisticated communications set-up so I'm getting a steady stream of messages, news briefs, and of course we're picking up secret naval information and orders. Besides Victor Sykes, who is not only fluent in Spanish, but also speaks French, German and Italian, I have a man on loan from one of the oil companies who speaks a number of the Arab languages, also a PO who has recently completed a Russian language course.' He was still looking down at the messages in his hand. 'That Russian cruiser was sighted visually just south of Spartivento at 16.03. She was steaming at thirty knots plus. The course and speed of the other ships I mentioned suggest that they will rendezvous with her fourteen miles east of La Mola shortly after midnight. So it's like I said, we haven't much time.'

'Time for what?' I was losing patience with him. 'It's Soo I'm worried about. I want to know where she is, whether she's all right, and I want her back – safe.'

He didn't say anything, his hands clasped tight on the wadge of papers, his shoulders stooping forward. God! he looked tired, as though the weight of the world was on his shoulders and it was too much for him. 'There's a signal here says a D-20 class destroyer, two frigates and some fast attack craft have just left Barcelona. They'll be joined by a couple of subs.' Even his voice sounded tired. 'There's some French warships about to sail from Toulon. They're too far away, of course, and they're not members of Nato. The Italians are even further. The earliest any of those ships can be off the entrance here is 03.00. That'll be at least two hours too late.'

'Why are you telling me this?' But I knew why. I had been right about his role. 'You're going to stay here. Is that what you're saying?'

He shrugged, an almost Gallic gesture, the palms of his hands spread.

Silence then, both of us thinking our own thoughts. He got slowly to his feet and began pacing up and down. Could I still persuade him? 'If you could pretend to leave. A gesture. Enough at least to get them to return her . . .'

He turned on me then, his voice rising on a note of anger as he said, 'Don't be a fool, man. You're not dealing with amateurs.' And he added, 'You don't know Pat. I do. He's cold-blooded, ruthless. That's his nature, and all his adult life he's lived in the cold-blooded, ruthless world of violence and terrorism.'

'But he let you go,' I said. 'That's what you told me, sitting right here at your desk. You said he dropped you overboard up-tide of the buoy, so you'd drift down on it. And he promised you wouldn't tell anyone who he was.'

He nodded, standing in the centre of the cabin, a silhouette against the light so that I couldn't see the expression on his face. 'Yes.' His voice was toneless. 'He gave me my life, and I made a promise.'

'Why? The blood tie? The fact that you share the same father. Is that why he saved your life?'

'No.' And after a moment he went on slowly, 'No, I don't think it was that, more a matter of putting me in his debt. I've never been a part of Pat's world, so I can't be sure, but I have an idea that, besides the ruthlessness,

285

there's a primitive sense of loyalty. You do somebody a good turn, then you're in credit with him and some day you can make a claim on him.' He glanced at his watch. 'I'll find out about that soon enough. Won't be long now.'

'You're expecting him?'

'Yes.'

'So what are you going to do?'

He sat down opposite me again and I thought for a moment he had reached a decision. But all he said was, 'Have you any idea of the average age of this ship's company?' He was interrupted again. More messages. He flicked through them, nodded briefly to Stanway, turning back to me and saying, 'Well, have you? The average age.' He slapped his hand on the table. 'You won't believe this, but it's not quite twenty-three and a half. That's the *average* age of everybody, officers, senior rates, the lot. They're kids, most of them, with mothers and fathers, girlfriends, quite a few of them married, and I'm responsible. Not just for them, for their lives, but to all those people I've never met.'

'All right,' I said. 'So what *are* you going to do?'

'What can I do?' He got suddenly to his feet. 'You don't seem to realise – this potty little island is the centre of the world. Just for the moment. For the next few hours.' He started to pace up and down. 'There are warships converging on it, the whole apparatus of military confrontation beginning to be put in motion. The heads of half a dozen of the world's most powerful countries will be consulting their advisers, despatching envoys with cautionary notes, even talking to each other direct, and all because of a little jumped-up peasant farmer called Ismail Fuxá, a bunch of disaffected locals and a couple of hundred highly trained professional soldiers, commandos probably, and almost certainly from an Arab country. In these circumstances, speed and ruthlessness, a willingness to take chances – hit the other fellow before he knows what's happening. God! I've had plenty of instruction on this. If you strike fast enough and hard enough you can change the face of the world. And you're asking me . . .'

The loudspeaker interrupted him. 'There's a boat coming out from Cala Llonga, sir. The speedboat again, I think.'

He picked up the mike. 'Very well. It should be a man named Evans. Have him met at the ladder and if it is bring him straight to my cabin.'

'Very good, sir.'

He turned back to me. 'You're worried about your wife, and so am I. But just try to get this clear in your mind – you, me, Soo, all the boys on this ship, we're just pawns in a game that is being played on a world board.' He turned away, staring out to the lights of the waterfront. 'It will all depend now on whether I can persuade Pat.' He gave a little shrug. 'Frankly I doubt it. This must surely be the biggest thing he's ever been involved in.' He looked at his watch. 'Cape Spartivento is about two-forty miles from here – eight hours' steaming, something like that, and it's nearly nine already. Five hours gone. By midnight a whole fleet of ships could be gathering off the entrance here. An hour after that they could be steaming in past Villa Carlos, and if they were able to do that unopposed . . . Then it would be a case of possession being nine-tenths of the law. International law, that is, and Fuxá has appealed to Moscow for help. Belatedly Spain has called upon her EEC partners to assist in maintaining her sovereignty here.'

He was running over it again for his own benefit, not mine. 'And on our side –' He was at the port hole. '*Mahonnaise!* That's what Richelieu's chef called his version of the local *allioli*. You know what that was for?' He was talking for the sake of talking. 'For the banquet. The French were holding a banquet here at Mahon after their victory over Byng. We'd held the islands for almost fifty years, from 1708 till 1756. *Mahonnaise!*' he said again. 'Poor Byng!' His voice had dropped to a whisper. 'We were here for another nineteen years, from 1763, and then yet again for four very important years during the Napoleonic Wars. That was when Nelson was supposed to have stayed up there at Golden Farm.'

He turned back to me, smiling sardonically. 'You see, I've been well briefed on the naval background. Grand Harbour, Mahon, Gibraltar, a string of naval strongholds stretching across the Western Mediterranean. We've held them all, and I wouldn't be surprised if there aren't quite a number of people back home, people who are in a position to influence events, who still hanker after them. So you see –' He hesitated. 'What I'm trying to make you understand, Mike, is that we're all just pawns – all of us who are here on the spot where it's happening. Pat included. I don't know what he gets out of it, but there's nothing you or I could offer him –' He swung round at the sound of the loudspeaker again. 'Yes?'

'It *is* Mr Evans, sir. I'll send him up, shall I?'

'Is he on his own?' Gareth's voice sounded suddenly nervous.

'There's three of them altogether, but he's the only one who's come aboard and he's asking to see you personally.'

'Then have him sent up right away.'

'Very good, sir.'

The loudspeaker clicked off, Gareth standing by his desk fiddling with a ruler. Was he scared of the man? The spate of words he had been pouring out to me was in itself a sign of nerves. 'Better let me do the talking.' He was on edge and I wondered how much of a hold this half-brother of his had on him. The years at *Ganges*, then on that houseboat in the mud gut at Felixstowe Ferry. And Evans – he must be very sure of himself, to come on board this ship.

The knock came sooner than I had expected. Gareth sat himself down abruptly at his desk. 'Come in.'

It was Davison. 'Mr Evans, sir.'

'Show him in. Then draw the curtain and wait outside.'

He seemed taller, the face more craggy, and the neck solid as a stone column. He wore no hat, his dark hair

288

rumpled, and his shirt and the camouflage jacket were open at the neck. He was smiling, but no warmth in it, just an indication that he was prepared to be reasonable – or was he nervous, too, was there a certain insecurity under that tough exterior?

'Come in, Pat.' Gareth had risen to his feet. 'Sit down.' He waved him to a chair. 'Mike Steele you know.'

'Yeah, we've met before.' He sat down, smiling at me, his voice low key. 'How's the boat behaving?' But he didn't expect an answer for he turned to Gareth, the smile gone from his face. 'Well, when do you leave?' And he added, 'It better be soon. Very soon.'

Gareth sat down opposite him. 'Didn't they tell you, about the engines?'

'Don't give me that crap.'

'We have condenser trouble.'

'I said, don't give me that crap.' The voice had hardened. 'The oldest gimmick there is – can't move because the engines don't work.' He laughed, his voice a sneering mockery. 'Considering why you're here, it's hardly likely their fucking Lordships would have let you to sea with engines that were on the blink. So you get your fancy marine engineer on the blower and tell him to start up.'

'Unfortunately, you're wrong about the engines.' The trembling of his lower lip somehow made the statement unconvincing. 'You should know how mean things can be in the Royal Navy. This is an old ship and she was fitted out in a hurry.'

'So that you, and the rest of them on board, could be blown to hell. You always were a soft option, boy. You sit here for another two or three hours . . . Look, the bastards who give the orders, they aren't going to be here to hold your hand when Fuxá gets the support he's asked for and all hell breaks loose.' He leaned suddenly forward, his voice softer, more urgent. 'Don't be a sucker. You're expendable, the whole lot of you. Nobody cares about you. So be sensible. And if you want to stick to that fiction about the engines, then there's a tug and two other ships waiting out there to give you a tow.'

'If I go at all I'll go under my own steam. Not under tow. And what I do depends on my orders.'

There was a long silence after that, the two of them staring at each other, and in that silence I heard my own voice, sounding like a stranger, as I said, 'And what about my wife?'

There was no answer, both of them apparently locked in their own thoughts.

'Where is she?'

Evans turned slowly and looked at me. 'Not far away.' He said it so reasonably, as though kidnapping a woman was the most ordinary thing in the world. 'I'll come to her in a moment.' He glanced at his watch. 'It's nine forty-seven. I'll give you until ten p.m. to sort your engines out and get under way. Fifteen minutes. Okay?' He had risen to his feet.

'And if I don't?' Gareth hadn't moved from his chair and the silence stretched between them as they stared at each other like a pair of gladiators.

'It's been a long time,' Evans said. 'Must be four years now.'

'Just on five.'

'Yeah. Well, you would remember, wouldn't you. Moira wrote me you'd been picked up. Sent me a copy of the *East Anglian* with a picture of you tied to the buoy.' His mouth stretched to something close to a grin, the teeth bared. 'And now they've landed you with something that looks to me like a bloody suicide mission.' He leaned forward again. 'Look, boy, you owe it to yourself, to the men you've got cooped up in this tin can they've given you – get out now, before it's too late.'

Gareth stared at him as though hypnotised.

'Well, say something, for Christ's sake. What's it to be? Stay here and get pulverised to nothing, or up your hook and get to hell out before it's too late?'

290

A funny little half-smile showed on Gareth's face. He shook his head. 'Come off it, Pat. You're not here just to try and save my life again. You're here because you know damn well the presence of one of HM ships in Mahon harbour makes the whole thing impossible. Your plan of operations depends on two things for success – surprise and unimpeded access to the harbour here. The first you've achieved. In fact, your people exploited the element of surprise so well that you were able to seize control of all the key positions at this end of the island. What you didn't expect was that there would be a Nato warship anchored in Port Mahon. Your coup now needs the backing of a major power and I doubt very much whether you'll get it as long as this tin can, as you call it, remains anchored here. At least that's my reading of all the flurry of signals my Communications Office is picking up.'

His voice had become stronger, more authoritative as he developed his argument. Now he leaned forward, both elbows on the desk, his eyes fixed on his half-brother. 'My advice to you – it's the same advice as you've just been giving me – get out now, while you can.' Abruptly his right hand came up, jabbing a finger. 'Time is against you, man. You know it. I know it.'

'You'll be smashed to hell, boy.'

'Maybe. But I don't think so.' Somehow his voice managed to carry conviction. 'By dawn you'll be faced with crack Spanish troops and the arrival of the first of their naval units.'

'And how will they get into Mahon? We'll blast them out of the water with those big guns on La Mola. As for troops – what troops? They can't land . . .'

'Paratroops,' Gareth said quietly. 'I've just heard they'll be taking off about an hour before dawn.'

'Thank you. I'll pass the information on. But I think Madrid may have second thoughts. Landing paratroops anywhere on Menorca would amount to invasion of the new republic's territory, and with the powerful support we shall then have –'

'That's provided you can get *Medusa* out of the way,' Gareth cut in. 'That's why you're here, isn't it?' And he repeated his previous argument: 'Because you know damn well that support won't be forthcoming so long as there's a Nato presence in Port Mahon.'

'So you won't listen to reason.' The line of the man's mouth had hardened, so had his voice. There was anger in it now as he said, 'Then I'll have to use another form of persuasion. The woman. We're holding her hostage for your departure.' He turned to me. 'Your wife, Steele. You haven't said much so far, but I'm telling you now, if you don't want her death on your hands, you'd better start persuading young Gareth here to get the hell out of Mahon.'

'Where is she?' I asked.

'I told you, not far from here.'

'Was it you who broke into the house and took her?'

He shook his head. 'Not me. Two of my crew. You met them the day you agreed to swap *Thunderflash* for that fishing boat of yours. They say she fought like an alley cat.'

'Is she all right? Is she hurt?'

'They had to tie her down, that's all.' He was looking straight at me. 'No, she's not hurt. Not yet.' He turned back again to Gareth and added, 'But she will be if you don't get out of here fast.'

'I have my orders.'

'Then get some new ones. Tell them there's a woman hostage and you're in love with her. You *are* in love with her, aren't you?' Gareth's eyes flicked in my direction and he passed his tongue over his lips. Evans was grinning, knowing now that his information was correct. 'You can have her back the instant you're clear of Port Mahon. I'll hand her over to Steele here. That suit you?'

Gareth half shook his head, his hands locked, the fingers

moving. I thought I detected a new mood, one of indecision. Evans saw it, too, and it was then that I heard him say, 'Look, Gareth, the people I'm with aren't squeamish, you know. Nor am I. But *they're* real hard. You know what I mean?'

Gareth half shook his head again, his eyes slitted as though wincing in advance of what he seemed to know was coming.

'Good. I think you do.' Evans swung round on me. 'But for your benefit I'll spell it out. If your wife's lover –' the words were spoken quite viciously, so that it was obvious he got a vicarious pleasure out of his shock use of them – 'doesn't shift his ship out of here within quarter of an hour, you could be getting her back in bits and pieces. Okay?' He got to his feet.

I had an instant ghastly picture in my mind of Soo laid out on a wooden slab while a man stood over her with an axe, her arms stretched out and pinioned ready for the blow. I felt sickened, and glancing across at Gareth I saw his face was ashen. What must have been going on in his mind at that moment I cannot think, Soo's life balanced against those years of being trained to carry out the orders of his naval superiors, and all the time the knowledge that forces beyond his control were moving inexorably to a point of crisis. And if he gave in to Evans's demands I had the feeling he would be doing so on the basis that, whatever he did, he and his men were doomed to extinction.

Evans glanced at the clock on the wall, then at his watch. 'Okay, so you're on local time. It's now 21.53. If you're not fetching your anchor by 22.10 –'

'I can't do it. Not to an exact deadline.' Once again he was arguing that the state of the ship's engines made an immediate move impossible. I don't know when he decided to do what he finally did, but it must have been at about this point, and he must have been something of a natural actor – maybe that was the Celt in him – but he did manage eventually to convince Evans there was a problem with the engines. I think what finally did it was an open discussion over the telephone with Robin Makewate, his Marine Engineer Officer, which ended with him saying, 'Half an hour then. I'll have them standing by the anchor at 22.15. I want power on that one engine by 22.15 at the latest. Without fail, Robin . . . Yes, that's an order. Do it how you like, but get one of them going by then or we're in trouble.'

He put the phone down and turned to Evans. 'That's the best I can do. I presume you didn't come on board without making some provision against my detaining you here?'

'Correct. VHF contact.' He patted the sagging pocket of his camouflage jacket. 'If I don't report in on the hour . . .' He gave a little shrug. 'But don't worry, I'll be on to them in a minute. Meantime, you want to know how we hand the woman back. Since you've got Steele here, and she's his wife, it better be to him.'

They discussed it between themselves, no reference to me and Soo treated as though she was some sort of parcel that was proving difficult to deliver. In the end it was agreed that Evans and I should be landed on Bloody Island to await the frigate's departure. As soon as it was out past the island of Lazareto, Evans would radio his base contact and Soo would be delivered to me in exchange for Evans. 'I'll have the Sergeant of Marines issue you with a gun,' Gareth said to me. 'You'll have to sign for it, of course, and somehow it will have to be returned.' He turned back to Evans. 'I take it you're not armed.'

Evans laughed. 'Not much point, one man against a whole ship's company.'

Gareth nodded and dabbed a number on the intercom system. 'Have Sergeant Simmonds report to my cabin and tell the First Lieutenant I want a word with him.' He went to the curtain and pulled it back. 'Escort Mr Evans to the head of the ladder,' he told Davison. 'He'll be sending his boat back to Cala Llonga. And have our own launch stand by to take both these gentlemen across to Bloody Island.

After that have it brought on board and stowed.' He turned to Evans. 'Whilst you're out in the open I suggest you take the opportunity to report in to your base that you're okay.'

Evans stood there for a moment, frowning, his eyes fixed on Gareth who had already turned back at the sound of a voice calling him over the intercom. It was Mault and he told him, 'I want the ship closed up ready for sea, Number One. We'll be getting under way as soon as MEO can give us the necessary power.'

'We've received new orders, have we?' Mault's voice was a mixture of curiosity and doubt.

'You've just received *my* orders, Number One, so get on with it.' There was a crisp finality in the way he said it that even the thickest-skinned could not fail to understand. 'We'll be out of here by 22.15 at the latest.' He switched off before his second-in-command could ask any more awkward questions and turned back to Evans. 'When you report in, tell your people to bring Mrs Steele down to Cala Llonga ready to take her out to Bloody Island. I don't know how far away she is, but I'd like her down on the beach there before we sail.'

Evans nodded. 'No problem. We'll have her waiting for you there. Then you can see her and identify her through your glasses. Okay?' And he added, 'There's some countries I been in where death is a way of life, as you might say. So don't fool around with me, either of you, see.' He turned on his heel then and left the cabin just as Sergeant Simmonds arrived.

Gareth told him to take me down to the armoury and issue me with whatever weapon he thought most suitable for holding a dangerous man hostage for half an hour or so. He was quite close to me when he said that and he gripped hold of my arm. 'Don't let him jump you. Just keep your distance and the gun on him the whole time.' His fingers were digging into me, his hand trembling. God help me, I thought, he was scared of the man. 'Just keep your distance,' he said again. 'All the time you're alone

295

with him on the island. Particularly at the moment of exchange. If it gets to that, if they actually bring her out to the island, then he'll have those two thugs of his to back him up, so don't let your eyes stray. He'll be waiting for that, the moment when Soo moves towards you.' And he added, 'Both of you held as hostage would complicate things.'

His hand relaxed his grip on my arm. He turned and picked up his cap. 'I'm going up to the bridge now. When you're armed, you can join Pat at the gangway. By then the launch will be waiting to run you over to the island. And remember – watch him, every moment.'

CHAPTER TWO

'Zulu One Zero, this is Zulu One. Come in, Zulu One Zero. Over . . . Yes, I've been put ashore as agreed on the island. You can bring the woman down as soon as the frigate starts to fetch its anchor . . . Yes, of course they did. It's the husband. That fellow Steele . . . Sure he's got a gun, one of those Stirling sub-machine pistols, but I don't know how good he is with it . . .' He glanced across at me, his teeth gleaming in the light of my torch. 'That's right, wait till you see the frigate's stern light disappear beyond Lazareto, then put her in the speedboat. You can come out for me soon as the Colonel reports he is locked on. Okay? . . . Good. Out.'

He turned to me, his teeth still showing white in that strange smile of his. 'Relax, for Chris'sake. Another half-hour and with any luck you'll have your wife back and I'll be gone.' He slipped the radiophone back into the pocket of his jacket and came down from the ruined wall on which he had been standing. I backed away, watching him, and he laughed as he came towards me. 'Think I'm going to jump you? No way. I've seen the silverware in that room of yours above the chandlery.' He walked right past me, out into the open where he had a clear view of the frigate. The launch was just going alongside and at the same moment all the upper-deck lights that gave the outline of the ship such a fairy look went suddenly out.

He walked past the dig, out to the northern end of the hospital's long seaward-facing block. From there the frigate was no more than three cables away and we could hear the voices of the men on the fo'c's'le as they waited for the order to weigh anchor. Evans lit a cigarette, his features picked out in the flare of the match. 'Suppose Gareth boy takes his tin can out and you don't get your wife back – what then, eh?' He blew out a stream of smoke, watching me.

I didn't say anything. The man was built like a tank, all hard bone and muscle. How many shots would it take to kill him? I had never fired a machine pistol before and I tried to remember what I'd been told. Was it high they fired, or low?

'Well?' He was grinning at me, but his eyes were cold and calculating in the torchlight, as though he were trying to make up his mind whether I was capable of shooting him down in cold blood.

A searchlight stabbed out from somewhere by the radio mast on the high point of La Mola, the beam blinding me. He could have rushed me then, but he had turned his head away and was staring out towards the frigate, now a black shape in silhouette. The clank of the anchor cable sounded loud in the stillness as they shortened in. The clanking stopped and in the searchlight's brilliant beam I could see the chain itself hanging straight up and down from the bows. Shortly after that the hum of machinery told us they had got one of the two turbines going again.

'Any minute now,' I said, my voice sounding strained. I only said it to relieve the tension.

Evans was still staring intently at the ship and I heard him mutter, 'It's against all his training . . .' He swung round on me. 'You reck'n he'll take her out, or is he up to something?' He started towards me. 'If you and he . . .'

I told him to stay where he was, my finger back on the trigger. 'Don't make me fire this thing.'

I don't think he heard me, for he had turned and was staring out again across the dark water. 'Like I said, it's against all his training. And if he thinks he's going to lie off the entrance till you've got your wife back –'

'You've been over all that,' I said. 'Once those guns can be brought to bear . . .'

'The guns — yes.' He nodded. 'A direct hit and he'd be blown out of the water.' He shook his head, standing very still. 'To throw it all away for that woman.' He glanced round at me, the teeth showing white again. 'No offence, but Christ! I don't understand.'

'Then you've never been in love,' I said.

He laughed. It was more like a guffaw. 'A four-letter word or a three-letter word, what the hell? It's sex, isn't it, and my mother taught him about that on board the *Betty Ann*. Didn't he tell you?' The clank of the anchor chain started up again. 'In a mud berth.' He seemed to find that funny, laughing still as he watched the ship. 'Quite a girl, my mother. But to throw away his whole career, everything he's worked for . . . Or is he scared? Is that why he's getting his anchor up, scared of being blown to hell if he stays?'

He looked at me for a moment, then his gaze switched back again to the black shape of the ship, his body quite still, almost tense. The navigation lights were on now, the anchor just coming clear of the water. The frigate was beginning to move. 'Poor little bugger!' I heard him murmur. Then he turned on me suddenly. 'Suppose I don't let her go? You going to gun me down?' The searchlight was switched off and I heard him laugh, everything suddenly very dark. I stepped back, expecting him to rush me, and tripped over a stone.

'He's going astern,' Evans said.

I switched on my torch again. He hadn't moved, but now his head was turned back, his gaze fixed on the dim shape out there on the water. The frigate's bows were swinging, the stern coming towards us. The sound of the engines suddenly increased. Or was it just one engine? The sound died abruptly as the ship lost way. Was there really something wrong with her machinery after all? The sound increased again, the bows swinging. It was as though they were having difficulty with the steering. I could see the stern light, the ship again coming straight towards us and growing steadily larger.

Several times she started to go ahead, but each time she veered to port, finally entering the narrows on the north side of Bloody Island stern-first. It wasn't exactly the most direct route if he was making out to sea, but it seemed it was only at slow astern they could steer a reasonably straight course.

Evans followed them back along the north shore of the island as far as the dig. I kept about twenty paces behind him. By this time the frigate was so close I was looking straight into the bridge, and in the brief moments I dared take my eyes off him, I could actually identify individual officers. Gareth was there and I saw him slip out of the captain's chair and move to the front of the bridge. Mault followed him.

The next time I glanced at the bridge the two of them seemed to be arguing, and they had been joined by Peter Craig. Evans had now crossed the dig and was standing by the beacon, staring at the frigate, which was then level with us, the slightly waved metal side of her gliding past within biscuit-toss. I stopped, and as the bridge came level with me I saw Robin Makewatc had joincd thc other three. At that moment Mault turned and walked off the bridge.

I caught a movement out of the corner of my eye and half turned. Evans had shifted his position and was looking behind him, towards Cala Figuera. I heard it then, the buzz-saw sound of an outboard coming nearer. At the same time *Medusa*'s stern came clear of the narrows and began to swing towards us. There was a great threshing under the counter and she checked just in time, moving slowly ahead, her bows swinging all the time to port.

Evans left his post by the beacon and came towards me. 'I should have stayed on board.'

I motioned him to keep his distance, the gun pointed at his stomach. 'Why?'

'Then I'd have some idea what the hell's going on.'

The sound of the outboard died, but I was barely conscious of it, my eyes half on Evans, half on the frigate, which was now going astern again and swinging more sharply. In this way it turned itself completely round until it was lying just off the landing place with its bows pointing almost directly at the big hotel above our house. 'Has he really got engine trouble?'

I didn't say anything, wondering about that glimpse I had had of Mault arguing with Gareth on the bridge.

The frigate was beginning to go ahead again. I thought she was endeavouring to round the island and head seaward through the wider southern passage, but the bows started to swing again so that it looked as though the whole grey bulk of her would land up stern-first in the hospital ruins.

Evans was hurrying now as he skirted the dig, took the path to the landing place, then turned off on the track that circled the old hospital building. It was brighter here, the frigate outlined against the lights of Villa Carlos. Water swirled at her stern, small waves rushing against the rocks. Evans had stopped. I think, like me, he was too astonished to do anything but stare at the dark shape coming closer, the bows swinging clear, but the low flat stern, with its flight deck and hangar, closing the rocks just south of our boat landing. She was coming towards us with no check, the hum of the one engine, the suck of the prop, the waves beating at the shore, all getting louder.

The grinding crunch of her grounding on the rocks was a rising cacophony of sound that seemed to go on and on, the stern rising till it was so close it looked from where I stood as though Evans could step across on to the deck itself. Then suddenly everything was still, a quietness gradually descending over the scene, the propeller bedded against rock, the water subsiding to the stillness of a balmy Mediterranean night. 'The silly bloody idiot!' The anger of Evans's voice was tinged with something else.

Resignation? I wasn't sure. And there were other voices now, from on board the frigate. Men tumbling up from below, out on to the deck to see what had happened, and Gareth standing there in the open wing door of the bridge on the port side, standing still as stone as though shocked into immobility.

It was like that for a moment, a blurred picture of disaster recorded by the eye's retina and made strange by the darkness and the lights beyond, the ruined hospital standing over it all like the mirror image of the stranding. Then Gareth moved, the upper-deck broadcast system blaring orders. The lights came on again, the ship's outline illuminated for all the world to see that she was ashore, her stern smashed into the rocks. God! What he must be feeling!

I knew who it was running up from the landing point before she reached me. I heard her panting and at the same time Evans had whipped out his radiophone and was talking into it, passing the word that the frigate was aground.

'He did it on purpose.' She caught hold of my arm. 'I saw it, Mike. I was right there in the boat. Christ! I thought he was going to drive her straight over me.' Her mouth was wide, her teeth white in the frigate's lights and those big eyes of hers almost starting out of her head. 'Why? Why did he do it?'

'Where have you been?' I asked her.

'Looking for Soo. But why for God's sake?' She was staring at me. 'I didn't find her. I don't know where they've taken her. Nobody seems to know.' And she said urgently, 'What will happen to him? It's a court martial, isn't it – running your ship aground? The Navy won't stand for that.'

'Probably not,' I said. The ship's decks were alive with men now and Gareth was down at the hangar doors, Mault with him. The sense of activity and purpose was fascinating to watch as the hangar door was slid back to reveal the dark interior of it stacked with wooden cases and all sorts of weapons, some that looked like rocket-launchers.

That was when he grabbed her. Fool that I was, I hadn't registered the fact that he should have been standing in dark silhouette against the light. But instead of being in full view, he suddenly appeared out of the shadows to my right. I heard Petra gasp, and as I turned and flashed my torch, the blade of a knife flicked in the beam, a steely glint pointing straight at her throat, his face, hard as rock, right beside hers as she opened her mouth wide and began to scream, her left arm twisted up behind her as he frog-marched her slowly backwards.

He didn't bother to tell me to drop the gun. He knew I wouldn't shoot as long as he was holding her as a shield. 'Don't move.' The order was hissed at me through those big teeth. 'Stay where you are and she'll be all right.' He was backing on to the path leading to the landing. 'And tell your wife's lover, he's just signed his death warrant. Hers too.'

He kept Petra between himself and me all the way back to the track that ran past the tent and down to the landing place. I didn't dare move. I had a feeling he was a desperate man now and capable of anything, even cold-blooded murder if it served his purpose. And then the incredible happened. The flap of the tent was pushed aside and Lennie appeared.

He stood there, stretching and yawning. I don't know whether he was still drunk, or just half-asleep, but it took a moment for the scene to register with him. Then his eyes were suddenly wide with shock as he saw, first the ship, then Petra in the grip of Evans as he backed down the path.

He was like that for an instant, his eyes wide. Then they narrowed, and in the same instant he moved, an instinctive, almost reflex action, moved with extraordinary speed, so that Evans was quite unprepared, Lennie's fist slamming into his face, knocking him backwards. 'Out of the way, girl!' He was moving after Evans and she just stood there in a daze, blocking his path.

· It almost cost him his life. She moved, but too late, Evans pulling himself to his feet again and brushing past her in a crouching run. The knife flashed as Lennie lashed out at him, and the next thing I saw was the Australian staggering backwards, clutching at his face and blood spurting between his fingers.

The knife slashed again and he went down, a strangled screaming like a trapped rabbit. Then Evans turned and ran, dropping out of sight almost immediately as he made for the landing place. I didn't shout. I didn't go after him. My concern was for Lennie. I couldn't tell whether he was alive or dead. He just lay there on a bed of wild flowers at the edge of the path, blood spurting from the loose flap of his cheek, where the knife had slashed it open, and a dark patch beginning to spread over his shirt as blood welled up from somewhere not far from his heart.

Petra moved to my side, her eyes wild as she grabbed at my arm. She was sobbing. But then she was suddenly silent, squatting down, her bare knee bent against a rock, still as a statue, horror-struck as she stared at the blood on Lennie's face, the ghastly cheek flap. 'Oh, my God!' He was no longer screaming, his body quite still. 'Is he dead?'

I shook my head. Blood was welling out over his shirt and I thought I could detect a slight movement of his chest. 'You look after him,' I said. 'I'll see if the ship will take him.'

It was then, as I rose to my feet, that I heard the outboard start, the sound of it rising as Petra's inflatable shot into view, hugging the rocks. I glimpsed it briefly as Evans skidded it round the north-western bulge of the island. Then it was lost to view as he ran it under the beacon and into the narrows. I turned back to the ship then, and as I hurried up the path under the hospital walls, I met two naval ratings lugging a case of rockets. Others passed me as I ran to the frigate's stern, shouting for the Captain.

Nobody took any notice of me for a moment. They had rigged a gangway from the stern to the top of a flat rock close by the path, the scene chaotic as almost the whole crew swarmed like ants from ship to shore, humping equipment from the hangar, listening gear and telephones, as well as rocket-launchers and ammunition. Orders were being shouted, arms issued, cases ripped open and ammunition got ready.

In the end it was Peter Craig who answered my call for help and, after some delay, he managed to find the medical orderly who finally got Lennie on to a stretcher and carried him on board. I wasn't allowed to go with him. Craig was adamant about that. And when I asked for Gareth, he told me the Captain was in the Communications Office and there was absolutely no chance of my seeing him until the situation had clarified itself.

'They'll do what they can for him,' he assured me. 'We've no doctor on board. You know that, I think, but those two did a good job on John Kent. Looked after him until we could get him ashore. They'll do the same for your man, and we'll get him ashore and into the military hospital as soon as possible. That is,' he added, 'if any of us are alive by morning.'

He smiled at me a little uncertainly. 'Remember what I said to you on the bridge that night, about the Captain carrying a weight of responsibility few of the officers realised. Well, now they do. We're in the thick of it, and if you or I are around in the morning, then by God I'll stand you a drink.' He tried to smile again, to make a joke of it, but it didn't work. Instead, he clapped me on the back before hurrying off up the gangway to continue supervising the unloading.

Back at the camp I found Petra busy preparing a meal. I think she was doing it more to distract herself from what was happening than from any want of food. 'Is he all right?'

'He's alive,' I said. 'They'll get him ashore when things

305

have sorted themselves out. Some time tomorrow presumably. Meanwhile, I imagine they'll stitch him up as best they can.'

She poured me some wine. It was good dark Rioja, the colour of blood. I drank it down at a gulp. 'They're a bit preoccupied right now,' I told her, and at that moment, as though to emphasise the point, the lights that lit the outline of the frigate went suddenly out, everything dark again.

She nodded. All around us we could hear voices, the clink of metal on metal, the tramp of feet. 'They've started to dig in,' she said.

I nodded and poured myself some more wine. I was suddenly very tired. Tension probably. I had never really contemplated death before. At other times, when I had been in danger, it had all happened too fast. Even that time Ahmed Bey had been killed, it had been very sudden, the Italian boat coming at us out of the darkness, and later, the days at sea and the heat, the trek along the African shore, getting weaker and weaker, it hadn't been the same at all.

Now I had been given virtually the exact time of death, the rendezvous approximately midnight fourteen miles off the coast. Fourteen miles. Just over half an hour at full speed. Say another half-hour while they argued it out over radio. I was remembering suddenly that Gareth had said he had a civilian on board who was fluent in Russian. Probable time of engagement, therefore, would be around 01.00. And my watch showed it was already almost midnight.

An hour to live! Perhaps a little more. But not another dawn.

If the decision had been taken to occupy Mahon harbour, then the opposition of a puny and obsolete RN frigate would be brushed aside in a holocaust of missiles. The whole of Bloody Island would be blasted to hell. Evans was right. His half-brother and the crew of his ship were doomed to extinction. So was I. So was Petra.

I looked across at her, wondering if she understood. 'Have you got any more brandy?' I asked her. 'Lennie finished that bottle of Soberano.'

She stared at me dully, her mouth turned slightly down at the corners, the big capable hands gripped on the edge of the table. I think she knew all right, for after a moment she nodded and got to her feet, opening the lid of a store box and rummaging around inside. She came up with a bottle, looked at the label, and said, 'No Soberano. It's Fundador. Will that do?' She was suddenly smiling. She knew damn well anything would do. 'You going to get drunk?' She handed me the bottle.

I shrugged as I screwed the cap off. 'Possibly.'

She sat down again, finished her wine and pushed the glass across to me. 'How long have we got?'

'Long enough.' I wasn't going to tell her how long it would be. 'In any case, a lot can happen . . .' I poured us both a good measure. '*Salud!*' And I added under my breath, 'Here's to the dawn!'

We were on our second brandy, and I was wondering in a vague sort of way whether it would be better to die in a drunken stupor or whether the two of us should lie together and die naked with the warmth of our bodies to give us comfort at the moment of impacting oblivion, when there was the sound of footsteps outside the tent and a voice said, 'Mr Steele?'

'Yes?' I went to the flap and pulled it back. Petty Officer Jarvis was standing there. 'Captain says if you and the lady would care to go ashore, he'll have the launch sent round to the landing point.'

I looked at my watch. It was now well past midnight – 00.37. The Russian ships could already be off La Mola, approaching the entrance to Port Mahon. Any moment things would start happening and he was giving Petra and myself a way out. And yet I stood there, feeling as though I'd been struck dumb. It was a lifeline he was offering us and I hesitated. Having braced myself for what was about to happen, having come to terms, or something very near to it, with the fact that I was about to die and would not live to see the sun rise, the offered reprieve seemed an affront to my manhood. Perversely, I found myself on the point of refusing. It was as though I would be running away, revealing myself to be a coward. It was only the thought of Petra that stopped me. Or was it? Was I really a coward seeking justification, an excuse for acceptance?

'Please thank him,' I told Jarvis. My mouth felt dry. 'Tell him I accept his offer. I have to find my wife. Tell him that. And Miss Callis should undoubtedly be got off the island.' And I added, 'Is there any chance I can have a word with him before we leave?'

'I doubt it, sir. He's in the Ops Room. At least that's where he phoned me from. And I gathered from his manner things were a bit hectic. A lot going on, if you understand my meaning, sir.'

'Yes, of course,' I said. 'Only to be expected.'

'Five minutes, sir. The launch will be there in five minutes, probably less. Okay?' He didn't wait to see my nod, but hurried off back to the ship.

Petra was already searching around frantically for her archaeological material, scrabbling up notebooks, rolls of film, dumping them in a holdall. I grabbed a sweater and told her to hurry. 'We've no time to lose.'

'My thesis,' she said. 'There's a draft of my thesis somewhere. I must have it.' And then she stopped. 'Oh, my God! It's in the hypostile. I left it there. Won't be a minute.'

She was ducking out of the tent when I seized hold of her arm. 'Forget it,' I told her. 'They'll hit this island any minute now. Alive, you can redraft it. Dead, it won't matter anyway.'

She was trying to wrench herself free, but at my words she stopped struggling and stared at me, appalled. 'D'you mean that? D'you mean it's – now?'

'Any minute,' I said. 'There's a Russian cruiser, several other warships. They should be off the entrance now.'

She came with me then, pulling on a loose cardigan as we hurried down to the landing point. The launch was already there, two sailors holding it alongside the rock with boathooks, Leslie Masterton in the stern, the engine ticking over. He took Petra's holdall, helped her in, and as I followed her, he gave the order to push the launch clear.

'What's the latest news?' I asked him as we pulled away from the rocks.

'I don't know, sir. Everybody's at action stations –' He rolled the words off his tongue as though savouring them with excited anticipation. For a moment he concentrated on swinging the launch under the frigate's bows. Then, when we were headed for Cala Figuera, he added, 'But the Captain hasn't said anything. There's been no announcement. So I don't know anything really, nobody does. All we've been told is to stay on maximum alert until we're ordered otherwise. A lot of the boys are off the ship and among the ruins of that hospital. But you know that. Seems the Captain's expecting some sort of an attack.' He was strung up, the words pouring out of him. 'I've been allocated the launch.' He grinned. 'Didn't expect the opportunity of a run ashore.'

I glanced at Petra and she smiled. I think we were both wondering whether Gareth had done it purposely, an excuse for getting this pleasant kid out of the firing line. I pulled back the sleeve of my sweater and looked at my watch. It was already 01.11. Eleven minutes after the time I thought they might be steaming in through the entrance.

It was then that one of the sailors said quietly, 'Ship on the port bow, sir. Close inshore.' He pointed and I could see it then, a dim shape under the Villa Carlos cliff line momentarily outlined by the double red flash of the light on the point. It was a small vessel, moving slowly and very low in the water. 'Looks like that customs launch,' Masterton said and throttled back until we were barely moving. Even so, the vessel, heading in towards Mahon itself, would cut right across our bows. We lay there without lights, waiting. And when I suggested that we make a dash for it, the young midshipman said, without even hesitating to consider the possibility, 'Sorry, but my orders are to take no chances and return immediately if challenged.'

We could see the launch quite clearly now each time the Villa Carlos light flashed red. She was low in the water because she was crowded with people. Soon we could hear the sound of the engine. She would cross our bows at a distance of about two hundred metres, and lying quite still, with no lights behind us, there was just a chance we would remain unseen.

But then, as the launch was approaching the point where she would cross our bows and we could see that the pack of men standing on the deck were most of them armed, a string of lights appeared behind us on the road above Cala Lladró. We were suddenly in silhouette against them. Somebody on the customs launch shouted, several of them were pointing at us, and then there was the flash and crack of a rifle fired. I didn't hear the bullet whistle past. It was lost in the roar of our engine as Masterton gunned it and swung the wheel, turning the launch round and heading back towards Bloody Island. I caught a glimpse of some sort of struggle on the deck of the customs launch. There was the crackle of small-arms fire, spurts of flame, splinters flying off the woodwork of our stern, a glass window shattered, and little geysers bouncing past us as bullets slapped the water close alongside.

The moment of shock passed, the customs launch receding into the distance until it was finally lost in the dark of Mahon's harbour. There seemed no reason then why we shouldn't resume our course for Cala Figuera, but when I suggested this to Masterton I found myself faced, not by a kid, but by Midshipman Masterton, a budding officer to whom orders were orders. He had been told to take no chances and return if he was challenged. He had been challenged. Not only that, he'd been fired on, and though

I argued that the customs launch was now out of sight and no danger, he said, 'I don't know who they were on that launch, but they were armed and they opened fire. Before we can make your quay at Cala Figuera they could be ashore and somebody on the phone to the military.'

Nothing I or Petra could say would change his mind. The nice cheerful face had suddenly become obstinate, his manner indicating the implacability of naval training. I think he was quite capable of initiative, but not when he had been given specific orders. 'I'll have to report back.' He said that twice. 'Then, if I'm instructed to proceed . . .'

But he received no such instructions. We ran straight alongside *Medusa* and it was the First Lieutenant, looking down on us from the bridge wing, who received his report. 'Are you sure it was the customs launch?'

'I think so, sir.'

'And crowded with men. How many would you say?'

'Can't be sure, sir.' Masterton's voice was pitched a little higher now that he was being de-briefed by his senior officer. 'Fifty. Sixty. Quite a lot, sir.'

Mault asked me then. 'What do you say, Mr Steele?'

'No idea,' I replied. 'It was too dark. But she was low in the water so I should think Mr Masterton's estimate is about right.'

'Good.' He seemed pleased, but when I suggested that we could now proceed to Cala Figuera, he shook his head. 'Sorry. No time now. We may need our launch.' And he ordered Masterton to land us, then return and tie up alongside pending further orders. I tried to argue with him, but he turned on me and said, 'If you're so urgent to get away from here . . .' He checked himself, then leaned out and said, 'Has it occurred to you, Mr Steele, that if it weren't for you and that wife of yours we wouldn't be in the mess we are?' He stared down at me, then turned abruptly and disappeared inside the bridge, leaving me wondering how he knew about Soo. Had Gareth let it slip out, arguing with the man as he backed the frigate through the narrows, or later when he'd put her on the rocks?

I was thinking about that as the sailors pushed off and we manœuvred round the rocks and into the loading point. Five minutes later we were back at the tent and as I held the flap back for Petra, I noticed the lights of at least half a dozen vehicles moving west along the main road from Villa Carlos. They were evenly spaced and looked like a military convoy. I thought perhaps they were re-inforcements for the defence of the airport, or perhaps for a dawn offensive towards Ciudadela. Their real significance never occurred to me.

In the dim interior of the tent it was as though we had never left it, the chairs, the table, the unwashed plates, the glasses and the bottle of Fundador. 'Damn that bastard Mault.' I reached for my glass, which still had some brandy in it. I was angry and frustrated, and when Petra said, 'It's not his fault, everybody must be very tense by now,' I told her to go to hell, downed the rest of my drink and walked out. I wasn't only angry with Mault, I was angry with myself. I should have handled it better. I should have insisted on seeing Gareth. I had the chance then, whilst we'd been tied up alongside, but I'd been so shattered by Mault's words, his obvious hostility, that I hadn't thought of it. And there was an element of truth in what he had said. That's what made it so hard to swallow. Putting his ship aground had been the one action Gareth could take that would effectively make Soo totally ineffective as a hostage, the one way he could save her life and at the same time carry out his orders to stay in Mahon under all circumstances. The only other thing he could have done was to put to sea, and that was out of the question.

Thinking about it, I almost fell into a newly dug slit trench. A Scots voice cursed me for a clumsy bastard, a hand gripping hold of my ankle. 'Luke where ye're fuckin' goin', laddie. There's some of us doon here that are still alive, ye noo.'

I was in the graveyard area and there were four of them sprawled on the ground with a couple of hand-held rocket-launchers. From where they lay they could see into the steep-sided little bay draped with the pale glimmer of villas that was Cala Llonga. I asked them if any vessel had put out in the last half-hour. But they had seen nothing, so clearly the customs launch had come either from Lazareto Island or from the La Mola peninsula itself. Perhaps even from Cala Pedrera on the other side of the Mahon entrance.

I squatted there talking to them for several minutes. Two of them were leading seamen whom I had met on the bridge during the trip out from Malta, one of them had brought me kai that night. But they couldn't tell me anything I didn't already know. They had had a word with the Captain, they said, just after midnight. Apparently Gareth had made a tour of all the positions established round the island and in the hospital ruins, but it had been more of a morale booster. He hadn't told them anything very much, only warned them that if they were attacked, it would all happen very quickly. He had also said jokingly that if they weren't attacked, they'd probably be stuck out there all night. 'I asked him straight oot,' the Scots lad said, 'wha' are we expectin' then, but he was no' verra communicative. He just said, if it comes, make cairtin ye've said yer prayers. An' he wasna jokin'. He was daid sairious.'

The time was then ten minutes short of two o'clock and still nothing had happened. I started back towards the tent, but just before I reached it, I saw a little group coming down the gangway from *Medusa*'s stern. With no lights, I couldn't see who they were, but they headed towards me along the path under the hospital walls, so I waited. It was Gareth, setting out on a second tour of inspection. Mault was with him, and Sergeant Simmonds. I don't think he saw me at first. He was walking with his head bent, not saying anything to his companions, as though lost in his own thoughts, and when I spoke his head came up with a startled jerk and he looked at me, tight-lipped and very tense. 'Sorry you didn't make it ashore,' he said.

I asked him what was going on in the outside world and he just shook his head. He would let me know, he said, as soon as he had any definite news. And he added that, until he knew for certain what the situation was, there was no question of his risking the launch in another attempt to take us into Cala Figuera. And when I pressed him, saying that something had to be done about Soo, he just looked at me and said in a voice that was dead and without emotion, 'Your wife is only one of many factors I have to take into consideration.' And he added, in that same dead tone, as though he were talking about something quite remote and impersonal, 'In the overall scale of things I'm afraid she ranks very low, however important she may be to you, and to me.' He muttered something about being in a hurry – 'A lot on my plate at the moment.' And he nodded briefly, brushing past me.

I went back to the tent then. Nothing else I could do. With no boat, Petra and I were marooned on the island, and we just sat there, waiting. It was long past the time when the warships that were supposed to be supporting Fuxá's coup d'état should have been entering Mahon harbour, and though I fiddled around with Petra's little radio, all I could get was dance music. God knows what was going on in the world outside of Bloody Island.

All around us there were the sounds of men settling in for the night in improvised trenches or in the stone walls of the hospital itself. And though I went out and talked to some of them, I couldn't find anyone who knew any more than we did. In fact, I suppose the only people who could have told us what was going on in the outside world were Gareth and his communications team. I learned afterwards that, apart from those two quick tours of the island's makeshift defences, he spent the whole night there, sifting endlessly through the mass of reports, signals, news-

314

flashes, and speculative comment from all around the world picked up by the ship's antennae.

Back in the tent again I found Petra sitting there, not drinking, not doing anything, just sitting there with a shut look on her face. I said something to her. I don't remember what. But she didn't answer. She had withdrawn into some secret world of her own. And then, suddenly, she got to her feet, a quick, decisive movement. 'I'm tired,' she said. 'God! I'm tired. No point in sitting here waiting for something to happen. I'm going to bed.'

I was desperately tired myself, my mind seemingly no longer capable of constructive thought. The picture of that room, the little dog, and Evans – the way he had talked about sending her to Gareth in bits and pieces. Christ! What a hell of a mess! All I could think of was the poor girl out there somewhere in the hands of those bastards.

In the end I found a spare sleeping bag and followed Petra's example. But before curling myself up in it, I went outside again. It was quite chill now, a whisper of a breeze coming down from the high ground above the harbour, the scent of wild flowers on the air, and as I stood there, relieving myself, I was conscious of the bodies all around me. It was very strange, hearing nothing, but knowing they were there, like the ghosts of all those buried dead.

But then the glow of a cigarette, showing for an instant under the hospital wall, brought my mind back to reality. Away to the right I could just make out the dim shape of a sailor standing in silhouette against the stars, and when I climbed to the top of a rock there was the outline of the frigate, stern-on and not a light showing. Somebody coughed, a hastily suppressed sound, and as I went back into the tent I heard a clink of metal on stone somewhere out beyond the dig.

It was almost four. Another hour and dawn would be starting to break. Perhaps it was the coffee, or perhaps I was just too damned tired, but I couldn't seem to sleep, my mind going round in circles, worrying about Soo, about the future, about what it would be like if she were killed.

Then suddenly I was being shaken violently and Petra's voice was saying, 'Wake up! Wake up, Mike! It's all over.'

'What the devil are you talking about? What's all over?' I sat up so abruptly my head caught her on the chin. The flap of the tent was drawn back, the sun blazing in. Blinking in the glare of it, I asked her what time it was.

'Just after ten and there's three Spanish warships steaming past us.'

I wriggled out of the sleeping bag, slipped my shoes on and went outside. They made a brave sight, two destroyers and what looked like some sort of a logistic ship, the sun blazing full on them, outsize Spanish flags streaming from the ensign staffs on the ships' sterns and the water of the harbour mirror-calm ahead of them, Mahon blindingly white above. The tanker was back in Cala Figuera, moving in to the fuel depot with the tug in attendance.

It really did look as though Petra was right and it was all over. But the Navy was clearly taking no chances, the frigate lying there against the rocks, silent and watchful, no movement on deck and only the hum of machinery to show that the inside of it was alive with men. No movement on the island either, only the occasional whisper of a voice to indicate that there were sailors there, standing to their weapons and waiting.

I clambered up on to the ruined wall above the dig, where I had an uninterrupted view eastwards towards La Mola. No sign of the Libyan freighter, the water flat calm and empty of anything except a small boat trawling for fish. The slit trench with the Scots leading seaman I had talked to in the night was quite close, but all they could tell me was that they had heard the freighter fetching its anchor sometime around three-thirty, just after they had seen the lights of a dozen or more vehicles moving away from La Mola along the road above Cala Llonga. They couldn't tell me whether the freighter had headed seaward or gone back to Mahon.

They were far more relaxed than when I had talked to them in the early hours. *Medusa*'s galleys had produced a hot breakfast for them at the usual time, the ground still strewn with mess tins and eating irons. They thought it wouldn't be long now before they were allowed to stand down.

I was still in my underpants and I went back to the tent to get myself dressed. Petra was cooking us some breakfast. I remember that very distinctly, the smell of bacon and eggs, and sitting there in the sunshine, neither of us talking. I don't know how many men there were around us, but the sense of hushed expectancy was almost overpowering.

Then suddenly the frigate's broadcast system was blaring out *Rule Britannia*, men erupting on to the deck, the island around us coming alive as word was passed to stand down, everybody talking at once, a roar of voices mingled with the high quick laughter that comes of nervous relief.

I joined a party lugging equipment and the debris of a meal down to the stern of the ship. There was an officer there, a man I hadn't seen before. He refused to let me on board and I was forced to scribble a note to Gareth on a message pad. But even as a seaman went for'ard to deliver it, I saw Gareth, dressed in what looked like his best uniform, scrambling down a rope ladder and jumping into the launch, which then headed for the harbour where the Spanish warships were anchored close off the Naval Base. I would now have to wait until he had paid his respects to the Spanish naval commander, and even then he might not feel able to send me ashore.

Shortly after that I walked out to the dig and stood by the red-flashing beacon, staring across the narrow strip of water to the steep rise of the land beyond with villas perched white on the slopes. Where would they have taken her? Pulling out suddenly like that, what for Christ's sake would they have done with her? They would hardly have taken her in that convoy of vehicles that had left from La Mola in the dark of night. Or would they?

I sat down on a rock, my mind going round and round, gnawing at the problem. And in the sunshine, with wild flowers in every crevice, I saw her as she had been back in Malta when I had first met her. A picnic on Gozo, her body lying on a rock all golden warm like the limestone of the buildings on the hill above caught in the slanting rays of a glorious sunset. And in that little trellis garden of her mother's, bougainvillaea and morning-glory, and the two of us dancing to that old portable gramophone, our bodies close and the moon full above the curved roof tiles. A world apart, the two of us hopelessly in love in the moonlight, not another thought in our heads, not a care in the world, our bodies tingling to the touch of our fingers, the ache for each other growing.

God in heaven! What had happened to us? To me? What had changed it?

Questions, questions, the result emotional torment and my heart reaching out to her. Surely to God two people who had been as close to each other as we had been then could make contact across the distance that now separated us. If I thought hard enough, if I could concentrate my mind sufficiently, surely I could evoke some response from her, some telepathic indication of where she was.

I was there by that beacon for a long time, alone with my thoughts, and right above me the Golden Farm to remind me of two other lovers. And then Petra came to say the launch had finally returned.

'Any message from the ship?' I asked her.

She shook her head and I stared at that narrow strip of water, wondering whether I could make it, picturing him back in his day cabin, his desk piled with urgent messages. In the circumstances, my note would hardly seem of great importance. Soo would either be dead or abandoned somewhere. Whichever it was, he had every reason to think a few more hours would make little difference.

I was in the tent, stripped to my underpants and stuffing my clothes, pipe, matches, keys, money, everything I might need ashore, into a plastic bag, when the flap was pulled back and I looked up to find Petty Officer Jarvis standing there. 'Captain's compliments, sir, and the launch is waiting to take you ashore.'

I shall always bless him for that. In the midst of all his problems he had read my note and understood my urgency, the depth of my feeling. I didn't attempt to see him. I just scribbled a note of thanks and handed it to Jarvis as he led me up the gangway on to the stern and for'ard to where the rope ladder was rigged. The same midshipman was in charge of the launch, and as we swung away from the frigate's side, I asked him what the news was. He looked at me, wide grey eyes in a serious face. 'News, sir? You haven't heard?' And when I told him it had been a long night and I had slept late, he grinned at me and said, 'They miffed off. The revolutionaries and those mercenaries who put that Fuschia chap in. The fleet, too – the fleet that was going to support the new government. It just faded off the radar screen. And all because of *Medusa*.'

'A Russian fleet, do you mean?'

'Yes, the Russians. The American Sixth Fleet is shadowing them.'

'Is that official?' I asked him. 'About the Russian and American fleets?' We had swung away from the ship's side and were heading for Cala Figuera, the note of the engine making it difficult to talk. 'Did you hear it on the news?'

He shook his head. 'I haven't had a chance to listen to the BBC, but that's what they're saying – saw them off all on our own, long before those Spanish ships arrived.' And he added, 'Now that he's back from seeing the Spanish admiral, I've no doubt the Captain will be making an announcement. I'd like to have heard that.' He gave an order to the helm, then turned back to me. 'You know him well, don't you, sir?' It was more a statement than a question and he didn't wait for me to answer. 'He's a super man. Never batted an eye all night, going the rounds, chatting and joking with everybody and all of us expecting to be blown out of the water any minute. Then, when it's all over, he has a thanksgiving in the wardroom.'

'When was that?'

'It was early, about 04.30. Just those on the ship. A few prayers, a hymn or two. All he told us then was that the situation had improved and we should give thanks to God.' The boy was smiling to himself, remembering the scene. '*Lead kindly light* . . . I can still hear him singing it in that fine voice of his. He's Welsh, you see.' And he grinned apologetically, embarrassed at being carried away and forgetting I would have known that. And when I asked him how the ship had come to land up on Bloody Island, he looked at me uncertainly, suddenly hesitant. But the excitement of events and his admiration for his Captain got the better of him. 'The buzz is he put her aground himself,' he said brightly.

'Deliberately?'

'I couldn't say, sir. I wasn't on the bridge. But that's what they're saying – so that there was no way they could shift us. We were committed then, you see, a Nato ship stuck there and prepared to fire at anything that didn't support the legitimate Spanish government and the Spanish King.'

I nodded. He wouldn't know about Soo, of course. None of them would, except Mault. At least I hoped he was the only one. For the time being anyway. The midshipman saw it solely in terms of naval tactics, the sort of move Nelson or Cochrane might have made, not realising that what Gareth had done was to take the one positive action that could nullify absolutely his half-brother's threats. God knows what it had cost him in mental anguish to take such a gamble, not just with Soo's life, but with his own, and with the lives of all his men. He had called Evans's bluff and he had won, and I was hearing it from this kid of a midshipman, who was standing there, starry-eyed and bubbling with excitement, as he told me how he had spent the first half of the night in charge of half a dozen

320

seamen on the hospital tower, acting as lookouts and armed with hand-held rocket-launchers.

It was hot as the launch slowed to run alongside our quay, the sun blazing out of a blue sky, the surface of the water oily-calm, and traffic moving on the steep road from the Martires Atlante to the Carrero Blanco. Everything looked so normal it was hard to believe that there had been several hours during the night when the future of Menorca had hung in the balance, the threat of hostilities looming.

And then I was ashore, the chandlery door open and Ramón coming out of the store in answer to my call. No, he had no news of the señora. I raced up the stairs. Somebody had cleared the place up, the maid I suppose. The telephone was still working. I sat down at the table by the window and rang the Renatos, but Manuela had no information about her. She suggested I ring the *Gobierno Militar*. Gonzalez had been there since early morning and might have heard something. But her husband was no longer there, and when I finally tracked him down at the *ayuntamiento*, he had heard nothing. I tried the *policia*, the *Guardia Civil*, finally in desperation I rang the Residencia Sanitaria. They had quite a few casualties in, but they were all men, including an Australian who had just been brought in from the English warship. When I asked how serious his injuries were, they said he had not yet been fully examined. If I liked to enquire a little later . . .

I said I would ring back in an hour's time, and then as a last resort tried to get through to Perez at the Naval Base, but the phone was engaged and when I finally did manage to reach his office, he was out and the officer who answered the phone had no idea when he would be back. I rang the Army then, out at La Mola, and to my surprise I was connected immediately with some sort of duty officer. He put me through to somebody in one of the casements, who said a woman had been seen with a group of the '*soldadi del revolución*', but where they had taken her he did not know. Needless to say he was not prepared to discuss what had happened the previous day nor even where she had been held.

All this took time and it was late afternoon before I had exhausted all possible sources of information and was forced to the conclusion that I would have to go out to Addaia, or wherever it was they had embarked, in the hope of finding somebody who had actually witnessed their departure. But first I needed a car. Mine had disappeared. I tried to borrow one, but everybody I rang was either out or their car was in use, and I couldn't hire one because my driving licence was in the pocket of my own car. In the end I persuaded the people who provided cars for tourists staying at the Port Mahon Hotel to let me have one of their little Fiats on the understanding that I applied immediately for a copy of my licence.

I tried the hospital again while I was waiting for one of their drivers to bring it round. After some time I was able to speak to one of the sisters, who told me Lennie's cheek had been stitched up and the knife wound in the chest, which had narrowly missed the heart, had pierced the lung. He was under sedation at the moment, so no point in my trying to see him. She advised me to ring again in the morning.

As I put the phone down Ramón called to me from below. I thought it was to say the car had arrived, but he shouted up to me that it was Miguel Gallardo's wife, asking to see me.

She was waiting for me in the chandlery, her large, comfortable-looking body seeming to fill the place, but all the vivacity gone out of her, a worried look on the round, olive-complexioned face, her large eyes wide below the black hair cut in a fringe. She had been trying to phone me, she said. About Miguel. She was speaking in a rush and obviously in a very emotional state. He hadn't been home for two nights and she wondered whether I had seen him or had any idea where he might be. She had been to the *Guardia*, of course, and the hospitals, but everything was so confused following all the happenings of the last two days . . . And I just stood there, listening to her, a sickening feeling inside me, remembering how her husband had driven up to that villa in his battered estate car. Christ! I'd forgotten all about it until that moment.

What the hell could I tell her? That Miguel, innocent and unsuspecting, had driven straight into a bunch of men loading arms and ammunitions from an underground cache and on the brink of a desperate coup? And then, as I stood there, speechless and unable to give her a word of encouragement, it hit me. That cellar, that hole in the floor. An oubliette. Oh, God!

I told her he might have had business somewhere, and in the circumstances he might not have been able to let her know he was delayed in some other part of the island. She nodded, drinking in my words, clutching at hope – and my own heart thumping. Would I know – if she were alive, or if she were dead? Would Miguel's wife, her hands folded and on the verge of tears, know if *he* were alive?

The car arrived and thankfully I escaped into the routine of taking it over. 'I've got to go now,' I told her. 'But I'll keep an eye open and if I see him . . .' I left it at that, the sickening feeling with me again as I offered her a lift. But she was all right. Her daughter had a shoe shop just by the Club Maritimo. She would take her home. Her hands were warm and pudgy as she clasped mine, thanking me profusely, her lips trembling. 'You will telephone me plees.' She was very near to tears now. 'If you hear anything. Plees, you promise.'

I promised, escaping quickly out to the car, close to tears myself as I thought of what might have happened. Evans wouldn't have taken any chances. He wouldn't have left her body lying about. And the villa of that absent German businessman was barely four miles from Addaia, ten minutes by car. Less if the *Santa Maria* had been shifted to the seaward end of the inlet and had been waiting for him at Macaret. The villa wasn't two miles from Macaret, and I had been so busy trying to find somebody in Mahon who might have seen her or know where she was that I hadn't thought of it.

I dropped the driver off at his garage on the Villa Carlos road, then took the shortest route to the waterfront, cutting down the General Sanjurjo to the Plaza España. It was getting dark already, the lights on in the shops and the narrow streets thronged with people, most of whom seemed there just to meet their friends and express their pleasure at the return to normality. And when I finally reached the waterfront even the Passo de la Alameda was full of people come to look at the Spanish warships anchored off.

There was considerable activity at the three Naval Base jetties, a coastal minesweeper coming alongside with what looked like a fishing boat in tow and a fishery protection launch pulling out. Standing off was a fierce little warship that I knew, the Barcelo-class fast attack patrol boat that Fernando Perez had taken me over one hot September day the previous year. All this, and the destroyers, with the *Manuel Soto*, the big white ferry from Barcelona, towering over the Muelle Commercial, was enough to give the Menorquins back their confidence. There was a lot of drinking going on in the port, an air of gaiety, and at the bottom of the Abundancia I had threaded my way through a crowd of about a hundred dancing in the street to a guitar.

Past the turning off to the right that led to the Naval Base and La Mola, I was suddenly on my own, the road ahead empty. Nothing now to distract my mind as I put my foot down, pushing the little car fast towards the crossroads and the turning to Macaret and Arenal d'en Castell. There is a garage on the right going towards Fornells. Its lights were on and I stopped there briefly to obtain confirmation from Señora Garcia that a convoy of vehicles had in fact passed along this road in the early hours of the morning. She had been woken up by several very noisy motor bikes ridden flat out and was actually standing at her window looking out when the line of vehicles passed. She had counted them – nineteen Army trucks and over thirty private cars, all heading towards Fornells. The *Guardia Civil* and the Army had already questioned her about the numbers and she had told them that all the vehicles had been crowded with men. I asked her if she had seen a woman in any of them, but she said no, it had been too dark.

Back in the car it seemed an age before I reached the crossroads. The scent of pines filled the night air. I passed the turning down to Addaia, swung left into a world of gravel and heath littered with the desolate dirt tracks of the tentative *urbanización*, and then, suddenly, there was the half-finished villa that Miguel had built and I had bartered for that catamaran. It stood four-square like a blockhouse on the cliff edge, the desolate heathland dropping away below it to the sea.

It was there for an instant in my headlights, the window openings of the upper storey still boarded up, a forlorn sense of emptiness about it. I didn't stop. He wouldn't have left her there. I was already on the slope of the dirt road we had driven down to leave Petra's Beetle at the Arenal d'en Castell hotel. The villa where we had watched them arming up was so crouched into the slope that I was almost past it before I glimpsed the wrought-iron gate in the low wall.

I slammed on the brakes, then backed. But when I got out of the car, I didn't go straight in. I just stood there, too scared to move. The windows, opaque in the starlight, were like blank eyes in a stucco skull and I was scared of what I'd find. The blackness of the heath, the sound of the sea snarling at the rocks, and the villa silent as the grave. What would they have done to her? For Christ's sake . . .

I braced myself and reached for the latch of the gate. Only one way to find out. But God help me, what *would*

I find? I tried to still the thumping of my blood, blot out my too-imaginative fears. I was never in any doubt, you see, that she was there. The house, with just its upper floor peering over the rim of the slope, its silence, its air of watchfulness – it seemed to be telling me something.

I jabbed my elbow against the largest window, the crash of glass loud in the night, the stillness afterwards more pronounced. I put my hand in, feeling for the catch. The window swung open. I had to go back to the car then for the torch I had left on the passenger seat. After that I moved quickly down through the villa's three levels and on down the steps into the cellar. I stopped there, the beam of my torch directed at the rack of bottles and the flat metal sheet on which it stood. Was that how we had left it? I couldn't be sure.

The rack was almost too heavy for me on my own, but emptying the bottles out of it would have taken time and by now I was desperate to know what waited for me in that rock passage below. The air in the cellar was still and very humid. I was sweating by the time I had managed to shift the rack clear and I stood there for a moment, gasping for breath and staring down at that metal sheet. I thought I could smell something. The dank air maybe. I took a deep breath, stooped down and pulled the corrugated iron clear of the hole.

I was certain then. It was the sweet, nauseous smell of decay. I called, but there was no answer.

I bent down, my head thrust into the hole, and shouted her name, the echo of it coming back to me with the soft slop of the sea. No answer, and the passage below empty for as far as the torch would reach. It was ten feet or more to the floor of it and no way of climbing out if I made the jump. I tried to remember what Lennie had done with the rope we had used. I was certain he hadn't had it with him when we had left the villa to run back to the car.

In the end I found it up in the top level, lying under a chest. He must have kicked it there just before we left. I grabbed it up and ran back with it down the stairs, back into that cellar, fastening it to the bottle rack as we had done before. In a moment my foot was in the first of Lennie's loops and I had dropped through the hole and was in the water-worn rock passage below shouting her name again. And when there was no reply, I followed my nose, the blood pounding in my veins as I turned a bend, the blowhole passageway narrowing to finish abruptly in the pale yellow of the matchboarding where we had heard the sound of their voices and the truck's engine as it backed up to the garage doors.

One of the lengths of boarding was splintered now. It had clearly been prised off and then nailed roughly back into place. But it wasn't the splintered boarding that held my gaze. It was Miguel's body.

He was lying just as he had fallen after being stuffed through the hole in the boarding, his eyes open and staring and the back of his head smashed in. There was blood mingled with the rock dust of the floor, smears of it on the fresh wood of the boarding, and his eyes reflected dully the light of my torch. The sight of him, and the smell . . . I turned away, feeling suddenly sick. And then I was hurrying back along the blowhole passage, doubt mingled with dread, wondering what they would have done with her. If they had killed her, then no point in bringing the body here. A weight tied to the feet, then overboard and the Balearic lobsters would do the rest.

I ducked past the rope and when I reached the second expansion chamber and could see the water-worn passage falling away and the scaffold poles rigged over the blowhole, I stopped. There was nobody there. I was shouting her name again, but it was a futile gesture, only sepulchral echoes answering me and the slop of the sea loud in my ears.

I was turning away when I thought I heard something. It was a high sound, like the scream of a gull. I stood there for a moment, listening. But all I heard was the sea, and nobody would go down into the cave itself without diving gear, for the entrance to it was deep under water and in a gale . . . And then it came again, high and quavering.

I flung myself down the slope, slamming into the scaffold poles and gripping tight as I leaned out over the hole, the beam of my torch almost lost in the expanse of water that flooded the cavern below. The tide seemed higher than when Lennie and I had looked down at it, the beach no more than a narrow strip and only the upper fluke of the rusty anchor above water. I didn't see her at first. She had retreated to the far end of the beach, her body pressed back against the rock wall of the cavern, so that all I could see of her was a vague shadow in the yellowing beam.

'Soo! Is that you?'

She was too far away and she had her hands up to her face. I couldn't be sure. I called again, but she shrank back, scared that one of the men who had held her captive had returned. It wasn't until I called my own name several times that she finally moved. She came across the beach very slowly, her face growing clearer and whiter as she approached, her black hair turned almost grey with rock dust, her eyes large and wild-looking. She wouldn't believe it was really me till I shone the torch on my face, and then she suddenly collapsed.

There was nothing for it but to go down to her. Fortunately the rope on the pulley was a long one, so that I was able to fasten one end of it round my body and use the other part to lower myself to the beach. She had passed out completely, her body limp, her eyes closed. There was a nasty bruise on her cheek and a gash on the back of her right wrist that had left the whole hand tacky with half-congealed blood. I bathed her face in sea water, the hand too, but it only caused the bleeding to start again.

The sting of it must have brought her round, for when I had scooped up some more water in my cupped hands, I came back to find her staring up at me. 'Who are you?' The words were barely audible, her body stiff and trembling uncontrollably.

'It's Mike,' I said and reached out for the torch, shining it on my face again.

'Oh, my God!' She reached out, gripping hold of me, her fingers digging into my flesh so violently they hurt.

I don't know how long I sat there on that wet uncomfortable beach holding her in my arms, trying to comfort her. Not long I suppose, but long enough for my mind to try to grapple with the future and what this meant to us. 'I love you.' She said that twice, like an incantation, her voice very quiet as though the words meant a great deal to her, and holding her tight, I thought, well, maybe we could try again.

I got her up and put her foot in the looped end of the rope, passing it round her body under the arms. I was just pressing her hands on to the standing part of it, imploring her to hold tight while I was hoisting her up to the scaffolding above, when she began to giggle. 'The barrel . . .' she murmured.

'Barrel?' I had been on the point of putting my weight on the tail end of the rope, but now I hesitated, letting go of it and shining the torch on her face. Her eyes looked enormous, the whites catching the light, and her mouth was open, bubbling with uncontrollable laughter.

It was reaction, of course. Not hysteria, just reaction from the strain of all she had been through in the last thirty-six hours or so. 'Don't you remember? That record. *And then the barrel . . .*' She had deepened her voice, tears welling in her eyes, tears of laughter.

And suddenly I remembered. 'Hoffnung. Gerard Hoffnung.' The silly saga of that barrel full of bricks.

'*And then I met the barrel coming down.*' Her laughter became a giggle again. 'For a moment I thought I was the barrel. If I pulled you off your feet . . . We could be yo-yoing up and down . . .' She put her hand to her mouth, stilling

329

her giggles. And after that she gripped the rope again. 'When I get to the top, don't let go, please.' She smiled at me, both of us remembering what had happened when the bricky had hoisted the barrel back up to the top of the chimney.

I hesitated, not sure whether I could trust her to reach for the scaffolding and haul herself out. But she seemed to have steadied herself. 'Okay,' I said. 'You're the barrel and you're going up.'

She was more of a weight than I had realised, and when her legs finally disappeared into the blowhole I began to wonder if I could hold her. Then suddenly I was on the floor, the rope slack in my hands. 'You all right, Mike?' Her voice, remote and strangely hollow, seemed to come from the roof of the cavern.

'Yes, I'm all right.' I got to my feet and stood there for a moment, letting the rope end down and getting my breath back. The height I had to hoist myself looked further than I had reckoned and if I couldn't make it . . . I swept the beam of my torch over the rock roof of the cavern where it came down to meet the water. Not a nice place to spend hours waiting for rescue, plagued by the thought that a gale might spring up from the north-west and the sea level rise. I knew then what it had been like for Soo, and she had lowered herself down on to the beach with no torch and no certainty that anybody would ever find her there.

I tied the end of the rope round my chest, put my foot in the loop and hauled down on the other end of it. For a moment I didn't think I would ever get off the ground, then suddenly I was swinging free, and after that it was a little easier. I didn't realise it at the time, but Soo was hauling too and it was her weight that made the difference.

It was when we were back in the first expansion chamber that she said, 'You know about Miguel?' The whisper of her voice trembled on the dank air.

'Yes.'

'You saw him?'

It wasn't something I wanted her to dwell on, so I didn't answer.

'I only had matches. Book matches from the Figuera Restaurant. I used five of them. Poor Miguel. He looked terrible. After that I had barely half a dozen left. I used the last after I'd lowered myself into the cave. I think if you hadn't come . . . It was so dark and damp, and the sound of the water . . . I think a few hours more and I would have gone for a swim. I couldn't have stood it much longer.' Her words came in a rush, her body trembling again. The smell was there in our nostrils and I think it was that more than anything that had brought back her fears.

We had reached the rope hanging from the hole in the cellar floor and when I had hauled her up the trembling had stopped. I took her back the way I had come and out through the door in the villa's top level. She stopped there, staring up at the stars, breathing deeply. I shall never forget that moment, the ecstatic smile on her face, the tears in her eyes. 'My God!' she whispered, her hand gripping my arm. 'I never realised what life meant before, not really. Freedom and the smell of plants growing, the stars, being able to see. And you,' she added, looking up at me, wide-eyed. 'Oh, God, Mike!' And she was in my arms and I was kissing her. 'Let's go somewhere,' she said. 'Not home. I'd have to cook something. I'm hungry. My God! I'm hungry. Let's pretend we've only just met. Let's go out somewhere and celebrate. Just the two of us.'

I knew she couldn't settle now, she was too keyed up, so I drove her to Fornells, to a favourite restaurant of ours that stood back from the waterfront. We knew the people there and she was able to clean herself up, telling them we had been exploring a cave and she had fallen down a hole.

It was past midnight when we left Fornells and she was asleep before we reached the old salt pans and the end of the shallow inlet. We had shared a bottle of Rioja *tinto* over the meal and she had had a large La Ina before it and two brandies with the coffee. She had every reason to sleep, but as soon as I turned the car on to the quay she was awake. Petra's inflatable was lying alongside and she saw it before I could switch the lights off. 'What's Petra doing here?'

I thought I detected a note of hostility in her voice, so I said nothing. Somebody must have recovered the boat from Cala Llonga, or wherever Evans had beached it, somebody from *Medusa* presumably. The lights were on in our flat upstairs, the chandlery door ajar, and as we went in Petra appeared at the top of the stairs. 'You found her.' She was looking down at Soo. 'Thank God for that. We've been waiting here – hours it seems, waiting and wondering. You all right, Soo?'

'Yes. I'm all right.' Her voice shook slightly.

'Who's with you?' I asked. 'You said *we*.'

I think I knew the answer, but when she said 'Gareth', Soo gave a little gasp and I cursed under my breath. It wasn't the moment. 'What the hell's he want?'

'You'd better come up,' Petra said. 'It's been a long couple of hours, and not knowing didn't help.' Her voice was a little slurred.

I told her to get Soo to bed and pushed past her, taking the stairs two at a time. I wanted to get shot of him, to save Soo the emotional strain of meeting him face-to-face. I didn't know what the effect on her would be.

He was in the front room, sitting in the wing chair I normally used with a glass in his hand and a bottle of brandy open on the table beside him. He was dressed in a white open-necked shirt and grey flannels, his face gleaming with perspiration, and his eyes had difficulty in focusing on me. 'Ah, M-Mike.' He hauled himself to his feet, clutching the back of the chair. He was very, very tight. He started to say something, but then he stopped, his eyes narrowing as he stared past me.

I turned to find Soo in the doorway, her eyes wide

and fixed on Gareth as he tried to pull himself together. 'Y'rorlright-th'n,' he mumbled.

She nodded and they stood there, the two of them, gazing at each other. Then abruptly Soo turned away, walking blindly into Petra, who had been standing just behind her in the doorway. 'Get her to bed,' I told her again, and she took Soo's arm and led her off to the bedroom. But she was back almost immediately. 'She's asking for Benjie.'

I'd forgotten about the dog. 'Tell her I'll get it for her.'

Gareth had subsided back into my chair, his arms slack, his eyes closing. 'Where did you find her?' he asked. And when I told him, he muttered, 'That's like Pat. Leave it to the sea, anything so long as he doesn't have to do it himself.' He hesitated. 'Impersonal,' he went on reflectively. 'Couldn't stand close contact, y'know. Didn't like to touch people, women especially.' And he added, 'Strange sort of man.'

Those last words were mumbled so softly I could barely hear them, and when I told him how he had seized hold of Petra and held a knife at her throat, he didn't seem to take it in, muttering something about he'd been thinking, his eyes half-closed.

I picked up the bottle and poured myself a drink. As I put it back on the side table, he reached out for it. 'B'n thinking,' he said again, leaning forward and staring down at his glass, which was half-full. 'Abou' what they did to poor ol' Byng.' He shook his head, picking up his glass. He stared at it for a moment, then put it down again, carefully. 'Had enough, eh?' He collapsed back in his chair. 'Byng. And now me. Know what they'll do to me?' He was leaning back, his black hair limp against the wing of the chair, deep furrows creasing his forehead, and his dark eyes staring into space. 'I b'n wress-wrestling all afternoon with a bloody form, man. S two three t-two – report on collision and grounding. I grounded my ship, y'see.' The eyes fixed suddenly on me. 'How the hell do I explain that?' And then, leaning suddenly forward, 'Bu' I di'n run.' He was peering up at me. 'I di'n run like poor ol' Byng. Shot him,' he added. 'On the quarterdeck of the ol' *Monarch* – in Portsmouth Harbour with the whole Fleet gawping at it.' And then he quoted, speaking slowly, groping for the words: *'Il est bon de tuer de temps en temps un amiral pour encrug-encourager les autres* – that's what Voltaire said. F-fortunately I'm not an admiral. *Tuer, non, mais . . .'*

He paused, staring at me sombrely. 'You ever b'n at a court martial?' He didn't wait for me to shake my head, but went straight on: 'That's what'll happen to me, y'know. They'll fly me to Portsmouth, an' just inside the main gate, ther'shpeshul room for poor buggers like me who've run their ships aground, an' you go back in with the prisoner's friend an' there's your sword with the b-blade pointing at you.' He shook his head angrily. 'An' all because I can't tell them the truth about why I ran *Medusa* ashore. All because of that devil Pat . . .' His voice trailed away. 'If Pat hadn't got hold of her . . . I can't tell them that, can I? So I'll be shot – figuratively, you un'erstand. They'd never . . .' His head was nodding. 'Never admit personal reason as legit-gitimate defence.' He reached out his hand to the side table, groping for his glass.

'That's the second bottle.' Petra had come back and was standing looking at him. 'I've given her something to make her sleep. She'll be all right now.' She nodded towards Gareth. 'After they'd recovered the inflatable he insisted on coming ashore with me. Said he wanted to see you. But I think it was Soo really. He wanted to make certain she was all right.' And she added, 'He's been here ever since – waiting. What are we going to do with him? He can't go back to his ship in that state. And he's worried sick about the future.' She touched my arm. 'Why did he do it, Mike? I was there. I saw it. He ran his ship aground – deliberately. Why?'

That was the question the Board of Enquiry was to ask him four days later. Not because Mrs Suzanne Steele was being held as hostage, they didn't know about that at the outset. Their primary concern was whether he could have achieved his purpose of holding fast in the approaches to Mahon without the need to ground his ship. But that was before they called Lieutenant Commander Mault to give evidence.

V

BOARD OF ENQUIRY

CHAPTER ONE

It never occurred to me that I would be involved. A Naval Board of Enquiry, Gareth explained as I took him down the stairs and out into the bright sunlight next morning, is much like that for any commercial shipping incident, except that the resulting report often includes a recommendation for court martial proceedings to be taken against those thought to be responsible. 'I shall, of course, be held solely responsible. And rightly.'

He stood there for a moment on the quay, looking out to the frigate half-merged in the shadowed bulk of the hospital ruins. 'I'll be relieved of my command and sent back for trial.' He said it slowly, a note of resignation in his voice. He looked dreadful in that dazzlingly crisp light, dark rings under his eyes, a worried look and his mouth compressed to a hard line. Then suddenly he smiled and his face lit up. 'Must be one of the shortest and most fraught commands anybody has ever had.' He shook his head, still smiling, and with a careful jauntiness walked across the quay to the waiting launch.

His last words to me before jumping in were, 'Tell her to forget all about me. I shan't attempt to see her again.' He thanked me then for putting him up for the night, gave me a quick, perfunctory salute, and seated himself in the stern.

It was Masterton who was in charge again. He looked up at me, waiting for me to follow. 'Well, don't let's hang around, Midshipman Masterton,' Gareth snapped at him. 'Get going.'

'Yes, sir. Sorry, sir.' The boy gave the order to cast off. 'My regards to Miss Callis please,' he called out to me brightly. Then he swung the launch away from the quay and headed out to the grounded frigate, where the port tug was already standing by to try to tow her off on the top of the tide.

That was Saturday and by mid-morning, with the help of one of the Spanish destroyers, *Medusa* was off the rocks and lying to her anchor some three cables off the Club Maritimo, not far from where the oil tanker usually anchored. Apart from the fact that her pumps had to be kept going and that extra pumps brought in from the Naval Base were gushing water over the side, she looked perfectly all right. However, divers were down most of the day examining the stern, and that evening I heard that both propellers were damaged and it was thought the port prop shaft had been forced out of alignment. She was expected to be towed to Barcelona for repairs within the week.

Wade phoned me from London on Sunday morning to ask if I had any news of Evans. His voice sounded relaxed, even friendly. And when I told him I hadn't the slightest idea where the man was, he laughed and said, 'No, I didn't expect you would. But did you gather any idea what his future plans were? You had a meeting with him on *Medusa*.'

'How do you know that?'

He ignored my question. 'I imagine the main point of that meeting was to use your wife as a lever to get Lloyd Jones to take his frigate out of Mahon. I'm not asking you for the details of that meeting,' he added quickly. 'That will be a matter for Captain Wheatcroft. What I want to know is, did Evans at any time during that meeting, or when you were on the island together, give any indication of what his plans were?'

'Of course not,' I said. 'Until the frigate went aground he was fully committed to the new government of Ismail Fuxá and to ensuring that the powerful aid it had asked for would not be hindered from entering the port.'

'Yes, but afterwards – after *Medusa* had gone aground?'

'The grounding and Miss Callis's arrival were almost simultaneous. You know about what happened after that, do you?' I asked him.

'Yes. But I'm not interested in that, only in whether he gave you any indication of what he might do next, where he would go?'

'There wasn't time.'

'All right, but earlier, when you and he were with Lloyd Jones in his cabin on *Medusa*.'

Again I told him there was no reason for Evans to even think about where he might go next. 'The discussion was about my wife and getting Lloyd Jones to take his frigate out of Mahon. He'd no reason then to think beyond the next few hours.'

'I see.' He was silent then, and the silence lasted so long I began to think we had been disconnected. Suddenly he said, 'You don't think he's still on Menorca then?'

'It hadn't occurred to me,' I said. 'Why?'

'That fishing boat you let him have – did you know it was sighted abandoned and on fire just outside Spanish territorial waters?' Another silence, and then he said, 'Oh well, doubtless he's pushed off with the rest of them.' And he added, 'Now if you'd been able to tell me he was hiding up somewhere on the island . . .' I could almost hear his shrug over the line as he went on, 'Pity! Looks as though somebody will have to start picking up the trail all over again.' And without another word he rang off.

Captain Wheatcroft, the officer sent out to head the Board of Enquiry, arrived that afternoon. With him on the same plane were his two Board members, a Commander Lovelock from Naval Plans, a marine engineering commander, and a smart little snub-nosed Wren Writer with black hair and rather bulging eyes. All four stayed at the Port Mahon Hotel, which had rooms to spare, some of their American guests having decided to get out. Also on the plane was a Commander Firth. Gareth had apparently served under him and having recently relinquished command of another frigate, he had been flown out to help and advise Gareth during the Enquiry – a sort of prisoner's friend. The Board began their sittings the following day, Monday, on board *Medusa*.

The morning was taken up with questions arising from her Captain's report of the grounding and the reasons for it, the afternoon with the evidence of one or two of the other officers, Lieutenant Commander Mault in particular. He was questioned by the Board for well over an hour.

I only heard about this, of course, later, after it was all over. I knew nothing about it at the time, but after Wade's phone call I was not altogether surprised when a midshipman, not Masterton, delivered a note from the Chairman of the Board calling me as a witness and requesting that I attend on board HMS *Medusa* at 10.00 hours the next morning. There would be a launch sent for me at 09.30.

Soo's immediate reaction when I told her was, 'Do they know about me?' and she added quickly, 'About my being held as a hostage?'

'Of course.' My own desperate enquiries had made that inevitable, and Miguel's body being found where she had been left to die had ensured maximum publicity.

'I know what they'll try and do. They'll try and prove he grounded his ship because of me. That's why you're being called.' Her large, dark eyes had a wild look. 'Can't you say he barely knew me, that when you were on board with Gareth and that wretched half-brother of his, he was making use of me just as he would any other hostage? I mean, so long as they don't know he was seeing me, then they'll have to accept that he put his ship aground because it was the only way he could be sure he wouldn't be towed out . . .' The words had been pouring out of her she was so tensed up, but I was shaking my head and slowly her voice died.

In the end I told her quite bluntly that what had happened was common knowledge. 'Things happen. That's life. And once they've happened they can't be undone.'

She nodded slowly, biting her lip. And then suddenly she began to cry. I tried to say I would do what I could. 'I've no desire to ruin his career, but if they bring it up I'm not going to pretend I'm a fool and didn't know.' And I added, 'A lot will depend on the sort of man Captain Wheatcroft turns out to be, how understanding he is of the emotional needs of naval officers, particularly somebody like Gareth.' But she wasn't listening. She had turned away, shaking her head, and with her hand to her mouth she ran to the bedroom and shut the door.

The Board of Enquiry had taken over the Captain's day cabin, the three members seated at a folding table that had been brought up from the wardroom, their blue uniforms with the gold bands on cuffs and shoulder straps solidly impressive. I was shown to a chair set facing them and after the preliminaries the Chairman went out of his way to put me at my ease by saying, 'This is not in any sense a court, Mr Steele, but you will understand, I am sure, that an expensive and valuable Navy ship has been set aground and we have to enquire into the circumstances of that grounding. For instance, was it an accidental grounding or was it deliberate? If the latter, then what were the reasons for the decision to set the ship aground?'

He was leaning a little forward, a long, fine-boned face with sharply pointed nose and high-domed forehead largely devoid of hair. 'I want you to understand – whatever your personal feelings – that the purpose of this Board is to resolve those two questions and report our findings. You will appreciate, of course, that the circumstances were very unusual – almost, I might say, unprecedented. And the odd thing is that you, a civilian, were on board, and to some extent involved, at several of the most crucial moments.'

Captain Wheatcroft had considerable charm, his manner friendly and altogether disarming, except that, as the questions developed, his voice, which was what I would call very establishment Navy, became more aloof and inquisitorial. He had me describe the frigate's movements from the time she raised her anchor to the time she grounded, and here I was able to avoid any reference to the glimpse I had had of an altercation between Gareth and his First Lieutenant. 'So you're suggesting the ship was out of control?'

'It looked like it,' I replied.

'Because he went stern-first through the narrows?' He didn't wait for me to agree, but added, 'He'd no reason to go through the narrows. He had far more sea room to the east of Bloody Island.' And then he said, 'I think I should tell you the evidence we have already heard makes it clear there was nothing wrong with the engines. That was a put-up job to justify the Captain's refusal to move his ship when he had been ordered to leave by the port authorities, and indeed by the self-styled president of the new regime himself. You know about that, I think?' And when I nodded, he smiled as though he had established a point he had been trying to make. 'You realise, of course, what follows from that?'

I nodded.

'So can I have a direct answer from you on the first question we are having to resolve – in your opinion was the grounding of the frigate *Medusa* deliberate? Yes or no, please.'

'Yes,' I said.

'Good. Now to the second question, Mr Steele, and this I think you may find some difficulty in answering. What in your opinion was the overriding reason for Lieutenant Commander Lloyd Jones's action in deliberately grounding his ship? And let me say here we already know that you were on board and here in this very cabin when a man named Evans arrived from Cala Llonga and was brought up to see him.' He glanced hurriedly through his notes. 'The three of you were together here, with nobody else present, for approximately ten minutes, perhaps a little longer. Now, would you kindly tell us exactly what was

344

said? Evans was holding your wife hostage, correct?'

'Yes.'

'Any particular reason why they should have seized your wife rather than somebody else's wife?'

I told him that perhaps it was because Lloyd Jones had personally met her. She wasn't a stranger to him. And I added, 'The circumstances were somewhat unusual and I was sure Evans would have heard about it.' I knew I was treading on thin ice here, and to avoid saying too much, I told him exactly what had happened the night of the barbecue.

'And you think, if Evans knew about that, it would be sufficient to make him single her out from all the wives in Mahon?' And he went straight on, 'You know, of course, that Evans is Lieutenant Commander Lloyd Jones's half-brother. Moreover, Evans had saved his life. That would surely be enough without bringing a woman into it?'

I didn't answer that. The man had been too well briefed, by Wade probably. He smiled and leaned back in his chair. 'Well go on, Mr Steele. You were going to tell us what exactly took place in this cabin when the Captain, you and Evans were closeted here together for over ten minutes.'

I gave him a brief account of what had been said, without referring to the vicious way Evans had tried to needle us both. But it wasn't Wade who had briefed him. It was somebody local, or else one of the officers, Mault probably, had leapt to conclusions, for he didn't wait for me to finish before saying, 'I'm afraid I must now ask a delicate and very personal question. I am sure you will understand why it is absolutely essential you give me a frank answer. What was the exact nature of the relationship between Lieutenant Commander Lloyd Jones and your wife?'

'I don't follow you,' I said.

'I think you do.'

'Are you suggesting there was something wrong with the relationship? They met for the first time at that Red Cross barbecue. I told you that. Within a fortnight Gareth

Lloyd Jones left for Gibraltar to take command of this ship. If you're suggesting what I think you are, then they knew each other for much too short a time.'

He looked at me quizzically. 'No offence, Mr Steele, but it doesn't take long, and it would explain, you see, why Evans would think that by seizing hold of your wife and threatening her life–'

'That's enough,' I said, pushing back my chair and getting to my feet. 'You've no right to make allegations like that on hearsay.' I don't know why, but I was angry, for Gareth as well as Soo. I felt he had been through quite enough without having this thrown in his face. And why should Soo's name be dragged into it, just because they were both human and had reacted quite spontaneously to something they couldn't help?

Standing there, I told Wheatcroft what I thought of him. 'You post a man to the command of a ship that's half volunteers, half throw-outs, tell him to do the impossible, and then when he does it, you come here chairing an enquiry that will send him to court martial, and you have the effrontery to suggest, as a means of destroying him, that he was having an affair with my wife.'

He smiled, oddly enough quite a warm smile. 'You say he wasn't having an affair, that there is no truth –'

'Of course I do.' And I added, 'I would hardly have gone on board his ship in Malta if I had suspected anything like that, would I?' I made it a question in the hope that he would believe me.

'So, if there was a court martial, you would categorically deny that there was any truth in the allegation?'

'Certainly.'

'You would be under oath remember.'

I nodded. I didn't trust myself to say any more.

'And that suggestion was never made by Evans when he was alone here with the two of you trying to persuade Lloyd Jones to leave Mahon?'

'It was made,' I said. 'As a try-on. Having grabbed my

346

wife, he was probing on the off-chance he could use her more effectively.'

'And it didn't work?'

'No.'

'It had no connection with the subsequent grounding?'

'Why should it if it wasn't true? In any case, Gareth –' and I used his Christian name then for the first time – 'was fixing it so that there was no way they could get him to leave port. Soo didn't come into it.'

'And your testimony as regards that will stand at the court martial?'

'If he's court-martialled, and I'm called to give evidence, then that's what I shall say.'

He stared at me a moment, then turned to the other two Board members. 'Any further questions, gentlemen?' And when they both shook their heads, he smiled and got to his feet. 'Then that's all, Mr Steele.' He held out his hand. 'Thank you for coming here to give evidence.' He called to the petty officer waiting outside and ordered him to see me off the ship. Then, turning to me again, he said, 'I'm hoping to have a little party here on board before I leave. Perhaps you and your wife would care to come – a small return for the trouble we have caused you.' He looked round at his colleagues. 'Tomorrow evening, don't you think?' They nodded and he said to me, 'Tomorrow evening then, six o'clock say. The launch will pick you up shortly before.'

It cannot be every day that the Chairman of a Board of Enquiry gives a party on the afterdeck of the very ship whose grounding he has been enquiring into. But the circumstances were exceptional, and so was Julian Wheatcroft's behaviour. No sign of the distant severity he had shown as Chairman of the enquiry. Now all the well-educated charm of the man was back in place as he greeted his guests on the flight deck. The borrowed deck pumps had been temporarily stilled, the ship relatively quiet, and it was one of those really lovely Menorcan evenings, the air warm and not a breath of wind.

I watched him as he greeted Soo, a little bow and a warm smile, his eyes travelling quickly over her body and fastening on her face, alert, watchful, sexually aware. The same watchfulness was there as she and Gareth greeted each other. It was obvious he was trying to make up his mind whether or not they had been lovers. She had assured me they had not, that it had been purely emotional. In retrospect, I see his problem. An emotional involvement did not concern him, only a physical one, particularly if the result were a child.

I had warned Soo that she would be virtually on show and that for Gareth's sake, if not for mine, she should be on her guard. In the event, she carried it off perfectly, greeting Gareth with an easy friendliness, offering him her cheek, smiling and happy-looking as she congratulated him on having survived such a difficult assignment. She did it with just the right touch of intimacy and warmth. I was proud of her, and watching Wheatcroft, I saw him relax, then turn away to say something to Lovelock, the commander from Plans, who had also been monitoring the meeting between Soo and Gareth. He nodded, the down-turned corners of his mouth twisting themselves into an unaccustomed smile. He, too, seemed suddenly relaxed.

It was a very small party, Gareth the only one of *Medusa*'s officers present, Soo and myself the only civilians. The other guests were the admiral commanding the Spanish fleet, his flag officer, and Fernando Perez from the Naval Base with his wife Ramona. Afterwards, when I talked it over with Soo, I found she had come to the same conclusion I had, that Wheatcroft's first objective in hosting such a very select little party was to take a look at her and check that it was safe for the Board to take the line it had virtually decided on.

His second objective was, of course, to make a short speech, largely for the benefit of the Spanish admiral and the commander of the Mahon Naval Base. For this he had arranged that Lieutenant Sykes should be waiting on deck so that the brief and very political speech he made was instantly translated into Spanish. And when he had finished, it was the Spanish admiral's turn to make a little speech.

Whether the admiral had been briefed or not I do not know, but at the end of his speech, when we were all applauding, he brought from his pocket an ornate little case, went across to Gareth, and taking out a bright ribbon with a decoration suspended from it, hung it round his neck.

Poor Gareth! He had clearly had no warning of this. He stood there for a moment, a flush on his face and his mouth opening and closing, no words coming. Finally, in desperation, he gave a naval salute and murmured one word, 'G-gracias.'

I thought that was the end of it. I think we all did. But then Julian Wheatcroft stepped forward again and said, 'There is something else I wish to say.' Victor Sykes was again translating the English into Spanish and I believe his continued presence to have been deliberate, ensuring as it did that the gist of everything that was being said would pass round the ship. 'Normally the findings of a Board of Enquiry are confidential and only revealed later when an announcement is made as to whether or not a court martial will result. However, the risks that Lieutenant Commander Lloyd Jones, his officers and men accepted and faced make the circumstances of *Medusa*'s grounding quite extra-ordinary.' He separated the words out so that they had the older, stronger meaning. 'And because I was very conscious that any recommendations I might make might be overturned, I've spent much of today in an exchange of signals with CINCFLEET and the Ministry of Defence. I may say that the Board was quite unanimous

in its view that court martial proceedings were inappropri-
ate in this case and I now have a directive –' and here
his voice became very formal and deliberate – 'from the
Secretary of State for Defence, approved personally by the
Prime Minister, that in the exceptional and unprecedented
circumstances of the grounding it has been decided to rule
out any question of a court martial.'

He paused there, then moved a step or two towards
Gareth. 'I, too, have a gift for you. It is not, I'm afraid, as
valuable or as beautiful as the decoration with which you
have been honoured by the King of Spain. It was given to
me just before I left London. It is from 10 Downing Street,
a personal letter from the Prime Minister to you, and
to all those serving on board HMS *Medusa*.' The long
envelope in his hand, he stepped forward, handed it to
Gareth, then took a step back and gave him a magnificent
salute.

There was a long pause, Gareth staring down at it, Welsh
emotion strangling any reply, actual tears in his eyes. It
was a moment we all shared, but having been with him
on various very crucial occasions, I could appreciate more
than any of the others on the flight deck the depth of his
feeling, the ordeal he had been through – not only facing
the prospect of imminent death for himself and the men
serving under him, but later in the loneliness of waiting
for his career to be terminated in a court martial.

Poor ol' Byng! I remembered his words, slurred with
drink, and now I saw him crying openly, the Spanish
decoration catching the last of the sun as he pulled himself
together and returned Captain Wheatcroft's salute.